# Religion and Reaction

# Religion and Reaction

## The Secular Political Challenge to the Religious Right

Susan B. Hansen

ROWMAN & LITTLEFIELD PUBLISHERS, INC.
*Lanham • Boulder • New York • Toronto • Plymouth, UK*

Published by Rowman & Littlefield Publishers, Inc.
A wholly owned subsidiary of The Rowman & Littlefield Publishing Group, Inc.
4501 Forbes Boulevard, Suite 200, Lanham, Maryland 20706
http://www.rowmanlittlefield.com

Estover Road, Plymouth PL6 7PY, United Kingdom

Copyright © 2011 by Rowman & Littlefield Publishers, Inc.

*All rights reserved.* No part of this book may be reproduced in any form or by any electronic or mechanical means, including information storage and retrieval systems, without written permission from the publisher, except by a reviewer who may quote passages in a review.

British Library Cataloguing in Publication Information Available

**Library of Congress Cataloging-in-Publication Data**

Hansen, Susan B.
  Religion and reaction : the secular political challenge to the religious right / Susan B. Hansen.
    p. cm.
  Includes index.
  ISBN 978-1-4422-1105-6 (cloth : alk. paper) — ISBN 978-1-4422-1107-0 (electronic)
  1. Religious right—United States. 2. Christianity and politics—United States. 3. United States—Church history—21st century. I. Title. II. Title: Secular political challenge to the religious right.
  BR516.H223 2011
  322'.10973—dc22                                      2011014881

∞™ The paper used in this publication meets the minimum requirements of American National Standard for Information Sciences—Permanence of Paper for Printed Library Materials, ANSI/NISO Z39.48-1992. Printed in the United States of America

# Contents

| | | |
|---|---|---|
| List of Figures and Tables | | vii |
| Preface | | ix |
| 1 | The Secular Challenge to the Religious Right | 1 |
| 2 | Explaining the Growth in Seculars in the United States | 19 |
| 3 | Religiosity, Public Opinion, and Political Involvement | 41 |
| 4 | Party Differences, Religious "Threat," and Voter Mobilization | 65 |
| 5 | Secular and Religious Right Organizations: Challenges and Alliances | 89 |
| 6 | Case Studies in Countervailing Power | 117 |
| 7 | Conclusion: A More Secular Future America? | 143 |
| Notes | | 163 |
| Index | | 193 |

# Figures and Tables

**FIGURES**

| | | |
|---|---|---|
| Figure 2.1. | Trends in Church Attendance and Religious Nonaffiliation, 1972–2008 | 24 |
| Figure 2.2. | Trends in Religious Beliefs, 1940–2009 | 25 |
| Figure 2.3. | Opposition to Atheism, 1972–2008 | 27 |
| Figure 2.4. | Gallup Poll: Willing to Vote for Religious Minorities | 27 |
| Figure 2.5. | Trends in Attitudes toward Sex Education, Premarital Sex, and Abortion, 1974–2008 | 38 |
| Figure 3.1. | Party Identification by Religiosity, 1980–2008 | 48 |
| Figure 3.2. | Self-Placement on Liberal/Conservative Thermometer, 1980–2008 | 49 |
| Figure 3.3. | Strength of Party Identification by Religiosity, 1980–2008 | 51 |
| Figure 3.4. | Thermometer Scores (0–100) for Gays and Lesbians by Religiosity | 52 |
| Figure 3.5. | Mean Scores on ANES Seven-Point Women's Equal Role Scale by Religiosity | 53 |
| Figure 3.6. | Mean Scores on ANES Index of Abortion Opinions by Religiosity | 53 |
| Figure 3.7. | Mean Level of Campaign Participation by Religiosity | 59 |
| Figure 4.1. | Mean Perception of Party Differences by Partisan Strength | 67 |
| Figure 4.2. | Proportion of Seculars by State | 77 |
| Figure 4.3a. | Predicted Candidate Differences on Abortion, by Religiosity and State Percent Seculars | 82 |

Figure 4.3b. Predicted Candidate Differences on Abortion,
           Catholics and Non-Catholics                                              83

## TABLES

| | | |
|---|---|---|
| Table 1.1. | Religious Beliefs and Practices among the Unaffiliated | 9 |
| Table 2.1. | GSS Data: Confidence in the Existence of God, 1988–2008 | 26 |
| Table 2.2. | Education and Religion, 2008 | 30 |
| Table 2.3. | Age and Religion, 2008 | 31 |
| Table 2.4. | Religious Beliefs by Birth Cohort, 1880–1980 | 33 |
| Table 2.5. | Cohort Effects, Demographics, and Religious Beliefs | 34 |
| Table 2.6. | Trends in Church Attendance and No Religion | 36 |
| Table 3.1. | Religiosity by Race, 1980–2008 | 44 |
| Table 3.2. | Demographics of Seculars, Moderates, and Traditionalists, 1980 and 2008 | 46 |
| Table 3.3. | Vote for President, Congress, and Third Parties, 1980–2008 | 50 |
| Table 3.4. | Opinions on Abortion Conditions by Religiosity, 2008 | 54 |
| Table 3.5. | Thermometer Scale Scores for Religious Groups by Religiosity | 55 |
| Table 3.6. | Political Activism by Seculars, Moderates, and Traditionalists, 1980, 2004, and 2008 | 57 |
| Table 3.7. | Multivariate Prediction of Campaign Activism and Voter Turnout, 1980–2008 | 60 |
| Table 3.8. | Multivariate Prediction of Campaign Activism by Religiosity | 61 |
| Table 4.1. | Perceptions of Policy Differences on Abortion and Seven-Point Issue Scales, 2004 | 68 |
| Table 4.2. | Perceived Party, Candidate, and Abortion Differences and Voter Turnout, 2004 and 2008 | 69 |
| Table 4.3. | Models Predicting Voter Turnout, 2004 and 2008 | 70 |
| Table 4.4. | Perception of Party and Candidate Differences, 2004 | 79 |
| Table 4.5. | Perceived Candidate Differences on Issue Scales | 85 |
| Table 5.1. | Major Religious Right Organizations | 92 |
| Table 5.2. | Secular Organizations and Allies Opposed to the Religious Right | 98 |
| Table 5.3. | Religious Affiliations of Party Convention Delegates, 2004 and 2008 | 110 |
| Table 7.1. | Religiosity and Policy Preferences by Race, Ethnicity, and Age | 147 |
| Table 7.2. | Policy Preferences of Seculars, Moderates, and Traditionalists | 161 |

# Preface

This book reflects my long-standing interest in the relationship between public opinion and public policy. My previous book, *The Politics of Taxation* (1983), explored a policy area where elites and citizens had very different preferences and priorities, and analyzed the institutional and strategic means by which elected officials were able to raise revenues despite widespread popular opposition to taxes. *Religion and Reaction* considers the growing discrepancy between an increasingly secular America and recent policy gains by the Religious Right.

Over the last few years traditional conservative Christian values have been reflected in policies ranging from the federal Defense of Marriage Act to state bans on gay marriage, restrictions on access to abortion, federal funding for abstinence education and faith-based public policies, and taxpayer-funded vouchers for students attending religious schools. These policy outcomes reflected the successful mobilization of the Religious Right at the grass roots, in state and local elections, in Congress, Republican Party politics, and the election of an evangelical president (George W. Bush) in 2000 and 2004. The rise of the Religious Right since the 1960s has attracted considerable attention from social scientists and the media. While other industrialized democracies have become more secular, controversies over religious values, interests, and policies have been increasingly prevalent in the United States.

Yet despite the policy gains by the Religious Right, public opinion appears to be moving in a more liberal and secular direction. Several scholars have noted declines in church attendance and religious affiliation, or have documented the growing presence of seculars within the

Democratic Party. But few expected seculars to gain much political influence. Lyman Kellstedt perceptively observes that although seculars now constitute about one-sixth of the population, "They are hard to reach; they don't sit around in secular pews."[1] But the Religious Right could build on an extensive church-based network to mobilize religious traditionalists and transform their concerns into votes and public policies reflecting conservative Christian values. Church attendance has emerged as a powerful predictor of voter turnout (and of voting for Republican candidates).

Political scientists have generally accepted the principle that organized interests have far more clout than the general public. The growth of the Religious Right could be considered a classic example of this phenomenon, and could well explain why conservative religious perspectives have often prevailed despite public preferences for more progressive or secular views, particularly regarding human sexuality and family structure. But is that the whole story? In the twenty-first century a new picture is emerging. The Religious Right is experiencing serious organizational difficulties and a crisis of leadership, and continues to be plagued by scandals. Younger evangelicals are motivated by very different issues than their elders, and also are developing more liberal perspectives on human sexuality and family structure. Trust in organized religion has diminished considerably, and Americans are increasingly skeptical of the role of religion in politics.[2]

Is the sleeping tiger of secularism beginning to stir? Kellstedt notes the "surprising" degree of voter turnout and Democratic support in 2004 by Americans with no religious affiliation, who had hitherto been less politically involved.[3] New secular organizations have emerged, in the states as well as in Washington, D.C., to engage in lobbying as well as grassroots mobilization. Some of these groups have pursued the strategy long favored by civil-libertarian organizations such as the ACLU: using the courts to challenge any entanglement of church and state, and to defend the rights of atheists as well as other religious minorities. Scientists and the medical profession were aroused to political action by many of the Bush administration's policies, such as denial of global warming, high-level federal appointments based on ideology or religiosity rather than scientific credentials, and suppression or distortion of scientific evidence during the policy process. Although bans on gay marriage passed in any direct-democracy state that put them on the ballot, public support for gay rights and gay marriage has continued to rise, and gay-rights activists have emerged as a major political force. While the general public still favors many restrictions on abortion, they continued to oppose repeal of *Roe v. Wade*, and the more extreme abortion restrictions or fetal-rights bills have lost at the polls in several states—including the solidly "Red" state of South Dakota.

I was increasingly struck by growing evidence of opposition to the Religious Right, among seculars as well as more moderate and liberal religious groups. And I was intrigued by the theoretical puzzle of how seculars might overcome the considerable organizational advantages of the Religious Right. My readings for a 2010 undergraduate course on religion and politics at the University of Pittsburgh included works by John Green, Lyman Kellstedt, Louis Bolce, and Gerald De Maio, all of whom had paid at least some attention to the growth in the numbers of seculars and their animosity to conservative Christians. So I decided that the political influence of seculars merited further investigation, from the perspective of both organizational theory and morality politics.

The morality-politics cycle emphasizes the role of threat to one's core values as a potent spur to mobilization. The resurgence of the Religious Right was stimulated in large part by the threats to their values posed by the social revolution of the 1960s. As a political scientist, I have long been impressed by the model citizenship of many religious conservatives: they register, vote regularly, volunteer in their communities, and are active in party and grassroots politics. They are well informed about at least some issues and judge candidates accordingly. Several recent studies have documented the contribution of religious involvement to American social capital. But could threats to secular values also contribute to increased political mobilization and issue awareness? Based on the survey evidence and case studies to be presented in this book, that is indeed the case.

I have a personal stake in this topic as well. As a feminist, a political and religious liberal, and a supporter of gay rights and reproductive freedom, I am personally opposed to most of the policy positions of the Religious Right. This book is certainly not intended as an attack on religion in general, or on the potential contributions to public discourse of religious views on moral issues. But many on the Religious Right seek to impose a particular policy perspective on Americans who may not share their values, and I believe this represents a serious threat to religious freedom and to American democratic principles. Seculars, civil libertarians, the Democratic Party, and the Religious Left have developed several strategies to combat the growing influence of the Religious Right over American politics and policy. I hope that the case studies and demographic trends documented in this book will contribute to the success of those efforts. Based on the demographic projections I make in the conclusion, a more secular American society of the future will not be bereft of values or moral principles, but will emphasize quite different values than those currently advocated by the Religious Right.

Many people have contributed to this project over the last two years. I am especially grateful to my students at the University of Pittsburgh, whose questions and concerns about religion, secularism, and politics have piqued my interest. My colleague B. Guy Peters first encouraged me to write about the changing role of religion in American politics. Colleagues David Barker, Jon Hurwitz, Kris Kanthak, and Heather Rice have shared their own research on religion and politics, and provided many helpful comments on chapter drafts. Graduate student researchers Marilia Mochel, Kristen Coopie Allen, Padi Hallam Joseph, and Brandon Lenoir helped immensely with data analysis and the tracking of sources and citations. John Green generously shared his data on state religiosity and the beliefs of Democratic and Republican convention delegates. My dear friend Kerry Ban was a good sounding board for my developing ideas, and reinforced my commitment to the American Civil Liberties Union. I have also benefited from helpful comments by anonymous reviewers for Rowman & Littlefield and political-science journals.

I am indebted to the General Social Survey[4] and the American National Election Studies[5] for much of the survey data used in this book. Any opinions, findings, and conclusions or recommendations expressed herein are my own and do not necessarily reflect the views of the funding organizations.

Last but not least, my patient and understanding husband, Fred, has provided ongoing intellectual and emotional support, probing questions about social-science jargon and methods, and his considerable computer expertise. Of course any errors, omissions, or misinterpretations are entirely my own responsibility. This book is dedicated to our granddaughter Lindsay Ellyn Christian, who will inherit the world we are making. We hope that American society will continue to provide the freedom of ideas and expression that will encourage her childhood curiosity and help her develop, as the Prayer Book puts it, "an inquiring and discerning heart."

SBH<br>
Pittsburgh, Pennsylvania<br>
March 2011

# 1

✝

# The Secular Challenge to the Religious Right

Conflicts over religion were prominent in the news in 2010:

- At one end of New York's Lincoln Tunnel, a billboard posted by the organization American Atheists displayed a Nativity scene but stated, "You know it's a myth. This season, celebrate reason!" At the other end of the tunnel, the Catholic League's billboard proclaimed, "You know it's real. This season celebrate Jesus."[1]
- In April 2010 a federal judge agreed with the contention of the Freedom from Religion Foundation that the annual presidential proclamation of a National Day of Prayer, a fixture since 1952, was unconstitutional. President Barack Obama said he intended to observe it anyway. But in December 2010 the Congressional Prayer Caucus accused President Obama of failing to mention "God" or "the Creator" often enough in his speeches.[2]
- Entrepreneurs announced plans for a theme park in Kentucky with an "authentic" replica of Noah's Ark, loaded with animals and actors, as the centerpiece of a Bible-based tourist attraction to be called Ark Encounter. The funders included the evangelical Christian ministry that had established the successful Creation Museum in Petersburg, Kentucky. The governor of Kentucky said that the state would subsidize construction of the new theme park because it would create jobs and bring in tourists. The American Civil Liberties Union threatened a lawsuit.[3]
- Federal Judge Virginia Phillips ruled on September 9 that the military's "don't ask–don't tell" policy for gay or lesbian soldiers was

unconstitutional. A vote to repeal this Clinton-era policy passed the Senate on December 18 by a 65–31 margin. Polls showed 67 percent of Americans favored repeal.[4]

To many observers, such controversies are further indications of the "culture war" identified by sociologist James Hunter in 1992, pitting conservative Christian orthodoxy against Americans with more progressive religious or secular views.[5] This conflict has deep roots in American history, exemplified by the Scopes trial in 1925 about the teaching of evolution. Media coverage of that trial, and subsequent court rulings, thoroughly discredited creationist arguments (although much of the general public still accepts them). Since the 1970s, however, conservative Christians have mobilized in the movement that became known as the Religious Right. "Values" issues (abortion, homosexuality, the status of women, religion in the schools) have dominated political discourse. By the early twenty-first century the Religious Right had won some significant victories: reelection of an evangelical president, appointment of many more judges sympathetic to religious expression, faith-based domestic and international policies, more restrictions on access to abortion, and bans on gay marriage passed in twenty-three direct-democracy states. Church attendance and religious beliefs have emerged as significant predictors of political attitudes and participation. Candidates for public office at all levels are now expected to express their personal religious beliefs on the campaign trail.

However, as this book will argue, the apparent policy successes of the Religious Right have generated significant opposition from younger Americans, seculars, and an emerging Religious Left. Secular perspectives have been mobilized at the grass roots as well as in Washington and in state capitals. Crucial alliances have been forged with the media, the scientific community, and the Democratic Party. The Religious Right has tried to fight back, but to an increasing extent on the grounds carved out by the defenders of secular values.

This argument will be based in part on trends in demographics, church attendance, and public opinion, all of which suggest an increasingly secular America. But political and policy outcomes are determined by how social trends and public preferences are mobilized, organized, and influenced by elites and parties. The Religious Right grew into a major force in American politics because of its solid organizational base in churches, Christian media, and the Republican Party. It has been far more difficult to mobilize seculars. But since the 1990s secular forces have found ways to address this organizational deficit and to put the Religious Right on the defensive, in the states as well as in Washington, D.C. Case studies of state and local conflicts over abortion, gay marriage, and evolution will compare the organizational effectiveness and political strategies of seculars and conservative religious groups. Republican victories in the 2010 midterm elections may allow the Religious Right to regain some lost ground, but long-term demographic trends favor secular viewpoints. The battles (especially in state and federal courts) are ongoing, and policy outcomes will continue to reflect the dynamics of political organization.

## SECULARS AND THE UNCHURCHED: A GROWING FORCE IN AMERICAN POLITICS

The resurgence of the Religious Right since the 1970s is largely responsible for the growing salience of religion in American politics. Scholars and journalists have documented the increased political influence, evolving organizational structures, leadership challenges, and policy impact of the Religious Right.[6] Religious or "values" issues (abortion, school prayer, gay marriage, creationism) are addressed in political party platforms, congressional debates, the media, and candidates' speeches. Political strategists, particularly in the Republican Party, have made use of values issues to mobilize voters. In 2004, the presence of gay-marriage bans on several state ballots, as well as grassroots mobilization efforts by Karl Rove, led to higher turnout by evangelical and conservative voters, and may have contributed to the reelection of George Bush.[7]

While the Religious Right has made significant gains in political influence, another trend has also emerged: an increase in the number of secular Americans who claim no religious affiliation. More and more people describe themselves as atheists or agnostics, and report few, if any, ties to organized religion. Although surveys show that Americans are still considerably more religious than people in other advanced industrial democracies, church attendance has been declining, especially among the young. Many of the unchurched still claim some belief in God or another form of Supreme Being, or define themselves as "spiritual." But there has been a notable increase in the proportion of Americans who are far more secular than religious, in terms of both beliefs and lack of involvement in any religious organizations.[8] Further, seculars (and many religious people as well) have been increasingly alarmed by the agenda, leadership, values, and tactics of the Religious Right.

The purpose of this book is to explore these emerging secular trends and to assess their political impact. Who are these people? Why are their numbers increasing? If they do not embrace traditional religious concepts, what political and social beliefs do they hold? What has been the secular response to political and policy gains by the Religious Right? And what might be the consequences of an increasingly secular society?

This book will also consider the problems and possibilities for organizing secular opposition to the Religious Right. The conventional wisdom among social scientists is that organized interests, whether these include businesses, labor unions, or churches, wield considerably more political influence than individuals or groups such as consumers or shareholders, who are far more difficult to mobilize. Conservative Catholics and active members of evangelical or fundamentalist churches thus constitute the social base of the Religious Right. Church offices, mailing and telephone lists, networks among clergy and congregations, religious radio and television programs, and targeted use of direct-mail appeals all helped to organize anti-ERA forces during the 1970s, and have been used effectively ever since on behalf of conservative candidates and issues. The Roman Catholic Church provided much of the infrastructure and financing of the pro-life reaction to the 1973 *Roe v. Wade* decision on abortion.

Unaffiliated seculars may indeed be more difficult to organize than regular churchgoers, and historically they have been much less politically active. Other social scientists who have taken note of secular trends may therefore have underestimated their political influence. As this book will argue, however, seculars have become much more politically engaged in recent years, in part because of their antipathy to the Religious Right. They have developed their own organizations as well as ties with some important allies: civil-liberties advocates, the scientific establishment, the mainstream media, the Democratic Party, the judiciary, and many on the Religious Left. Secular forces have also developed a range of strategies to counter the influence of religion on American culture and politics, and in several instances have been able to overcome the superior grassroots organization of the Religious Right.

The threat of competing values can also be a potent tool to spur organization, by seculars as well as by the faithful. For decades leaders of the Religious Right have denounced "secular humanists" who, in their view, have removed religion from the public square, taken prayer and the Bible out of public schools, degraded conventional morality, and undermined family values by supporting abortion and gay rights. They have also been highly critical of the media, the scientific establishment, and "activist courts" for questioning their beliefs, denigrating their values, and promoting unacceptable "alternative lifestyles."[9] Seculars have likewise demonized the viewpoints and leaders of the Religious Right, and its apparent political and policy successes have led seculars to take action to counter what some have termed the "medieval" policies of the "American Taliban."[10] These mutual misperceptions may in reality exaggerate the actual positions of both seculars and religious activists on a range of issues, but demonizing one's opponents is a proven tool for political mobilization.

## DEFINING AND MEASURING RELIGION AND SECULARISM

Before assessing the emerging challenges to the Religious Right, we must first define the people to be described as "seculars." Categorizing people according to religious beliefs (or lack thereof) is a nontrivial problem for social scientists, especially in a country as religiously diverse as the United States. The first mass surveys, such as the Gallup poll and the earlier versions of the American National Election Studies (ANES), used simple categories (Protestant, Catholic, Jew, Other, None) with which respondents were asked to self-identify. But such broad categories ignored the considerable denominational or theological variation within these groupings, particularly the divisions between mainline Protestants and evangelicals. "Evangelical" is itself a broad category, originally referring to the pietistic or Anabaptist churches that emerged from the Reformation, but now including a number of nondenominational, community, or "Christian" churches, as well as some Catholics and members of historic mainline denominations. Evangelicals are also distinct in theology and worship practices from fundamentalists, charismatics, and Pentecostals, and in the United States all such groupings of conservative Christians are further divided by race.[11]

Membership data has also been used to document Americans' religious affiliations. But such data can be problematic as well, since the religious groups who supply these data may define membership very differently. Does it require attendance? Contributing (even tithing)? Subscribing to particular beliefs? The age at which children can be considered full members also varies significantly among religions. The various denominations have different resources and standards for record keeping, and of course may also have incentives to exaggerate the size of their membership. If we can assume that these factors change little over time within religious groupings, membership studies can be useful as a means of categorizing trends in religious affiliation (rapid growth among Mormons and evangelicals, declines among mainline Protestants). Both membership and survey data suggest a growing number of Americans with no religious affiliation.[12]

But membership alone is less useful as a predictor of political attitudes or behavior. To supplement indicators of "belonging" based on religious affiliation, survey researchers in the 1980s began to add questions concerning specific beliefs: whether people considered themselves to be "born again," whether the Bible was the literal Word of God, whether people believed in God or Heaven or the devil. But it is not easy to translate arcane theological concepts into understandable survey-research questions or response options. Further, sociological studies of religion have found that many people sitting in the pews are unaware of, unsure about, or actively opposed to the official beliefs of that denomination. A recent study found that atheists were in fact considerably better informed about religion than church members.[13]

Church attendance may fulfill many social and psychological needs, or constitute an important aspect of family or community life, or reinforce ethnic identity. But it need not imply commitment to any or all of the beliefs espoused by that church's official creed. Thus many Roman Catholics may regularly attend weekly Mass, but contrary to official Church teachings, they may support abortion rights, the death penalty, or the ordination of women, and accept divorce or gay marriage. And regardless of the Apostles' Creed they recite every Sunday, many mainline Protestants (and their clergy) question core Christian doctrines such as the virgin birth, the Resurrection, or eternal life. Studies of the clergy have also found considerable variation within denominations as to whether assenting to a particular creed or theology is required for either clergy or laity.[14]

Membership data and opinion surveys have been of limited help in explaining politics and policy outcomes. Exactly how are religious affiliation, involvement, and particular beliefs linked to political mobilization or policy preferences? How much influence do clergy have on the people in the pews? Does involvement in a particular faith community change people's religious or political views? In the absence of good data pertaining to such questions, it was all too easy to conclude that, unlike in most European democracies, religion (defined as group membership or self-identification) had little political impact in the United States.[15]

Much of this changed, however, when groups that became known as the Religious Right became increasingly active in politics. After the failures of campaigns against Prohibition and the teaching of evolution in the 1930s, most conservative Christians kept their focus on concepts central to evangelical and fundamentalist religious traditions: individual piety and saving souls. Their reentrance into political activism, their growing numbers, and their increasing political influence have been well documented: the Cold War, the advent of direct mail, televangelism, the campaign against the Equal Rights Amendment (ERA), and the *Roe v. Wade* decision all contributed to an expanding public role for defenders of traditional Christian views. By the 1980s groups affiliated with the Religious Right included many conservative Roman Catholics and Orthodox Jews, as well as traditionalists within mainline Protestant denominations, and constituted a significant proportion of Republican Party voters, candidates, officeholders, and court appointees.

Intrigued by these developments, political scientists have developed new methods and measures to help explain them. The "old" religious analysis was based on belonging; the "new" religious analysis is based more on indicators of believing and behaving. ANES categories for religious group membership have been greatly expanded since 1980, and many new questions were added about religious involvement and personal beliefs in the ANES and the General Social Survey (GSS) as well. Survey groups such as Gallup and the Pew Forum on Religion and Public Life fielded new and more comprehensive surveys. Detailed community and case studies were undertaken of congregations as political as well as religious communities. Scholars documented geographical variation in religious involvement across regions and states, such as the well-known Red state/Blue state divide. Activities of the Religious Right in Congress, at Republican Party conventions and platform meetings, and in elections have received thoughtful scholarly attention. The Religion and Politics section became one of the largest within the American Political Science Association.[16]

This process is ongoing. Recently added ANES survey questions on individual piety (church attendance, being "born again") may have given undue weight to evangelical and fundamentalist traditions. By introducing new questions in both pilot studies and national election surveys, political scientists were able to document a "Religious Left" in 2006 and 2008 with very different beliefs and voting patterns than the Religious Right. In other words, the answers one gets depend to a considerable extent on the questions being asked about religion.[17]

However, the new focus on religion's political role, and new measures of religious beliefs and behaviors, have paid too little attention to seculars. Several studies have noted recent declines in church attendance and the increase in Americans with no religious ties.[18] But the reasons for these trends, and their political and policy implications, merit further examination. The central argument of this book is that seculars not only constitute a fast-growing section of the American electorate but have also become much more politically active in several arenas of power, and are mounting a major challenge to the Religious Right.

## WHO ARE THE SECULARS?

Any estimate of the number of "seculars" is dependent on the definitions used. Based on a battery of questions on religion, morality, and social issues, Bolce and De Maio classified the American electorate as 19 percent traditionalists, 69 percent moderates, and 12 percent seculars. They defined seculars as those who rejected scriptural authority, had no religious affiliation, never attended church or prayed, and said religion provided no guidance for daily life.[19] The 2004 Pew National Survey of Religion and Politics classified 16 percent of the U.S. population as unaffiliated, and subdivided this group into unaffiliated believers (5 percent), seculars

(8 percent), and atheists or agnostics (3 percent). Based on the Pew criteria, the proportion of people with "no religion" in several states as of 2000 was even higher: Alaska, 29 percent; Washington, 25 percent; Vermont, 22 percent; Colorado and Oregon, 21 percent. And in 2004, 14 percent of Democratic National Convention delegates were classified as unaffiliated—more than any other category except for less observant Catholics (16 percent) or mainline Protestants (15 percent).[20]

This book will use "secular" as an umbrella term to describe four somewhat distinct groups of individuals. The first group consists of atheists who actively deny the existence of any kind of God or Supreme Being. The second (and considerably larger) group consists of agnostics. In the tradition of the philosophers Immanuel Kant and David Hume, agnostics argue that key religious concepts such as the existence of the deity, the afterlife, or the soul cannot be examined by means of empirical observation or the tools of the scientific method, so there is no way to determine whether God exists.

The third group consists of people with no religious affiliation whatsoever. In national polls, they answer "none" when asked if they are identified with, or a member of, any religious group. Many of these may be atheists or agnostics, but as we shall see, the unaffiliated category also includes people who do exhibit some religious beliefs or behaviors. And the fourth group consists of people who may claim some nominal identification with a particular religious tradition, but attest that they "never" attend religious services (some surveys allow for ceremonial exceptions such as weddings or funerals).

These four categories are certainly not mutually exclusive. Many people who attend services regularly (perhaps for social, family, or political reasons) do not actually subscribe to the beliefs of that particular congregation or denomination. And undoubtedly many people who object to organized religion, and choose never to attend religious services, may yet have strong religious beliefs or spiritual orientations. Data from the 2008 Pew survey describes the religious beliefs and practices of the people they classified as unaffiliated (table 1.1). While most seldom or never attend religious services, a substantial minority report that they do believe in God, engage in prayer, or consider religion to be important in their lives. But their views of scriptures are decidedly secular, with 64 percent agreeing that the Bible was written by men and is not the Word of God. In response to a specific question about belief in God on the Pew survey, 11 percent agreed with the agnostic position "unsure if God exists" and 9 percent agreed with atheist position that "God does not exist."

Measurement issues further complicate the assessment of religious beliefs (or lack thereof). People may reject the somewhat pejorative labels atheist or agnostic even if those terms would appear to describe them.

Table 1.1  Religious Beliefs and Practices among the Unaffiliated

|  |  | Percent of Unaffiliated |
|---|---|---|
| Do you believe in God or a universal spirit? | | |
| | Believe in God; absolutely certain | 36 |
| | Believe in God; fairly certain | 24 |
| | Believe in God; not too certain/unsure | 10 |
| | Do not believe in God | 22 |
| | Don't know/refused/other | 8 |
| How important is religion in your life? | | |
| | Very important | 16 |
| | Somewhat important | 25 |
| | Not too/not at all important | 57 |
| | Don't know/refused | 2 |
| Frequency of attendance at religious services | | |
| | Once a week or more | 5 |
| | Once or twice a month | 5 |
| | A few times a year | 17 |
| | Seldom | 35 |
| | Never | 37 |
| Frequency of prayer | | |
| | Daily | 22 |
| | Weekly | 13 |
| | Monthly | 7 |
| | Seldom | 24 |
| | Never | 32 |
| Interpretation of the Bible | | |
| | Word of God, literally true word for word | 11 |
| | Word of God, but not literally true | 14 |
| | Book written by men, not the word of God | 64 |
| | Don't know/other | 10 |

Source: Pew Forum on Religion and Public Life, 2008 U.S. Religious Landscape Survey, based on the 16 percent of Americans who say they have no ties to any religious group.

Respondents may also tell a pollster that they believe in God, or think religion is important, because that is what they think they "ought" to say. It is thus a daunting task for social scientists to sort out what people do (or don't) "really" believe; indeed, many of us wrestle with these profound questions throughout our lives. A more reliable strategy may therefore be to focus on people's reported behavior: Do they identify as a member of a religious group? Contribute money to religious organizations? How often do they attend services? According to one recent analysis, the measures of believing and behaving in the 2004 Pew survey all reflect the same underlying factor, so church attendance (or lack thereof) is as good a proxy as any for distinguishing seculars from the religious.[21]

Yet behavioral measures are far from perfect either. Self-reports of church attendance (like self-reports of voting) are almost certainly exaggerated because of the social-desirability factor. However, considerable research in political science has found church attendance to be a powerful predictor of political attitudes and behavior, even within particular denominations.[22] Behavioral measures are also reasonably consistent over time and across different surveys, while assessments of particular beliefs are subject to the vagaries of question wording and the difficulties of translating abstract theological concepts into straightforward survey questions. As chapter 2 will show, trends over time in indicators of both believing and belonging point to increases in secularism.

In order to assess the political impact of such trends, the empirical analysis in chapter 3 will define seculars in terms of low frequency of church attendance as well as lack of interest in religion. Combined indicators of beliefs and behavior will also be used to describe religious traditionalists and moderates. As we shall see, seculars and the religiously involved differ considerably in their political views, stands on issues, and voting choices. They also have strongly polarized perceptions of each other. Further, this book is focused on the political role of organizations and strategies to address the practical difficulties of organizing the unaffiliated. A behavioral measure based on frequency of church attendance is therefore appropriate, and more theoretically useful for these purposes, than indicators of specific beliefs or attitudes might be.

## ORGANIZATIONAL CHALLENGES AND MORALITY POLITICS

Organized opinions bear far more political weight than those of isolated individuals. E. E. Schattschneider argued that many interests were "organized out" of American politics, and noted the strong class bias of associations; he estimated that "90 percent of the people cannot get into the pressure system."[23] The American political system was deliberately designed to include counter-majoritarian institutions (the Senate, courts, the Electoral College) that could outweigh the preferences of the mass public. The House of Representatives may be popularly elected, but powerful and well-funded lobbyists hold considerable sway over legislation. Even in states with direct democracy, interest groups and money strongly influence the outcomes of initiatives and referenda.[24] Reformers have struggled for years to limit the influence of money and of business interests over politics and elections.

Two major perspectives have been developed to explain the development of organizations. The economic or rational-choice approach emphasizes the relative costs and benefits of organization. Costs include time, money, and opportunity (time or money devoted to one purpose cannot be used for another). Of course, wealthier individuals can more easily bear the financial costs of organizational involvement. Another major challenge is the free-rider problem: why should a rational individual contribute time or money to a worthy goal if others are likely to do so? This is especially evident in the case of a public good such as public radio or television. Despite their endless fund-raising appeals, only about a third of listeners or viewers actually contribute; most assume the broadcasts will continue based on others' support, government or foundation funding, or business underwriting.[25]

Viable organizations must therefore find ways to overcome the free-rider problem. One way is to provide selective benefits just to members. National Rifle Association (NRA) members may or may not accept that group's efforts to block all gun regulations, but NRA membership also includes reduced costs for ammunition, time at rifle ranges, and children's programs (Little Eddie gun safety classes). Membership in the American Medical Association or the American Political Science Association includes journal subscriptions. The free-rider problem is also less likely if a group is small enough that shirkers can be readily identified and persuaded to pay up through social pressure or legal means. It is thus far easier to organize well-defined industry groups (manufacturers, energy producers) than customers or shareholders.[26]

Labor unions must also address the free-rider problem. They are far weaker in the twenty-two states with right-to-work laws, where workers in a union shop are not obligated to pay union dues. The union position is that since everyone in a union benefits from higher wages and job security, everyone should pay dues; union opponents claim that such "forced" membership violates individual rights to freedom of association. The Religious Right, because of its support for vouchers and charter schools, has supported right-to-work laws and other efforts to limit the influence of teachers' unions.[27]

Other costs of organization include identifying and communicating with members. The Internet may have reduced the need to pay for phone lines or postage, but website design and maintenance still cost money. Someone must locate and update e-mail addresses, or persuade people to contact a website (perhaps by offering "free" products or entry in a sweepstakes). This is a major advantage of organized religion; it is far easier to contact church members, to provide them with information on candidates or issues, and to try to direct their vote choices. These messages may come from the pulpit, from other church members, or from appearances by candidates at worship services or other church events. Naturally, churches and synagogues experience free-rider problems as well when it comes to fund-raising. They may therefore publicize lists of people who pledge or tithe, and try to use social pressure to convince all other attendees to contribute. The psychological or social benefits of group involvement may persuade some individuals to join or contribute. However, economic perspectives on the costs of organization cannot explain why some people *do* support public radio, or join public-interest groups like Common Cause, the League of Women Voters, environmental organizations—or churches.

An alternative to cost/benefit theories of organization is provided by the concept of a morality policy cycle based on threats to fundamental values.[28] In a democracy, citizens and elected officials are usually in agreement on these values. But a "shock" to this system, such as the Supreme Court's 1973 *Roe v. Wade* decision on abortion, may represent such a challenge to core beliefs that individuals have a strong motivation to respond, regardless of the costs in money, time, or opportunity. The grassroots right-to-life groups that sprang up after *Roe v. Wade* expected no financial gains or selective benefits from such involvement, but their members were deeply concerned that their religious beliefs, or concepts of family and motherhood, were threatened by legalization of abortion.[29] Since core values are at stake, compromise or incremental change is not a viable option as is usually the case with economic or regulatory policy. Intense conflict over morality issues may then result until a new consensus is reached.

The morality-politics cycle provides a useful perspective on the political development of the Religious Right. Social changes in American society and the political upheavals of the 1960s led to policy changes threatening to traditional religious values: the Equal Rights Amendment, the legalization of abortion, Supreme Court decisions limiting religious expression and local autonomy in public schools. The growth of national media (especially television) and the Civil Rights Act of 1964 brought the increasing secular values of the wider society into direct conflict with traditional congregations in the South and rural areas. Such "threats" to deeply held values became the focus of televangelism and fund-raising appeals, and evangelical preachers ranging from Oral Roberts to Billy Graham to Jerry Falwell bemoaned declining morality and rising rates of divorce, crime, and drug use.

Despite the rhetorical skills of such preachers, the growth of the Religious Right into a serious political force was greatly facilitated by its emerging organizational infrastructure. Evangelical and fundamentalist churches had already borne some of the costs of organizing to address threats to fundamental values. But evangelical churches had historically been small, located in the South and/or in rural areas, and divided among many different denominations (and divided by race as well). The advent of direct mail and televangelism in the 1960s, and the creation of Christian broadcast networks in the 1970s, greatly facilitated communication and fund-raising among these dispersed churches. Targeted appeals could be sent by computerized direct-mailing techniques, and millions of dollars were raised by these methods.[30] The emergence of megachurches, with thousands of members, also provided an organizational basis for promulgating conservative religious views, and produced leaders highly skilled in fund-raising and media management.[31] When issues such as abortion and the Equal Rights Amendment burst on the scene in the 1970s, opponents of these initiatives found an organizational base already in place. To better coordinate the mobilization of religious traditionalists, the Moral Majority was founded by Jerry Falwell in 1978. Its successor organizations (the Christian Coalition, Focus on the Family) likewise cultivated strong ties to local churches and their leaders, although they expanded their efforts beyond the fundamentalist church base of the Moral Majority.[32]

Conservative and Republican political elites soon realized that conservative Christians were a potential constituency with very low voting rates, but one likely to support much of their agenda. The Religious Right also found sympathetic allies within the Reagan campaign and the Republican Party, and began a concerted effort to recruit candidates, party officials, and judicial appointees who shared their views. Its supporters came to dominate the party organization in many states.[33] Further, the Republican Party has in recent years been far more cohesive than the Democrats in terms of both legislative voting and organizational structure.

Leadership is important for both the cost/benefit and morality-policy approaches to organizational development. Policy "entrepreneurs" can also use their charisma, media savvy, expertise, or personal wealth to reduce some of the costs of organization. Many leaders of the Religious Right, including Jerry Falwell (Moral Majority), Dr. James Dobson (Focus on the Family), Pat Robertson and Ralph Reed (Christian Coalition), and Chuck Colson (Prison Fellowship), developed formidable skills in communication, fund-raising, and organization building, and successfully convinced many others to support their causes. Leaders of organizations can highlight potential threats to deeply held values in order to persuade people to join their movement, contribute, or vote.[34] Thus Religious Right leaders such James Dobson and Don Willmon emphasize threats to the "traditional family," and Roman Catholic bishops articulate the risks that legalization of abortion poses to the church and to family life. Some wealthy individuals, such as the Koch brothers, have been less visible but have contributed generously to organizations and institutions supportive of the Religious Right. A major problem, however, is that if the leader, founder, or funder dies or is caught up in scandal, the organization may not survive.

The Religious Right thus had had considerable organizational advantages over seculars or the Religious Left. The "unaffiliated" by definition are harder to contact, mobilize, or solicit for contributions, and historically have been less likely to vote. But the morality-policy cycle helps to explain why seculars in recent years have begun to mobilize against increased religious influence over politics and public policy. In response to perceived threats to secular values such as individual freedom, church/state separation, women's rights, and gay rights, seculars have found ways to overcome the costs of organization and to mount effective challenges to the Religious Right. As chapter 3 will show, antipathy to Christian fundamentalism has been a significant spur to greater political involvement.

Chapters 5 and 6 will document secular organizational strategies in greater detail. First of all, atheists, agnostics, and free thinkers have established their own organizations, including umbrella organizations to coordinate their efforts. Second, seculars found some important allies, such as the American Civil Liberties Union and Americans United for Separation of Church and State. Such groups have sought to uphold religious freedom and practice (the free exercise clause of the First Amendment), but have also been fierce opponents of anything they consider to be an establishment of religion. Alliances with people holding liberal or moderate religious views have also been forged to combat specific challenges such as state initiatives to ban gay marriage or abortion.

Third, secular and civil-liberties groups have made effective use of legal strategies to challenge any comingling of church and state. And they have found considerable sympathy for their cause in the courts, including the U.S. Supreme Court, in a series of landmark decisions involving prayer in public schools, public financing of parochial schools, and the teaching of evolution. In fact, these successes have prompted strenuous efforts by the Religious Right to mount their own legal challenges and to recruit judges more sympathetic to traditional religious views.

Fourth, much of the media and the entertainment industry have a decidedly secular perspective. Newspaper reporters and television commentators tend to be less religious than the general population and skeptical of traditional religion. The media in its watchdog role is quick to cover any sex scandals or financial improprieties involving religious leaders (and there has been no shortage of these on the Religious Right in recent years). Sex, violence, gambling, and pornography are big business; the entertainment industry has strenuously fought against any forms of censorship of these by conservative religious groups, and has the legal resources and political clout to do so. And although right-wing radio and television (Rush Limbaugh, Fox News) still dominate the airwaves,[35] their perspectives have faced challenges from popular liberal media personalities such as Jon Stewart and Ellen DeGeneres.

Fifth, scientists have become important advocates for secular rather than religious viewpoints. As individuals, scientists tend to be more secular than religious, and highly skeptical of many religious claims. The scientific community has also provided expert evidence and testimony, in Congress and before the courts, to counter efforts by the Religious Right to introduce creationism into the public schools or traditional sexual morality into public policy. Scientific organizations have emerged to lobby for public policies based on science rather than ideology, religion, or business profits.

Sixth, the Democratic Party has become increasingly secular. To be sure, Democrats confront their own challenges in trying to build coalitions out of highly diverse constituencies. After the 2004 electoral loss, many Democrats considered strategies to counter Republican claims that they were antireligion, and to try to appeal to Democrats or independents who still had strong religious ties. But because of the presence of so many seculars among Democratic voters, campaign activists, and convention delegates, party platforms and campaign strategies usually avoid overt support for religious perspectives.[36] The Democratic Party thus provides another organizational base for seculars to counter the Religious Right's influence over the Republican Party.

Last but by no means least, the Internet is transforming the mobilization of interests. Websites, blogs, and social networking tools have all facilitated communication and fund-raising, and have thus reduced many of the costs of organization. Of course, religious groups are learning to use the Internet effectively as well, and the political impact of the Internet has yet to be determined.[37] But the Internet and social networking are especially appealing to the young and well educated, who also tend to be the most secular groups in American society. So the further expansion of the Internet into election campaigns and party politics is likely to benefit secular rather than traditional religious perspectives.

The organizational bases of secularism and its allies will be explored in more detail in chapter 5. But an indication of the increasing importance of secular organizations is that the Religious Right has been forced to respond to their challenges, by setting up its own media networks and Internet sites, and by establishing conservative legal foundations to counter the courts and the ACLU. The Religious Right has also established quasi-scientific "think tanks" to provide support for religious perspectives on homosexuality, intelligent design, and climate change, or, at minimum, to challenge scientific orthodoxy on these issues. Of course, the secular groups and their allies are quite diverse and must deal with their own internal conflicts over leadership, strategy, and issue priorities. But the

Religious Right is facing many of the same organizational tensions. Future outcomes may thus depend on which side is better able to organize its interests into politics and policy.

## PLAN OF THE BOOK

This chapter has described "seculars" at both the individual and organizational level. In chapter 2, survey questions asked consistently over time will be used to assess trends in religious beliefs, church involvement, and tolerance of atheists. Chapter 2 will consider some reasons why secular perspectives have been increasing in the United States since the 1970s and why younger, well-educated Americans are far more secular than their parents or grandparents in terms of religious beliefs, behavior, and the importance they attach to religion.

Chapter 3 will contrast the attitudes, political involvement, and voting behavior of seculars with those who identify strongly with organized religion (including both religious moderates and traditionalists). As we shall see, while church attendance was a strong predictor of both voting behavior and conservative views on social issues in the 1980s and 1990s, that relationship has weakened considerably since 2000. Although seculars are less likely to be strong partisans or involved in other organizations, their levels of political interest and activism have increased markedly since the 1980s, due in part to their negative views of "Christian fundamentalists." These results point to the growing political influence of seculars, not only within the Democratic Party, but also in the American electorate.

Chapter 4 turns to questions with both theoretical and political consequences: why have political elites become considerably more polarized on many political and social issues, and how aware is the general public of differences between parties or candidates? Political elites can be motivated to emphasize issue differences because of their effect on voter turnout. Chapter 4 will compare perceptions of party and candidate positions on abortion and other issues in 2004 in states with different religious environments and different levels of electoral competition. Frequent church attendees (regardless of denomination) are more likely to be aware of candidate or party stands on "values" issues such as abortion, especially in states with higher proportions of seculars. But seculars are more likely to perceive party and candidate differences across a broad range of issues, a possible explanation for their increasing political activism.

Chapter 5 moves from the individual to the social and organizational level in order to describe some of the major organizations that have emerged to defend secular values, the strategies they have used to do so, and the role of the media (both old and new). Seculars have also developed crucial alliances with civil libertarians, the scientific community, the Democratic Party, the Religious Left, and minority groups including feminists, Jews, and gays and lesbians. I will also discuss recent countermobilization efforts by the Religious Right to oppose these secular strategies and alliances.

Chapter 6 will examine three recent cases where seculars and the Religious Right have come into direct conflict, at the polls, in the courts, or in the policy arena, particularly in the states. These include the battle over Proposition 8 (banning gay marriage) in California in 2008, recent attempts in South Dakota to ban almost all abortions, and challenges to the teaching of evolution in the public schools of Dover, Pennsylvania. The morality-policy cycle and the organizational perspectives developed in chapter 5 will be used to explain the outcomes of these instances of countervailing power.

Chapter 7 will consider future prospects as both seculars and the Religious Right continue to battle for political influence, policy outcomes, and the hearts and minds of Americans. In the short run, the Religious Right still has considerable organizational advantages, and retains influence within the Republican Party, the courts, Congress, and many state legislatures. Democratic strategists must somehow appeal to the party's activist secular supporters as well as to the many Democratic and independent voters who retain strong ties to organized religion or to traditional social values. However, the Religious Right is also confronting serious internal strains, and the emerging Tea Party movement is causing sharp divisions among Republicans. Electoral and policy outcomes will continue to reflect the organizational balance of power.

In summary, this book will investigate the social and political implications of declining church attendance and increasingly secular views on religion and social values. Long-run demographic trends tend to favor seculars, who also benefit from their alliances with science, media, and many on the Religious Left. Despite the organizational advantages of the Religious Right, seculars have become much more politically involved and influential in several areas of American society. The results of the 2010 elections notwithstanding, seculars are likely to play an even larger political role in the future. Their political mobilization, much of it in opposition to the Religious Right, therefore merits serious consideration.

What would a more secular America be like? Many on the Religious Right foresee disastrous outcomes. Francis Schaeffer's influential 1984 book *Bad News for Modern Man* blamed "secular humanists" for a variety of social ills: divorce, rampant sexuality outside the bonds of marriage, teen pregnancy, the AIDS epidemic, crime, violence, failing schools. God and the promise of an afterlife (or eternal damnation) provide the moral basis of society, and if faith in these declines, immorality can only increase.[38] Leaders of the Religious Right regularly invoke threats of family breakdown and immoral behavior (including homosexuality) in order to mobilize the faithful and to advocate morally restrictive policies.

However, this book argues for a more optimistic conclusion. In a more secular society, values will still be important for politics, but a different set of values than those espoused by the Religious Right. Church attendance may continue to decline, but other forms of social capital are emerging from use of the Internet and social networking. Religious commitment may still encourage both civic and political involvement, but the increased political activism of seculars and their allies will help to maintain the separation of church and state that has been a hallmark of American democracy and a guarantor of individual freedom.

# 2

✣

# Explaining the Growth in Seculars in the United States

This chapter will consider trends since the 1970s in American religious involvement and beliefs. Most of the analysis will be based on data from the General Social Survey (GSS) administered by the National Opinion Research Center at the University of Chicago. The GSS collects information on demographics and opinions about a series of social and political issues, based on face-to-face interviews with randomly selected national samples of noninstitutionalized U.S. adults. Since its initiation in 1972, most of the core GSS questions have remained the same, which makes it possible to track changes in U.S. public opinion over time.

Based on a number of these indicators, secular perspectives have increased in the United States since the 1970s. Church attendance is down, and many more people claim that they have no religious affiliation or that religion is not important in their lives. Although most Americans still say they pray regularly and believe in God, tolerance for atheists and expressions of atheist viewpoints has increased. Many more Americans now support the Supreme Court's ban on school prayer and Bible reading than when the *Engel v. Vitale* decision was first announced in 1963. Public confidence in organized religion has fallen markedly. Attitudes on several controversial social issues (premarital sex, sex education in the schools, equality for women, gay marriage) have also moved in a more liberal direction. However, attitudes toward abortion and toward evolution have changed very little since the 1980s. Less religious and more liberal viewpoints are considerably more prevalent among younger Americans born in more recent decades.

Secular thought is hardly a new phenomenon; at least a few "free thinkers" have been found throughout American history. Several prominent social theorists have argued that secularization is an inevitable component of modernity, science, industrialization, and economic development. Although secular attitudes and low levels of church attendance have long been widespread in Western Europe, high levels of religiosity have persisted in the United States until recently. What has changed, and why? This chapter will use GSS data to consider social and demographic explanations for recent increases in secular beliefs and religious involvement, specifically trends in education, racial and ethnic diversity, and income. Chapter 3 will turn to American National Election Studies (ANES) data to explore differences between seculars and religious Americans in public opinion, partisanship, and political involvement.

## A BRIEF HISTORY OF SECULAR THOUGHT

Medieval and early modern Europe was almost completely dominated by religious worldviews.[1] These were predominantly Christian and (until the Reformation) Roman Catholic, although remnants of pagan practices persisted in some remote areas. Scholarship and intellectual life were limited to monasteries and convents. During the Reformation Martin Luther, John Knox, John Calvin, and their followers mounted a major challenge to the Roman Catholic Church's teachings, hierarchical church structure, and political dominance, based to a considerable extent on their interpretations of original Christian precepts and practices. The Reformation and Counter-Reformation produced centuries of bloody warfare and led to the Inquisition, but challenges to the Vatican and to Catholic dogma garnered significant popular and political support in many countries.

Even before the Reformation, scholars in monastery libraries had begun to read and translate the writings of Greek, Roman, and Muslim scientists and philosophers. This work gained circulation as trading networks expanded throughout Europe and the first universities were established. The Renaissance, however, set in motion factors that would ultimately produce serious intellectual and social resistance to a religious worldview and to Christianity itself. The beginnings of modern science, based on empirical observation, experimentation, and mathematics, challenged many traditional Christian precepts and quickly drew the enmity of the Vatican. The prototypical confrontation between religion and science was the challenge to the biblical Eurocentric view of the universe posed by the work of the astronomers Kepler, Copernicus, and Galileo, later supported by the mathematics of Newton and Leibniz. The Vatican forced Galileo to recant and placed him under house arrest in 1633, but the genie was out of the bottle, and astronomy and natural science continued to challenge religious viewpoints. By the late twentieth century the Vatican had largely made its peace with the scientific worldview. In 1992 it formally admitted that Galileo was right after all when it finally lifted its Edict of Inquisition against him and installed a statue of Galileo on its grounds.[2] Ironically, opposition to scientific claims concerning evolution and climate change is now led by evangelical Protestants, not Catholics.

Medieval theologians and philosophers had tried to construct proofs for the existence of God, but by the Renaissance, philosophy had diverged from theology. Blaise Pascal (1623–1662) famously described faith as a wager, a hedge against an unknown and unknowable future. David Hume (1711–1776) argued convincingly that since philosophy could not prove the existence of God, it should no longer try to do so.[3] There might have been a Prime Mover or Creator, but a loving and merciful God who responded to prayers, rewarded the just, and intervened in human history appeared to be increasingly implausible, as Voltaire (1694–1778) and other European intellectuals so strenuously argued after the devastating earthquake in Lisbon in 1755.[4] Religious perspectives on this natural disaster were further discredited when the Jesuits opposed the reconstruction of Lisbon and argued that the earthquake was a just punishment for the sins of its inhabitants. Even Portuguese Catholics could not accept such reasoning, and the Jesuits were expelled from that country in 1758.[5]

A secular worldview thus has a long intellectual tradition in the West. Secular rather than religious perspectives came to dominate in the arts, science, psychiatry, literature, and popular culture.[6] Social theorists such as Max Weber, Friedrich Nietzsche, Emile Durkheim, and Sigmund Freud all argued that religion would decline in importance in modern industrial societies.[7] After World War II, these arguments appeared to have validity in most of Western Europe: church attendance declined, and surveys showed that fewer and fewer people subscribed to traditional religious beliefs concerning the existence of God, Heaven, or Hell. However, religion continued to play a major role in voting behavior and party alignments, and Christian Democratic parties retained widespread popular support in countries with sizable Catholic populations.[8]

The United States also has a long-standing tradition of "free thinkers" who questioned or rejected established religious views. Some early free thinkers suffered public opprobrium; Roger Williams was expelled from the Massachusetts Bay Colony, and the American Revolution pamphleteer Thomas Paine, author of both *Common Sense* and a diatribe against religion, died in penury. But some nineteenth-century critics of religion, such as Robert Ingersoll and Mark Twain, were highly popular authors and speakers.[9] By the time of the founding of the American Republic, many political philosophers, scientists, and even statesmen (including a number of the Founding Fathers) considered themselves to be deists, theists, or agnostics. Despite recent claims to the contrary, the United States was originally not defined as a "Christian nation," and the Constitution (unlike the Declaration of Independence) avoided any reference to the Creator.[10] Instead, Article 6 forbade any religious test for holding public office. The First Amendment guaranteed freedom of religion, and Congress was not allowed to provide official recognition or financial support (establishment) for any religion.

Except for a few deists or religious skeptics, nearly all Americans were identified with religious communities when French historian Alexis de Tocqueville visited the United States in 1832. He described a predominantly Protestant nation in which religion played a far more active role than in Europe.[11] But even in 1832 there were a few Jews in New York and New England, a strong Catholic presence in Maryland, and Native American religious traditions that managed to survive the brutal migrations, wholesale slaughter, and forced conversions imposed on them. Much greater religious diversity developed after the waves of nineteenth- and twentieth-century immigrations. Many native-born Protestants reacted strongly to this perceived threat, and organized political parties and government policies to limit the political influence of the growing numbers of Catholics, Jews, Asians, or Mormons. Amendments were added to many state constitutions to forbid any public financial support for parochial schools.[12]

Nineteenth-century scholarship on archaeology, linguistics, biology, geology, and church history called into question many aspects of the King James Bible and of traditional religious beliefs. By 1900 such scholarly evidence was generally accepted in universities and in the more liberal seminaries serving most mainline Protestant denominations, but it scandalized the faithful as evidence of the inroads of secularism. In response, the branch of Christianity now described as fundamentalist originated in the early twentieth century with the publication of a series of pamphlets called *The Fundamentals.* These reaffirmed traditional Christian views of the virgin birth, the Resurrection, Jesus' miracles, the literal truth of Scripture, and the imminent Second Coming of Christ. The World Christian Fundamentals Association, founded in 1919, spearheaded political opposition to the Social Gospel and to Darwin's theory of evolution.[13]

## RELIGIOUS RESURGENCE IN THE UNITED STATES

After the Scopes trial in 1925 and the repeal of Prohibition in 1933, religious conservatives largely abandoned efforts to influence public policy. Evangelicals and fundamentalists returned to their historical focus on saving souls (although in the Bible Belt strict liquor laws prevailed and evolution was seldom mentioned in biology classes).[14] As Catholic and Jewish immigrants became assimilated, religious group membership was expected to have less and less influence over Americans' attitudes or vote choices. Most American social scientists were so convinced of these trends that few questions on religious beliefs or behavior were even included in public-opinion surveys. One exception was pollster George Gallup, himself an evangelical Christian, who regularly asked Americans about their church attendance and belief in God.[15]

Even in the late twentieth century, Americans could be described as far more religious than Europeans. Except perhaps for the Irish, Americans reported the highest rates of church attendance, belief in God, the devil, Heaven and Hell, frequency of prayer, and agreement that religion provided significant answers to the problems of daily living.[16] Membership in mainline Protestant churches had declined, as did Roman Catholic numbers after Vatican II. However, membership increased in other churches, especially among Pentecostals, Jehovah's Witnesses, and the Latter-day Saints (Mormons). Roman Catholic membership stabilized because of the influx of predominately Catholic Hispanic immigrants.[17] A sizable number of nondenominational or "community" churches sprang up in the fast-growing suburbs or exurbs. These and the new megachurches tended to reflect more evangelical or fundamentalist views of Christianity, with an emphasis on biblical literalism, social conservatism, and adult "born-again" conversion experiences.[18]

Somewhat to the surprise of many social scientists, during the 1970s religion reemerged as a major factor in American politics. The resurgence of the Religious Right has been well documented as a function of opposition to taxes on religious educational institutions, the 1973 *Roe v. Wade* decision, and the Equal Rights Amendment.[19] Conservatives and Republican leaders soon realized that evangelicals and fundamentalists represented a sizable number of potential voters who could be mobilized in opposition to the liberal legacy of the 1960s. With their encouragement, groups such as the Moral Majority and the Eagle Forum emerged to support traditional viewpoints on political and social issues. Ronald Reagan actively courted the Religious Right, and the 1980 Republican Party platform (reversing previous positions) opposed both abortion and the Equal Rights Amendment.

Throughout the 1980s the Religious Right gained influence within the Republican Party, and came to dominate candidate recruitment and selection in a number of states. Reverend Pat Robertson came in a surprise second in the 1988 Republican Party caucuses in Iowa. Although their successes in Congress were limited, groups supporting the Religious Right turned their focus to state and local offices. An increasing number of religious conservatives were elected to state legislatures and school boards, where they fought to ban controversial books, opposed sex education, tried to reinstitute school prayer, and pushed for the teaching of creationism.[20] And with the election of George W. Bush in 2000, an Office of Faith-Based Initiatives was opened in the White House, and religious groups became eligible for an increasing range of government funding for social services. President Bush supported abstinence-only sex education and opposed gay marriage and most research on stem cells; he appointed proponents of those views to high-level medical and scientific positions in his administration. The Supreme Court, in its *Gonzales v. Carhart* decision in 2007, upheld a congressional ban on late-term abortions. But these actions also generated furious political opposition as well as legal challenges.[21]

## EVIDENCE OF GROWTH IN SECULAR PERSPECTIVES

Paradoxically, the expanding political role of conservative religious groups and the salience of "morality" issues (abortion, homosexuality, drug use, gaming, the status of women, extramarital sex) has been accompanied by considerable growth in secular trends. Figure 2.1 shows the in-

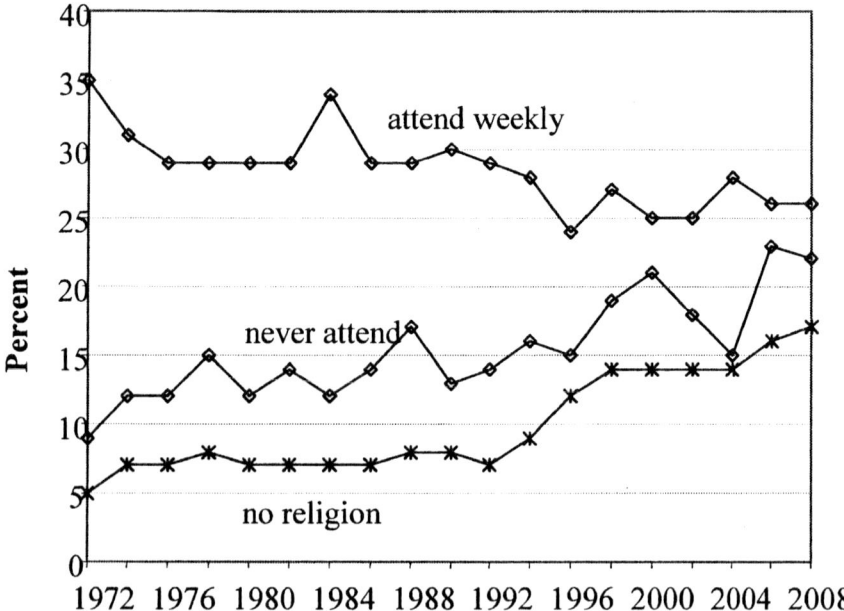

Figure 2.1. Trends in Church Attendance and Religious Nonaffiliation, 1972–2008 (GSS)

crease in the proportion of Americans who report no religious affiliation and say they never attend worship services. According to data from the General Social Survey (GSS), those with no religious ties increased from 7 percent of Americans in the 1970s to 17 percent by 2008, while those who said they never attended services grew from 13 to 21 percent.[22]

Figure 2.1 also shows that people claiming weekly attendance at religious services declined from 35 to 26 percent, although even these percentages may be inflated because of the social-desirability factor. Social pressures may also discourage people from admitting that they are atheists or agnostics. A survey conducted by *Skeptic* magazine found that a majority of self-defined atheists feared social repercussions from the workplace, community, or within the family.[23]

Gallup polls since the 1930s (figure 2.2) suggest that most Americans retain core religious beliefs in God or in life after death. This is in sharp contrast to European data from the World Values Survey, which indicate considerable declines in those beliefs even in Catholic countries (Ireland is the only exception).[24] Yet, as figure 2.2 shows, the proportion of Americans saying that religion is "very important" in their lives declined from 70 percent in 1968 to 54 percent in 2008.

Assessing trends in religious beliefs is problematic because it is not easy to translate abstract theological concepts into survey questions. The

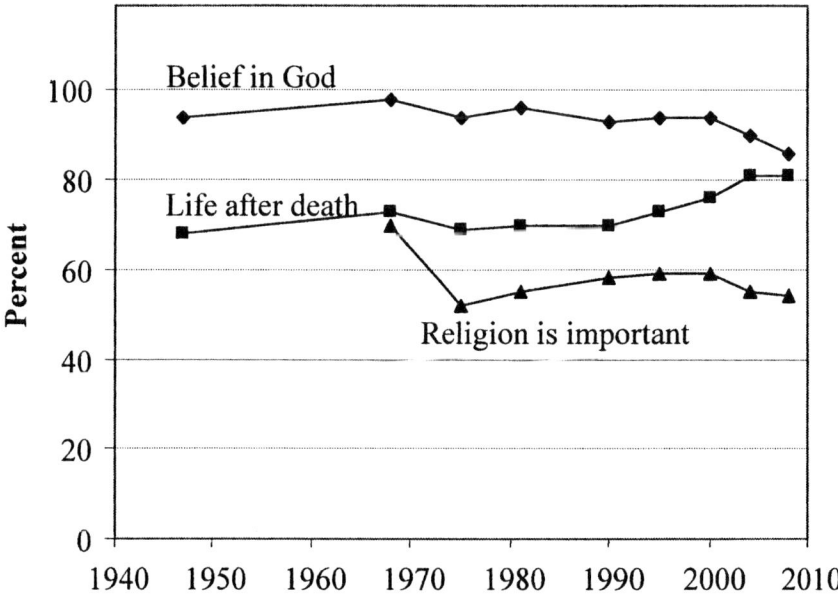

Figure 2.2. Trends in Religious Beliefs, 1940–2009 (Gallup Poll)

Gallup and World Values surveys just cited gave respondents only limited options to questions on religion: yes/no/not sure. However, since 1988 the GSS has provided respondents with a greater range of choices to express "what you believe about God." Table 2.1 shows little change in views between 1988 and 2008, with over 60 percent of respondents agreeing that "God really exists, and I have no doubts about it." But among those born after 1980, certainty of belief declined and the proportion of atheistic or agnostic responses increased. A 2010 Pew survey showed only 53 percent of Americans born since 1981 expressing faith without doubts.[25]

These trends in skepticism and nonaffiliation have been accompanied by some growth in tolerance of nonbelievers. GSS data (figure 2.3) show that in the 1970s, 37 percent of Americans would ban a book "against churches and religion" from public libraries; by 2008 only 23 percent agreed. Similar declines are seen in the percentage who would bar persons expressing such atheistic views from making a public speech or teaching in a college or university.[26]

Since the 1930s the Gallup poll has asked Americans whether they would vote for members of various marginal groups (women, blacks, Jews, Catholics) for president if a "qualified member of that group were nominated by your party." "Atheists" were added to the Gallup list in 1958, and as figure 2.4 shows, willingness to vote for an atheist increased from only 18 percent in 1958 to 49 percent in 1999. However, support for atheists as president has consistently ranked lower than for any other marginal group in these Gallup surveys.[27] That same pattern appears in ANES surveys asking respondents to rate their feelings toward various groups using "thermometer scores" (100 equals warm or positive feel-

Table 2.1  GSS Data: Confidence in the Existence of God, 1988–2008

|   | 1988 | 1998 | 2008 | |
|---|---|---|---|---|
|   |   |   | Born before 1980 | Born after 1980 |
| 1 | 1.5% | 3.2% | 2.8% | 4.0% |
| 2 | 3.6% | 5.1% | 4.5% | 6.6% |
| 3 | 7.4% | 10.0% | 9.4% | 12.6% |
| 4 | 5.1% | 4.6% | 2.9% | 5.1% |
| 5 | 19.0% | 13.8% | 16.8% | 17.3% |
| 6 | 63.3% | 63.3% | 63.6% | 54.4% |

*GSS question*: Please look at this card and tell me which statement comes closest to expressing what you believe about God:
1. I don't believe in God.
2. I don't know whether there is a God and I don't believe there is any way to find out.
3. I don't believe in a personal God, but I do believe in a higher power of some kind.
4. I find myself believing in God some of the time, but not at others.
5. While I have doubts, I feel that I do believe in God.
6. I know God really exists and I have no doubts about it.

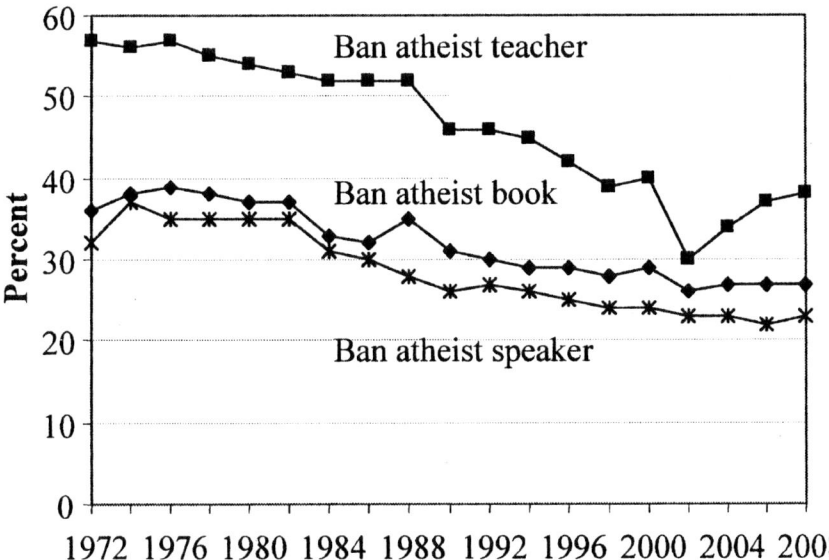

Figure 2.3. Opposition to Atheism, 1972–2008 (GSS)

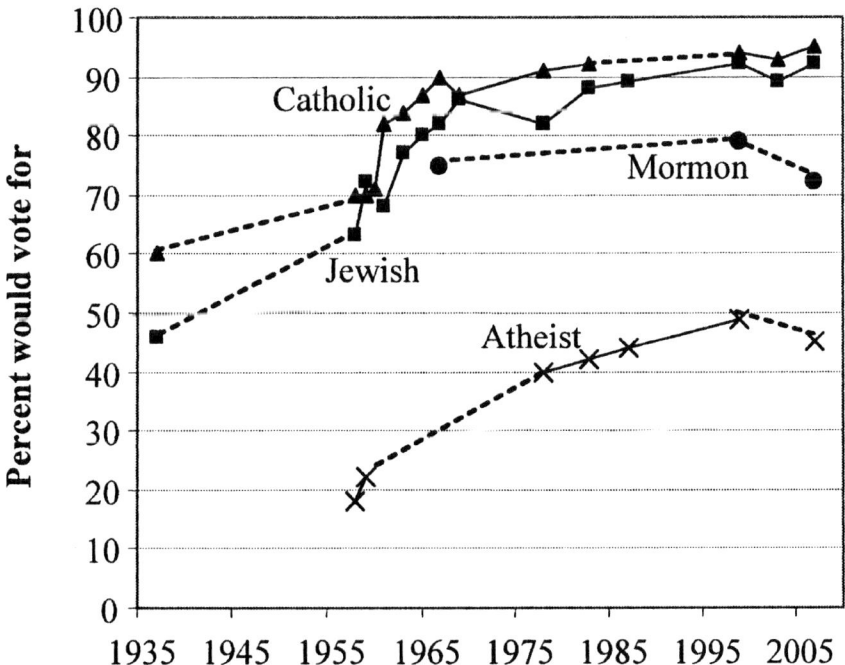

Figure 2.4. Gallup Poll: Willing to Vote for Religious Minorities

ings, 50 is neutral, 0 equals negative feelings). In 2008 atheists received the lowest average thermometer rating (40) of any groups, ranking below even other unpopular groups: illegal immigrants (average of 44), gays and lesbians (50), or Muslims (52).

Another possible indicator of increasing tolerance is a GSS question asking respondents whether they considered their own religion to be "fundamentalist, moderate, or liberal." The question wording may be somewhat problematic since it is not clear what "liberal" or "fundamentalist" religion means to the respondents, although the Merriam-Webster dictionary definition of "liberal" includes "broad-minded; not bound by authoritarianism or orthodoxy." The percentage claiming to be "fundamentalist" has been unchanged since the 1970s (about 29 percent) but the "liberal" religious perspective increased from 19 percent to 32 percent in 2008. By contrast, both the GSS and ANES surveys show that the proportion of Americans claiming to be liberal in terms of political ideology has declined over the same time period, while political conservatism has grown.[28]

## EXPLAINING THE GROWTH IN SECULARISM

Of course, most Americans still claim belief in God, sizable numbers report weekly church attendance, and the Gallup data suggest that an atheist has little chance of being elected president. But the data just presented indicate a steady increase since the 1970s in secular perspectives, religious nonaffiliation, and tolerance of atheism or viewpoints opposing religion. Are these secular trends a function of demographic and social change? How have party leaders and the media influenced public opinion? Or is secularism a reaction against the increasing prominence of conservative religious perspectives on politics and public policy?

Several demographic factors might account for these trends. First is education; the proportion of Americans with at least some college has increased steadily over the last few decades. Second is generational change; young adults tend to be less religious than their elders, and religiosity is considerably more prevalent among Americans born and socialized before World War II. Third, the United States is far more religiously and ethnically diverse today than in previous decades, and such diversity could make tolerance and moral relativism a political and social necessity. On the other hand, increased religious diversity could also be perceived as a threat to traditional Christianity and lead to political efforts to protect those beliefs.

Alternatively, these trends in public opinion may reflect changes in the cues given by political elites and the media. Politically aware citizens and strong partisans and media are especially likely to respond to such cues.[29] Especially since Watergate, American media have become increasingly skeptical of religious as well as political authority. Exposure of scandal and malfeasance by prominent officials is a central function of media in its watchdog role, and uncovering juicy scandals is also a good way to sell newspapers, generate TV audiences, and perhaps even win a Pulitzer Prize. Media coverage of religious scandals (of which there has been no shortage over the last few years) could well account for some increase in public skepticism regarding religion and religious beliefs.

Party elites can also influence public opinion. Party leaders are strongly motivated to find issues and candidates that will appeal to voters, win elections, and generate legislative majorities. The Republican Party has made effective use of "morality" issues to mobilize religious conservatives, and as "wedge" issues to attract independents and Democrats who share their views on abortion and gay rights. But these positions and the public policies supporting them have also driven seculars, skeptics, and religious liberals out of church and into the Democratic Party. Church attendance has declined much more among political liberals and moderates than conservatives, and Christian fundamentalists began to be regarded in highly negative terms only after the Religious Right became more closely identified with the Republican Party.[30] Thus political as well as demographic factors have contributed to increases in secularism. Links among secularism, parties, and public opinion will be considered in more detail in chapter 3, and the role of the media in chapter 5. The remainder of this chapter will use survey data from the General Social Survey (GSS) to evaluate how demographic and social changes have affected trends in secular viewpoints.

### Education, Age, Income, and Secular Perspectives

Religious beliefs are in many respects a function of education. As table 2.2 shows, based on 2008 GSS data, people with no more than a high-school education are considerably less likely to have doubts about God's existence and much more likely to take the Bible literally as the Word of God. They are more likely to view their own religion as fundamentalist, are much less tolerant of allowing an atheist to speak in public or teach in college, and are more willing to ban books questioning churches or religion from public libraries. By contrast, well-educated Americans are much more supportive of the Supreme Court's decision to ban prayer and Bible reading in public schools, and have less confidence in organized religion.[31] But belief in an afterlife is high regardless of education. Religious behavior, however, shows more tenuous links to education. The well educated are actually somewhat more likely to attend church weekly, and only slightly less likely to say they pray on a daily basis. The proportion claiming a strong religious affiliation also does not vary by education. Fourteen percent of those with graduate degrees claim no religious affiliation, compared with 8 to 10 percent of people with high school or less.

We would also expect religious beliefs and behavior to vary by age, in part because older Americans tend to have less education. But regardless of education, as people grow older and prepare to "meet their Maker" in death, we might also expect an increase in prayer, church attendance, and belief in God and Heaven. The American population also includes an increasing proportion of senior citizens, and their religiosity might counterbalance the more skeptical views of younger groups.

Table 2.3 shows that daily prayer, weekly church attendance, and certainty about God's existence indeed increase with age. Older Americans are more likely to describe their religious affiliation as strong, to take the Bible literally, to describe their church as fundamentalist rather than lib-

**Table 2.2  Education and Religion, 2008**

|  | Education | | | | |
| --- | --- | --- | --- | --- | --- |
|  | < HS | High school | Some college | BA/BS | Post-grad |
| No religion | 8 | 10 | 11 | 13 | 14 |
| Never attend church | 19 | 15 | 14 | 13 | 15 |
| Attend weekly | 28 | 28 | 28 | 32 | 31 |
| Bible = Word of God | 55 | 35 | 29 | 17 | 11 |
| Daily prayer | 60 | 56 | 56 | 53 | 49 |
| God exists | 73 | 66 | 65 | 54 | 48 |
| Believe in afterlife | 75 | 72 | 85 | 81 | 77 |
| Oppose school prayer ban | 72 | 63 | 58 | 44 | 36 |
| Religious fundamentalist | 42 | 31 | 29 | 19 | 16 |
| Religious liberal | 17 | 24 | 26 | 37 | 43 |
| Oppose atheist: | | | | | |
|   College teacher | 69 | 48 | 35 | 27 | 20 |
|   Library book | 55 | 31 | 21 | 15 | 8 |
|   Public speaker | 52 | 27 | 17 | 12 | 9 |
| Confidence in organized religion—% responding "a great deal" | 35 | 28 | 24 | 25 | 24 |

Source: GSS

Table 2.3  Age and Religion, 2008

| Age | 18–25 | 26–40 | 41–64 | 65+ |
|---|---|---|---|---|
| No religion | 17 | 13 | 8 | 5 |
| Never attend church | 29 | 24 | 19 | 18 |
| Attend weekly | 13 | 20 | 27 | 42 |
| Bible = Word of God | 29 | 29 | 33 | 37 |
| Daily prayer | 43 | 50 | 63 | 69 |
| God exists | 48 | 60 | 63 | 70 |
| Believe in afterlife | 79 | 80 | 81 | 79 |
| Oppose school prayer ban | 45 | 53 | 63 | 70 |
| Religious fundamentalist | 24 | 26 | 32 | 28 |
| Religious liberal | 39 | 33 | 31 | 28 |
| Oppose atheist: | | | | |
| College teacher | 35 | 38 | 52 | 72 |
| Library book | 24 | 26 | 35 | 50 |
| Public speaker | 22 | 21 | 31 | 49 |
| Confidence in organized religion—% responding "a great deal" | 29 | 25 | 29 | 39 |

Source: GSS

eral, to disapprove of the court's school-prayer decision, and to express confidence in religious leaders and institutions. They are considerably more likely to disapprove of books or public speeches critical of churches or religion, or of letting an atheist teach in college. But we see little impact of age on belief in an afterlife.

Norris and Inglehart argue that in industrial and postindustrial societies, religiosity is very much a function of income (or lack thereof). Their cross-national analysis, based on the World Values Survey, found that poorer and economically more vulnerable people are more likely to pray frequently and to say that religion is important, and they found a similar pattern in the United States based on that same survey.[32] They also report higher levels of religiosity in societies with more unequal distributions of income than in European welfare states, where generous social programs ameliorate the risks of unemployment, child rearing, or illness. However, GSS data show that with the exception of frequency of prayer, none of the other indicators of religious behavior or beliefs discussed in this chapter show much relationship with income.[33]

## Social Change and Religious Beliefs: Cohort Effects

American society has changed considerably over the last few decades, and people born in the 1970s or 1980s were socialized in a very different world than those who came of age in earlier generations. A series of Supreme Court rulings moved religious observance from the public to the private sphere; school children after 1962 were unlikely to experience daily prayer or Bible reading in public-school classrooms. The overall level of education has increased; median school years completed rose from 11.3 in 1972 to 13.4 in 2008, and the proportion of Americans with graduate degrees rose from 4 to 13 percent. Income inequality has increased, as has the minority percentage of the population.[34] As will be discussed in more detail in chapter 5, media analysis of both religious and political institutions has become more skeptical, with ample coverage given to scandals. If American society is becoming more secular, we should see evidence of such trends in a cohort analysis comparing the beliefs and practices of people born in different decades.[35]

Table 2.4 indeed shows a number of changes between the earliest cohort (those born between 1880 and 1919) and more recent ones. Weekly church attendance has declined markedly across cohorts, while the proportion of Americans with no religious affiliation has increased from 4 to 26 percent. Only 26 percent of those in recent cohorts claim a strong religious affiliation, compared with 53 percent of those born before 1920. Fewer people in recent cohorts are convinced of God's existence, regard the Bible as the Word of God, or engage in daily prayer. Support for the court's ban on school prayer has increased, as has tolerance of atheist expression in books, public speaking, or college teaching. The number of those expressing a "lot of confidence" in religious institutions has declined from 42 to 29 percent. The exception is belief in an afterlife, which has actually increased somewhat over recent decades. Many young people who have rejected traditional Judeo-Christian notions of Heaven and Hell have embraced alternative religions (Buddhism, spirituality) that emphasize doctrines such as reincarnation or communication with the deceased.[36]

What accounts for these changes across cohorts? Do they simply reflect the increase in education levels over the last few decades? Or are some of these trends likely to be attenuated as the population ages? In the United States income levels have risen since the 1970s, and the proportion living below the official poverty level has declined. But inequality in income and wealth have increased as well, and wages and family incomes have stagnated since the 1990s.[37] The relationship between income and religiosity should therefore be stronger for later rather than earlier cohorts.

Table 2.4  Religious Beliefs by Birth Cohort, 1880–1980

| Birth Cohort | 1880–1919 | 1920 | 1930 | 1940 | 1950 | 1960 | 1970 | 1980 |
|---|---|---|---|---|---|---|---|---|
| God exists | 73 | 71 | 68 | 66 | 63 | 62 | 59 | 52 |
| Life after death | 78 | 78 | 81 | 80 | 81 | 81 | 80 | 84 |
| No religion | 4 | 4 | 6 | 9 | 11 | 15 | 20 | 26 |
| Strong religion | 53 | 50 | 46 | 42 | 40 | 37 | 31 | 26 |
| Never attend | 13 | 13 | 13 | 15 | 16 | 21 | 21 | 26 |
| Attend weekly | 40 | 38 | 34 | 29 | 24 | 22 | 19 | 15 |
| Daily prayer | 75 | 70 | 63 | 61 | 57 | 54 | 48 | 44 |
| Bible = Word of God | 45 | 40 | 37 | 31 | 31 | 33 | 30 | 31 |
| Oppose school-prayer ban | 72 | 71 | 69 | 60 | 54 | 52 | 50 | 44 |
| Fundamentalist | 30 | 31 | 34 | 31 | 31 | 32 | 29 | 25 |
| Religious liberal | 23 | 23 | 23 | 25 | 26 | 26 | 31 | 35 |
| Oppose atheist: | | | | | | | | |
| College teacher | 78 | 66 | 56 | 40 | 35 | 37 | 34 | 31 |
| Library book | 55 | 42 | 36 | 25 | 24 | 26 | 22 | 31 |
| Public speaker | 55 | 39 | 31 | 21 | 20 | 22 | 19 | 24 |
| High confidence in organized religion | 42 | 34 | 31 | 26 | 24 | 23 | 25 | 29 |

Source: Pooled GSS data, 1973–2008

Changes in race and ethnicity should be also considered. African Americans and Hispanics tend to attend church more frequently and to have more conservative religious beliefs than white Americans, and the proportions of both of these groups have grown since the 1970s.[38] Since the GSS did not include a question about Hispanic background until 2000, we will only be able to compare whites and African Americans in earlier time periods.[39]

If changes in religious beliefs and practices indeed represent general social trends (cohort effects), they should be evident regardless of an individual's age, education, income, or ethnic background. Multivariate statistical techniques will be used to analyze the relative influence of age, education, income, race, and cohort effects on Americans' religious beliefs and practices. Age is measured in years, education in years of school completed, family income in quintiles of constant dollars, and cohort by birth decade.

Table 2.5  Cohort Effects, Demographics, and Religious Beliefs

| | Years included | Age | | | Education | | | Cohort | | | Income | | | Race | | | Constant | $R^2$ |
|---|---|---|---|---|---|---|---|---|---|---|---|---|---|---|---|---|---|---|
| | | b | SE | t | b | SE | t | b | SE | t | b | SE | t | b | SE | t | | |
| God exists | 1988–2008 | 0.009 | 0.000 | 2.83 | -0.099 | 0.008 | **-12.09** | -0.012 | 0.031 | 0.40 | -0.013 | 0.015 | 0.90 | 1.012 | 0.297 | **12.71** | 1.47 | 0.04 |
| No religion | 1972–2008 | 0.004 | 0.003 | 1.16 | 0.052 | 0.009 | **5.70** | 0.357 | 0.032 | **11.21** | -0.086 | 0.014 | **-6.07** | -0.589 | 0.076 | **-7.78** | -3.78 | 0.06 |
| Church attendance | 1972–2008 | 0.006 | 0.003 | **1.91** | 0.065 | 0.008 | **8.23** | -0.212 | 0.028 | **-7.61** | 0.065 | 0.011 | **5.84** | 0.951 | 0.059 | **16.02** | 8.33 | 0.04 |
| Daily prayer | 1983–2008 | 0.018 | 0.003 | **6.70** | 0.002 | 0.006 | 0.27 | -0.020 | 0.025 | -0.78 | -0.051 | 0.009 | **-5.47** | 0.777 | 0.037 | **20.83** | 17.13 | 0.07 |
| Bible = Word of God | 1984–2008 | 0.002 | 0.001 | 1.12 | -0.053 | 0.002 | **-23.16** | 0.002 | 0.013 | 0.16 | -0.023 | 0.004 | **-5.69** | 0.264 | 0.018 | **14.98** | 10.85 | 0.09 |
| Ban school prayer | 1984–2008 | 0.015 | 0.003 | **5.87** | -0.139 | 0.008 | **-17.37** | -0.034 | 0.026 | -1.29 | -0.015 | 0.011 | -1.37 | 0.690 | 0.067 | **10.25** | 3.96 | 0.06 |
| Fundamental/ liberal religion | 1972–2008 | -0.004 | 0.004 | 1.16 | 0.110 | 0.008 | **14.31** | -0.077 | 0.037 | **-2.09** | 0.075 | 0.011 | **6.74** | -1.452 | 0.062 | **-23.43** | 3.59 | 0.09 |
| Ban atheist teacher | 1972–2008 | 0.008 | 0.002 | **3.63** | -0.194 | 0.007 | **-29.61** | -0.229 | 0.022 | **-10.44** | -0.049 | 0.011 | **-4.52** | 0.272 | 0.051 | **5.31** | 13.90 | 0.12 |
| Ban atheist book | 1972–2008 | 0.009 | 0.002 | **3.61** | -0.203 | 0.007 | **-28.87** | -0.104 | 0.024 | **-4.37** | -0.109 | 0.011 | **-9.91** | 0.454 | 0.061 | **7.39** | 6.82 | 0.11 |
| Ban atheist speaker | 1972–2008 | 0.007 | 0.002 | **2.99** | -0.200 | 0.007 | **-27.99** | -0.146 | 0.024 | **-6.10** | -0.122 | 0.011 | **-10.68** | 0.379 | 0.058 | **6.55** | 7.31 | 0.12 |
| Confidence in organized religion | 1973–2008 | -0.002 | 0.001 | **-2.97** | -0.006 | 0.002 | **-3.28** | -0.052 | 0.006 | **-9.23** | 0.005 | 0.003 | 1.78 | 0.059 | 0.017 | **3.48** | 29.91 | 0.01 |

Source: GSS
Statistically significant t-values (p<.05) in bold

The cell entries in table 2.5 show the relative impact of these independent variables on the various indicators of religious beliefs and behavior.[40]

The results provide considerable evidence of statistically significant cohort effects, even with controls for age and education, for several indicators: lack of religious affiliation, frequency of church attendance, lack of confidence in organized religion. Tolerance of atheist teachers, speakers, or library books has tended to increase over time, but the effects are largely related to individuals' level of education. But we see no evidence of independent cohort effects for views of the Bible, frequency of prayer, or certainty of belief in God (although the latter question has only been included on the GSS since 1988).

Level of education is strongly related to all of these indicators of religious belief and behavior, especially to views of the Bible, religious liberalism, expressions of atheism, and acceptance of the ban on school prayer. Regardless of age or cohort, the better educated are more likely to attend church weekly. Older people (regardless of cohort or level of education) are more likely to pray frequently, to oppose expressions of atheism, and to describe their own religion as fundamentalist rather than liberal. Yet even after education, income, and age are taken into account, race remains a highly significant predictor of American religiosity. African Americans pray and attend church more frequently and hold more conservative religious beliefs. They are also less tolerant of public expressions of atheist viewpoints and more likely to oppose the Supreme Court's ruling on school prayer.

As table 2.5 indicates, higher-income people are more likely to attend church weekly and to describe their own religion as liberal. But American society has become considerably more unequal since the 1970s; has the impact of income on religiosity increased over time, as Norris and Inglehart suggest? To test this hypothesis, the effects of income, race, age, and education on church attendance and religious nonaffiliation were calculated separately for 1972–1984, 1985–1998, and 2000–2008 (cohort effects were not included because of the shorter time periods). As table 2.6 shows, the regression coefficients and t-values for income are somewhat larger since 1985 than in earlier years. In the twenty-first century higher-income people were more likely to attend church frequently and somewhat less likely to claim no religious affiliation. These results suggest that increasing income inequality could indeed have contributed to trends in religiosity, although other social changes since the 1980s might also account for these trends.

Table 2.6 shows that the coefficients for race have grown somewhat larger over time, indicating that the religious practices of whites and African Americans are increasingly divergent. Additional analysis showed that Hispanics (who can be of any race) tend to be more religiously obser-

Table 2.6  Trends in Church Attendance and No Religion

|  | Age | | | Education | | | Income | | | Race | | | Constant | $R^2$ | N |
|---|---|---|---|---|---|---|---|---|---|---|---|---|---|---|---|
|  | b | SE | t | b | SE | t | b | SE | t | b | SE | t | b | | |
| **Church attendance**** | | | | | | | | | | | | | | | |
| 1972–1984 | 0.026 | 0.002 | **15.66** | 0.044 | 0.012 | **3.67** | 0.043 | 0.020 | **2.21** | 0.645 | 0.105 | **6.15** | 1.53 | 0.03 | 13,965 |
| 1985–1998 | 0.026 | 0.002 | **14.95** | 0.073 | 0.012 | **5.89** | 0.069 | 0.015 | **4.56** | 0.915 | 0.082 | **11.21** | 0.50 | 0.04 | 17,852 |
| 2000–2008 | 0.024 | 0.002 | **10.83** | 0.080 | 0.014 | **5.95** | 0.109 | 0.020 | **5.57** | 1.354 | 0.110 | **12.31** | -0.46 | 0.05 | 10,184 |
| **No religion**** | | | | | | | | | | | | | | | |
| 1972–1984 | -0.036 | 0.003 | **-12.07** | 0.086 | 0.019 | **4.63** | -0.082 | 0.030 | **-2.72** | -0.477 | 0.140 | **-3.41** | -1.49 | 0.05 | 13,971 |
| 1985–1998 | -0.031 | 0.002 | **-12.71** | 0.057 | 0.014 | **4.10** | -0.108 | 0.022 | **-4.92** | -0.535 | 0.145 | **-3.69** | -0.89 | 0.04 | 18,024 |
| 2000–2008 | -0.028 | 0.002 | **-12.48** | 0.028 | 0.014 | **1.97** | -0.085 | 0.023 | **-3.70** | -0.704 | 0.119 | **-5.91** | 0.11 | 0.03 | 10,241 |

** OLS was used to predict church attendance; logit to predict no religion (1 = none, 0 = all others)
Source: GSS
Statistically significant t-values (p<.05) in bold

vant and conservative than non-Hispanics. Since Hispanics constitute the fastest-growing segment of the U.S. population, their growing numbers could give more weight to religious than secular views in future years. However, as will be discussed further in chapter 7, younger Hispanics are already adopting the more secular views of most other young Americans.

Norris and Inglehart claim that "levels of social and economic security in any society seem to provide the most persuasive and parsimonious explanation" for secularization, but they also note that pockets of poverty and of religiosity may persist even in wealthy nations. Nevertheless, tables 2.5 and 2.6 show only modest contributions of income to most trends in American religious beliefs and behavior; age, education, race/ethnicity, and cohort effects are considerably more important. Events such as terrorism, natural disaster, wars, or recessions may also lead to a short-term increase in insecurity and religiosity; reported church attendance in the United States did increase somewhat after the 9/11 terrorist attacks.[41]

## THE CULTURE WAR AND TRENDS IN PUBLIC OPINION

Decline in church attendance, increases in nonaffiliation, and growing doubts about religious beliefs, are certainly deeply troubling to the many Americans who remain religious and strongly committed to their churches. But also troubling to religious conservatives is evidence that they are losing the "culture war." Attitudes toward several hot-button social issues have certainly liberalized since the 1970s. The GSS does not include time-series data on views concerning homosexuality, but other surveys show a remarkable shift in Americans' attitudes. ANES data show that mean "thermometer scores" for gays and lesbians increased considerably, from the lowest rating for any group (mean of 30) in 1984 to 52 in 2008. Recent polls indicate that support for gay rights and gay marriage has also risen sharply.[42] Although thirty states continue to ban gay marriage, it is now legal in six states and the District of Columbia. When the don't ask–don't tell policy concerning gays in the military was repealed in December 2010, the decision was supported by 67 percent of Americans.[43] Despite concerted efforts, the Religious Right has not been able to counter the liberalization of American attitudes toward sexual behavior and sexual orientation.[44]

The GSS provides data on other controversial social issues. As figure 2.5 shows, Americans in 2008 were far more likely than in the 1970s to support sex education in the public schools and to agree that premarital sex was permissible. However, two other hot-button issues have proved stubbornly resistant to these liberal cultural shifts. Figure 2.4 indicates that public attitudes toward abortion have been remarkably stable since

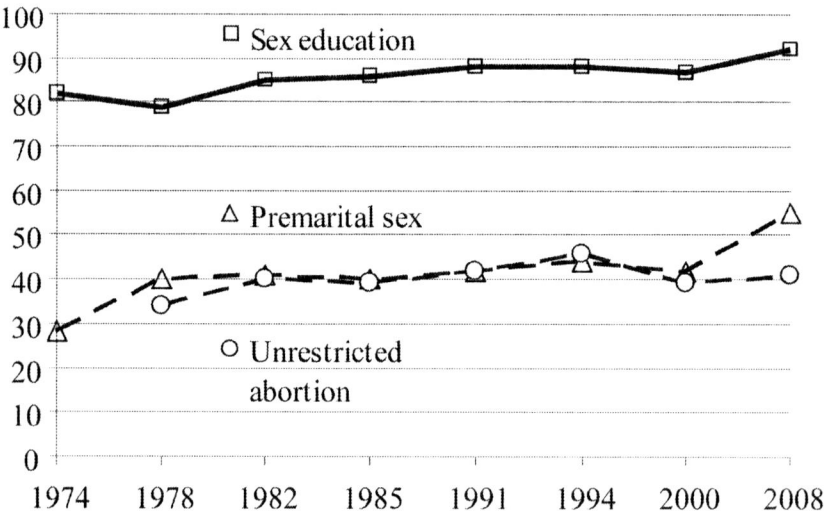

Figure 2.5. Trends in Attitudes toward Sex Education, Premarital Sex, and Abortion, 1974–2008 (GSS)

the 1970s, but with a slight decrease since 1994 in Americans who say women should be able to have an abortion "for any reason." Gallup poll data likewise show an increase in the proportion of Americans who define themselves as pro-life rather than pro-choice, from 33 percent in 1975 to 51 percent in 2009. In both years, however, exactly the same proportion of Americans (22 percent) would make abortion illegal.[45] Gallup data also indicate that attitudes toward evolution have hardly budged since 1982, when Americans were about evenly divided as to whether they accepted evolution or creationism. A 2004 GSS question showed that approximately half of Americans still reject any notion that "people are descended from animals."[46]

## CONCLUSION

By midcentury the consensus view among American intellectuals was that the United States was destined for the same secular trends as in Europe. Sociologist C. Wright Mills predicted in 1959 that "the sacred shall disappear altogether, except possibly in the private realm."[47] "The sacred" has hardly disappeared, but the GSS survey data reviewed in this chapter point to a striking paradox: even as the Religious Right has become increasingly influential in American politics, church attendance has declined and secular perspectives have become more prevalent, especially among younger people.

The presence of significant cohort effects certainly does not imply that all Americans are becoming more tolerant of expressions of atheism or more skeptical of organized religion. Many remain devoutly religious and feel deeply threatened by secularism. Atheists and nonbelievers still face social stigmas, legal discrimination, and political marginality.[48] As the morality-policy cycle predicts, policy "shocks" can spur both greater religiosity and political activism by those whose core beliefs are challenged. Individuals, institutions, and political and religious elites involved with the Religious Right have reacted to counter secular trends in law and public policy. And in some areas they may have succeeded; attitudes toward abortion and evolution have not shifted in the direction that demographic changes (increased education, declines in church attendance or religious affiliation) might predict.

The GSS data also reveal significant changes in the religious and political views of younger cohorts. These results thus challenge the conclusion by Hout and Fischer that the decline in religious affiliation has *not* been accompanied by more secular attitudes. But their study was based on GSS surveys only through 2000, and did not consider trends among more recent cohorts. Hout and Fischer also argued that political factors affected the increase in nonaffiliation: liberals were far more likely than conservatives to develop weaker ties to organized religion because it had become more closely linked to the conservative social agenda.[49] Chapter 3 will provide additional evidence of the impact of religious conservatism on the political mobilization of seculars. Chapters 4–6 will examine in more detail the political and organizational efforts, by both the Religious Right and secular forces, to respond to changes in Americans' religious beliefs and to influence their opinions on social and moral issues. The concluding chapter will consider the future religious and political implications of the ongoing demographic trends described in this chapter.

# 3

# Religiosity, Public Opinion, and Political Involvement

The previous chapter analyzed trends since the 1970s in religious beliefs and behavior in the United States. Data from the General Social Survey showed declines in church attendance and increases in the proportion of Americans without religious affiliation. An analysis based on birth cohorts showed that except for belief in life after death, recent generations are considerably more secular than earlier ones, even after changes in age, education, and ethnicity are taken into account. If these trends continue, the United States may come to resemble other European democracies in terms of religious beliefs and practices.

This chapter will assess the impact of these secular trends on public opinion, political involvement, and voting behavior. The Democratic and Republican parties have become increasingly polarized on a range of social issues, reflecting in part the growing influence of the Religious Right within the Republican Party and of seculars within the Democratic Party.[1] While the general public may not be as polarized as political elites, seculars have more divergent views and voting patterns than the most religious Americans. However, although church attendees are still more involved in partisan politics and social organizations than seculars are, the gap in political mobilization has narrowed considerably since 1980. Antipathy to the Religious Right has emerged as a significant factor explaining campaign activism by religious moderates as well as seculars.

I will first develop a consistent categorization of religious involvement to define seculars, moderates, and traditionalists. Trends in these groups since the 1980s will then be compared in terms of demographics, party identification, public opinion, and voting patterns. While seculars, moderates, and religious traditionalists come from somewhat different social backgrounds, all these groups have been affected by ongoing changes in American society, particularly the increase in minorities and more liberal views on the role of women and gays. I then turn to an analysis of trends in political involvement. Considerable evidence has documented the advantages of the Religious Right for mobilizing their members. If religious commitment indeed encourages political activism, secular viewpoints are less likely to be heard. A comparison with religious moderates and traditionalists will show that seculars now constitute a sizable proportion of the politically interested, active, and aware. Their opinions thus carry considerably more weight at the polls and within the Democratic electorate than in the 1980s.

## COMPARING SECULARS, MODERATES, AND TRADITIONALISTS

To understand trends in the political involvement of both religious and more secular Americans, we need indicators of religious beliefs or practices that are reasonably consistent over time. We also need consistent indicators of political attitudes and behaviors. For these purposes, the American National Election Studies (ANES) provide comprehensive national surveys in every presidential election year, with a considerably more detailed focus on politics than the General Social Survey. ANES data, 1980–2008, will therefore be used in this chapter.

As discussed in chapter 1, one of the most straightforward measures of religious commitment has been frequency of church attendance. Questions concerning that have been regularly posed by Gallup polls, the General Social Survey, Pew surveys, and the American National Election Studies for many decades. Church attendance has been shown to be a powerful predictor of both turnout and vote choice in recent elections. Attendance at worship services is also an ideal measure from the organizational perspective that this book emphasizes; frequent attendees gain social skills, learn about religious and social issues from pastors and fellow congregants, and are tied into information networks that can link their values and their votes.[2]

Yet relying only on church attendance as an indicator of religiosity has drawbacks as well. People are likely to overreport how frequently they attend church, and the impact of church involvement varies considerably across churches and denominations. As noted in chapter 1, many who never attend services still have some religious beliefs. A better alternative, therefore, is to combine church attendance with some indicator of the centrality of religion to one's life. Bolce and De Maio used

ANES data combining these two factors in order to document trends in religious beliefs and behavior.[3] I will follow their approach, making use of ANES questions that have been reasonably consistent since 1980: frequency of church attendance, whether or not respondents think religion constitutes an important aspect of their lives, and their views of biblical truth.

Seculars, therefore, will be defined as respondents who say they never attend services and who also say that religion is not important in their lives. Some of these do report nominal ties to some religious group, but as noted in chapter 1, ANES religion codes have changed considerably over time, and the question wording does not consistently distinguish among religious affiliation, membership, or preference. Seculars will be contrasted with respondents classified as traditionalists, who attend church on a weekly basis, regard religion as very important, and believe the Bible is the Word of God and literally true—all defining characteristics of much of the Religious Right, including both fundamentalists and evangelicals.[4] All others, including those who attend religious services occasionally, attach only moderate importance to religion, or do not accept the Bible as literally true, will be defined as religious moderates. This is a large and diverse group, including most mainline Protestants, some evangelicals, the majority of Hispanic and non-Hispanic Roman Catholics, denominations identified with the Religious Left, and Jews. Others have analyzed the demographics, religious beliefs, and political views of these intermediate groupings in more detail.[5]

The main focus of this chapter will be to contrast those who have largely rejected religion with those who are most strongly committed to traditional religious views. ANES indicators that have been consistent over time point to the same conclusion suggested by the GSS measures described in chapter 2: an increase in the proportion of seculars, from 12 to 18 percent. The proportion of religious traditionalists has also increased, from 28 to 34 percent. The result is an electorate more polarized along religious lines, since the moderate proportion declined from 61 percent in 1980 to 46 percent in 2008.

Table 3.1 contrasts the racial and ethnic distribution of seculars, moderates, and traditionalists within racial and ethnic groups in 1980, 1992, 2004, and 2008. Among white ANES respondents, the proportion of seculars has doubled since 1980, while the proportion of moderates has declined; the proportion of white traditionalists has not changed over the last three decades. Bolce and De Maio confined their analysis to whites only, arguing that whites' beliefs and political behavior have changed considerably since 1980.[6] However, as table 3.1 shows, African American and Hispanic religiosity has undergone changes as well; there were a few more seculars, fewer moderates, and considerably more traditionalists

Table 3.1  Religiosity by Race, 1980–2008

|  |  | Seculars | Moderates | Traditionalists |
|---|---|---|---|---|
| Whites | 1980 | 14% | 61% | 26% |
|  | 1992 | 17% | 57% | 26% |
|  | 2004 | 19% | 56% | 25% |
|  | 2008 | 26% | 49% | 26% |
| African Americans | 1980 | 3% | 54% | 43% |
|  | 1992 | 4% | 49% | 46% |
|  | 2004 | 6% | 51% | 43% |
|  | 2008 | 6% | 43% | 52% |
| Hispanics | 1980 | 2% | 76% | 22% |
|  | 1992 | 5% | 68% | 26% |
|  | 2004 | 8% | 64% | 30% |
|  | 2008 | 13% | 52% | 35% |

*Source*: ANES

among both groups by 2008. Religious polarization has thus increased among minorities as well as whites.

Hispanics were historically overwhelmingly Roman Catholic, but in recent decades many more Hispanics have turned to Protestant denominations. Evangelicals, Pentecostals, Jehovah's Witnesses, and Mormons have all aimed missionary activities at Hispanics, with considerable success in the United States as well as in Latin America. However, a sizable proportion of Hispanics remain Catholic, and the proportion of Catholics in the American population would have declined considerably if not for the growing Hispanic presence.[7] A few (mostly younger) Hispanics can now be classified as seculars.

African Americans have long been the most religiously involved segment of the American population. Until the 1970s most African Americans identified with Methodist or Baptist denominations, although usually the African American variants thereof. Mainline Protestant churches remained highly segregated by race, despite some outreach efforts and strong clergy support for the civil-rights movement. But in recent years African Americans (similar to Hispanics and whites) have moved in large numbers to more fundamentalist and/or nondenominational churches. Pentecostals and Jehovah's Witnesses have successfully recruited many African Americans as well. Catholic parishes have also attracted some people of African descent, particularly Haitian and Dominican immigrants.[8] As their economic fortunes improved, many African Americans and Hispanics have been attracted to churches that preach the "Prosperity Gospel," combining traditional Bible-centered Christianity with the promise that faith and tithing will lead to personal riches on Earth as well as eternal life.[9]

Although overall levels of religiosity, including church attendance and biblical literalism, remain high among African Americans, a few more can now be defined as seculars. Before the civil-rights movement, African American churches were often the only social and organizational option open to the black community, and church affiliation (regardless of one's beliefs or personal preferences) was often a political or business necessity. As other economic and social options became available, more younger African Americans made use of nonchurch or non-Christian (such as Black Muslim) associations.[10] However, although African Americans retain conservative social and religious beliefs and high levels of church attendance, their voting patterns (unlike those of white traditionalists) have been consistently Democratic.

## DEMOGRAPHICS AND DENOMINATIONS: SECULARS, MODERATES, AND TRADITIONALISTS, 1980–2008

The GSS data summarized in chapter 2 indicated seculars to be considerably younger and better educated than the religiously involved. Table 3.2 shows additional contrasts in the social characteristics of seculars, moderates, and traditionalists as defined above, based on ANES data for 1980 and 2008.

Gender differences among these three groups are striking in both 1980 and 2008. While traditionalists are disproportionately female, seculars are more likely to be male. Trends in racial composition are striking as well; all three groups are much more diverse in 2008 than in 1980. In fact, non-Hispanic whites are now a minority among those categorized as traditionalists. Seculars are also considerably younger than traditionalists; fully half of the latter are over age fifty-two. All groups were less likely to be married in 2008 than in 1980, but seculars in both periods were more likely to be single or divorced. Twenty-two percent of traditionalists were homemakers in 1980; this decreased dramatically to 9 percent in 2008. Thus even religious conservatives have been affected by changes in the status of women and their growing presence in the labor force.

In terms of education, all groups in 2008 included a substantial proportion of respondents with high-school degrees or less. This is likely due to the presence of more minorities, which could also explain decreases in the proportions of homeowners since 1980. Traditionalists in 2008 were some-

Table 3.2  Demographics of Seculars, Moderates, and Traditionalists, 1980 and 2008

|  |  | Seculars | | Moderates | | Traditionalists | |
|---|---|---|---|---|---|---|---|
|  |  | 1980 | 2008 | 1980 | 2008 | 1980 | 2008 |
|  | Percent of sample | 12 | 18 | 61 | 48 | 28 | 34 |
|  | Male | 56 | 53 | 45 | 46 | 32 | 34 |
|  | Female | 44 | 47 | 55 | 54 | 68 | 66 |
|  | Median age | 39 | 43 | 44 | 45 | 49 | 52 |
|  | Percent homeowner | 66 | 57 | 68 | 59 | 76 | 68 |
| Marital Status | Married or widowed | 57 | 55 | 71 | 62 | 79 | 61 |
| | Single | 26 | 18 | 16 | 18 | 9 | 17 |
| | Divorced or separated | 14 | 23 | 12 | 19 | 11 | 21 |
| | Partners | 4 | 4 | 1 | 2 | 0 | 1 |
| Ethnicity | Other race | 96 | 73 | 83 | 52 | 78 | 38 |
| | African American | 3 | 8 | 10 | 23 | 18 | 39 |
| | Hispanic | 1 | 14 | 4 | 22 | 3 | 21 |
| Family Income | 0–16th percentile | 11 | 14 | 16 | 20 | 23 | 23 |
| | 17–33rd percentile | 16 | 18 | 15 | 18 | 17 | 22 |
| | Middle third | 35 | 42 | 35 | 39 | 39 | 35 |
| | Upper third | 39 | 27 | 34 | 23 | 19 | 19 |
| Occupation* | Professional/manager | 36 | 34 | 26 | 37 | 19 | 26 |
| | Clerical/sales | 17 | 28 | 19 | 25 | 17 | 28 |
| | Skilled/service | 32 | 28 | 35 | 28 | 37 | 30 |
| | Farm/laborers | 5 | 4 | 5 | 5 | 5 | 5 |
| | Homemakers | 11 | 6 | 15 | 5 | 22 | 11 |
| Education | HS or less | 29 | 43 | 46 | 46 | 52 | 52 |
| | HS +/AA | 45 | 29 | 38 | 32 | 36 | 31 |
| | BA | 16 | 20 | 10 | 15 | 9 | 12 |
| | Post-grad | 10 | 8 | 6 | 7 | 3 | 5 |
| Religious Affiliation | Mainline Protestant | 24 | 14 | 37 | 36 | 27 | 45 |
| | Evangelical Protestant | 10 | 5 | 26 | 21 | 43 | 31 |
| | Roman Catholic | 10 | 16 | 26 | 28 | 23 | 20 |
| | Jewish | 6 | 2 | 4 | 3 | 1 | 3 |
| | Other | 0 | 1 | 3 | 4 | 4 | 0 |
| | None | 50 | 63 | 4 | 8 | 2 | 1 |

*2004 data, 2008 coding not comparable

Source: ANES

what more likely than in 1980 to be college graduates or to have advanced degrees, and to be in professional or managerial occupations. Their income distributions have also become more similar to moderates. As the analysis in chapter 2 indicated, frequent church attendance is more, not less, common among Americans with higher incomes and levels of education. Stereotypes of the religiously observant as poorly educated, credulous folks from the Bible Belt or the backwoods are clearly outdated, although seculars still have an edge in education, family income, and occupational status.

Ongoing social changes in America have affected traditionalists and moderates as well as seculars in terms of racial diversity, marriage rates, and the status of women. Twenty-one percent of traditionalists were divorced or separated in 2008, compared with 11 percent in 1980, and in both years seculars were less likely to be married. A question on a respondent's sexual orientation was not asked on ANES surveys until 2008 and, not surprisingly, those identifying as gay, lesbian, or bisexual were more likely to be seculars. As of 2008 traditionalists were significantly more likely than seculars to be older, female, married, low income, and a member of a racial or ethnic minority. However, all three groups today are socially quite diverse in terms of education, race/ethnicity, and range of occupations.

Table 3.2 shows the distribution of seculars, moderates, and traditionalists across the major religious classifications used by the ANES. Comparisons on this dimension over time are somewhat problematic because subcategories of fundamentalists, evangelical Protestants, Jews, and other religions were only added to more recent ANES surveys. However, the Protestant classifications can be approximated using the detailed coding of religious denominations provided by the ANES in both years.[11]

Not surprisingly, a significant number of evangelical Protestants (both white and African American) are traditionalists, but many evangelicals are classified as moderates as well, and mainline Protestants constituted the largest single category of traditionalists in both 1980 and 2008. A sizable proportion of traditionalists were Catholic in both 1980 and 2008. About a quarter of Catholics claimed to be biblical literalists, although that is not official Church doctrine, and a significant number of mainline Protestants also shared beliefs in biblical literalism. In 1980 fully half of seculars reported some religious affiliation, predominantly mainline Protestant, but by 2008, 63 percent were unaffiliated. As of 2008 the ANES included distinctions among Orthodox, Conservative, and Reform Judaism. A few Orthodox Jews are coded as traditionalists, but the actual numbers in these categories are very small. Jews in both years were predominantly classified as religious moderates, and the Jewish proportion of seculars declined from 6 percent in 1980 to 2 percent in 2008.

## PARTIES, IDEOLOGY, AND POLARIZATION

Since 1980, the Democratic and Republican parties have certainly diverged, based on voting patterns in Congress, party platforms, and ratings by ideological groups. The religious profiles of the major parties have become more polarized as well, reflecting the relative influence of seculars among the Democratic Party coalitions and the Religious Right among Republicans.[12] On the basis of religious background as well as demographics, we would expect increasing divergence in political views among seculars, moderates, and traditionalists.

Consider first trends in party identification, based on the ANES seven-point scale, ranging from "strong Democrat" to "strong Republican." Figure 3.1 (based on whites only) suggests considerable polarization, driven largely by the increase among traditionalists who identify as Republican. Seculars since 1992 have been consistently more Democratic, but both secular and moderate categories include a sizable number of independents.

Ideology shows a similar pattern (figure 3.2), based on whites' self-placement on an ANES seven-point scale ranging from 1 (most liberal) to 7 (most conservative). Seculars are more likely to identify as liberal and traditionalists as conservative, and the differences have increased since 1992. But that spread is due mostly to the considerable increase in conservatism among traditionalists. Seculars tend to be closer to the middle of the road than to the liberal end of the ideological spectrum.

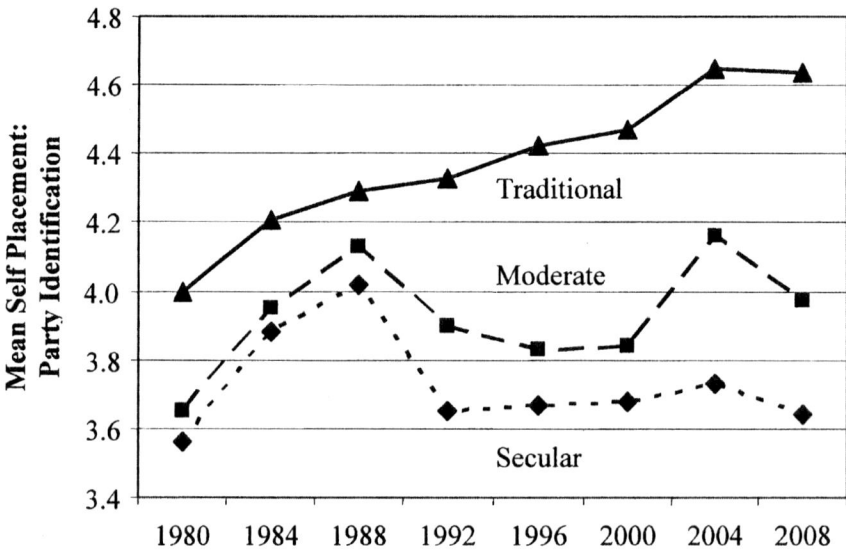

Figure 3.1. Party Identification by Religiosity, 1980–2008 (ANES)

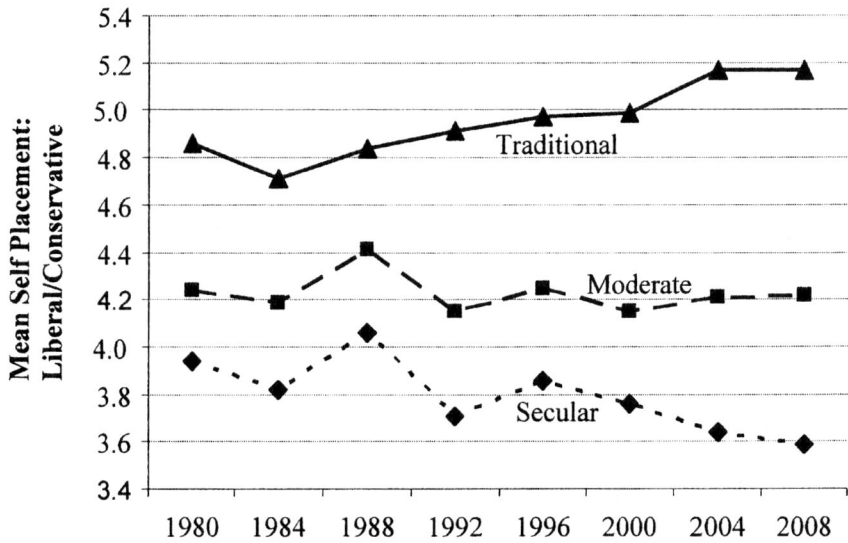

Figure 3.2. Self-Placement on Liberal/Conservative Thermometer, 1980–2008 (ANES)

Even more than partisanship or ideology, voting behavior has become polarized along religious lines. Table 3.3 shows votes by white Americans only, since ANES surveys show that African Americans, regardless of religious orientation, have consistently given Democrats 90 percent or more of their votes for president and Congress since 1980. Republicans Ronald Reagan and George H. W. Bush actually received the majority of seculars' votes in the 1980s, but since 1992 seculars have strongly favored the Democratic candidate. In 2008 a majority of white moderates supported McCain, along with 77 percent of white traditionalists. Seculars have also consistently favored Democrats for both House and Senate, although not to the same degree as for president. By contrast, since 1980 white moderates have become more Republican in voting for both the president and Congress, and white traditionalists even more so (well over 70 percent in 2008).

Furthermore, white seculars constitute an increasing proportion of the total Democratic votes for Congress; 30 percent of the House vote in 2008 compared with 17 percent in 1980, and 31 percent of the Senate vote in 2008 compared with 19 percent in 1980 (based on ANES data, although their surveys do not cover all fifty states). Seculars may not consistently define themselves as liberal, or as Democratic Party identifiers, but (unlike white moderates or traditionalists) they are increasingly Democratic in terms of voting behavior.

However, table 3.3 also shows that seculars have been more likely than moderates or traditionalists to support third-party candidates,

Table 3.3  Vote for President, Congress, and Third Parties, 1980–2008 (whites only)

|  | 1980 | 1984 | 1988 | 1992 | 1996 | 2000 | 2004 | 2008 |
|---|---|---|---|---|---|---|---|---|
| *Republican percent of major party vote for President* | | | | | | | | |
| Seculars | 55 | 57 | 53 | 28 | 30 | 34 | 44 | 37 |
| Moderates | 62 | 64 | 59 | 43 | 46 | 49 | 57 | 52 |
| Traditionalists | 69 | 69 | 66 | 67 | 63 | 70 | 72 | 77 |
| *Republican percent of vote for House* | | | | | | | | |
| Seculars | 38 | 42 | 38 | 33 | 40 | 38 | 38 | 42 |
| Moderates | 49 | 49 | 54 | 54 | 57 | 49 | 53 | 51 |
| Traditionalists | 57 | 52 | 54 | 53 | 67 | 67 | 70 | 73 |
| *Republican percent of vote for Senate* | | | | | | | | |
| Seculars | 35 | 49 | 48 | 43 | 40 | 38 | 38 | 42 |
| Moderates | 48 | 53 | 59 | 54 | 51 | 44 | 54 | 60 |
| Traditionalists | 62 | 53 | 57 | 65 | 62 | 67 | 69 | 73 |
| *Vote for third-party candidates* | | | | | | | | |
| Seculars | 24 | 2 | 2 | 24 | 16 | 8 | 3 | 3 |
| Moderates | 11 | 1 | 1 | 20 | 8 | 4 | 2 | 2 |
| Traditionalists | 5 | 1 | 1 | 13 | 7 | 2 | 0 | 2 |

Source: ANES

especially John Anderson in 1980 and Ross Perot in both 1992 and 1996. They even gave 8 percent of their votes to Ralph Nader in 2000, which could well have affected the outcome of the election. Many seculars thus reject political as well as religious orthodoxy. While minor-party candidates are more likely to attract votes among citizens who are disconnected from social institutions, churches constitute an important institutional base that has helped to sustain the two-party system and voting patterns over time.[13]

Figure 3.3 shows trends in strength of partisanship, 1980–2008, based on a scale ranging from 1 (independent or apolitical) to 4 (strong partisan). Both moderates and traditionalists are now more likely to consider themselves strong partisans than in the 1980s, but seculars' partisanship has fluctuated over time and by 2008 was quite weak. This lack of strong partisan commitment could well account for the propensity of seculars to back third-party candidates. It also means that the Democrats cannot always count on votes from seculars in either the primary or general elections.

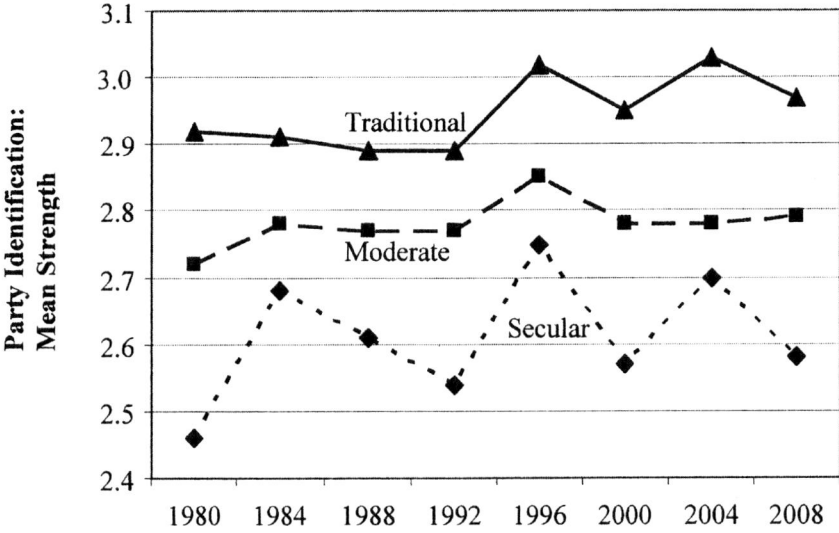

Figure 3.3. Strength of Party Identification by Religiosity, 1980–2008 (ANES)

## OPINIONS ON SOCIAL ISSUES AND RELIGIOUS IDENTITIES

Recent debates about religion and morality in the United States have centered on hot-button social issues, such as abortion, the role of women, and the status of gays and lesbians. Political elites have certainly polarized on these issues since 1980, as indicated by the Democratic and Republican party platforms and by party-line voting in Congress.[14] Are citizens also divided on these controversial issues along religious lines?

The degree of polarization varies considerably by issue. Consider first opinions concerning gays and lesbians (figure 3.4), based on an ANES thermometer score (0 equals negative feelings, 50 is neutral, 100 equals warm feelings toward some group or institution). Social acceptance of gays and lesbians has increased considerably since the ANES first asked the question in 1984, and the trend has been upward among religious traditionalists as well as seculars. However, the groups were even farther apart in 2008 than in 1980.

The 2008 survey included more specific questions concerning gays and lesbians, and not surprisingly, seculars were far more likely than traditionalists to support gay marriage or civil unions (60 versus 16 percent, respectively) and gay adoption (70 versus 29 percent). Differences also emerge in support of gays in the military (87 versus 68 percent) and laws barring economic discrimination against gays or lesbians (79 versus 63

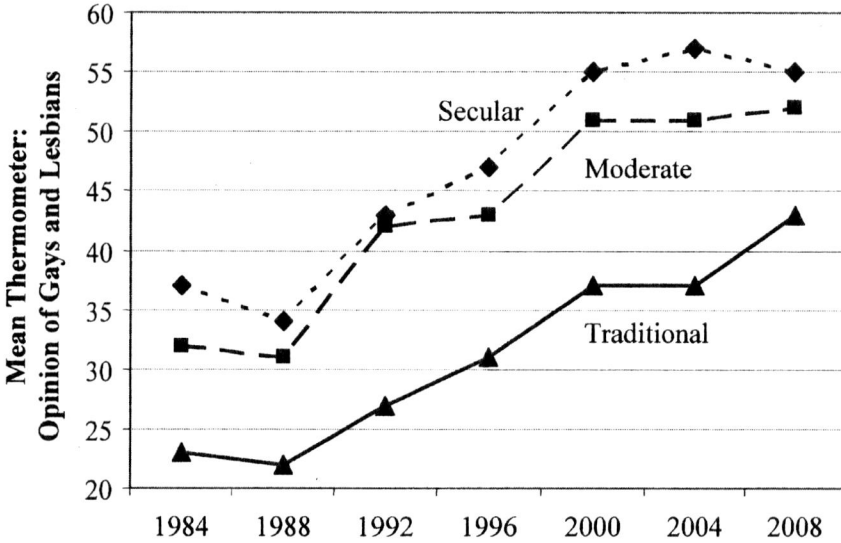

Figure 3.4. Thermometer Scores (0–100) for Gays and Lesbians by Religiosity (ANES)

percent), but it is striking that a strong majority of religious traditionalists are now willing to accept these policies. Previous ANES surveys did not include these specific questions but, as discussed in chapter 2, Gallup polls and other surveys also show increasing acceptance of gays and lesbians since the 1980s.

Since 1980, ANES surveys have asked respondents to place themselves on a seven-point scale ranging from 1 ("Men and women should have equal roles") to 7 ("Women's place is in the home"). Opinions concerning the status of women have liberalized since 1980 among all three religious groupings (figure 3.5). By 2008 a strong majority of Americans agreed that men and women should have equal roles, and this opinion prevailed among traditionalists as well as seculars. However, while secular and moderate males and females agreed on this question, traditional males were considerably more likely than traditional females to believe that women belong in the home.

By contrast, opinions on reproductive rights have been mostly stable since 1980. Figure 3.6 uses the fourfold set of responses offered by the ANES surveys and shows the trend averaged across these.[15] Seculars are far more likely to agree that "By law, abortion is a woman's choice," although by 2008 fewer seculars were willing to take this position. This reflects in part the growing proportion among seculars of African Americans and Hispanics, who tend to hold more conservative views on social issues. A majority of moderates and traditionalists would accept abortion

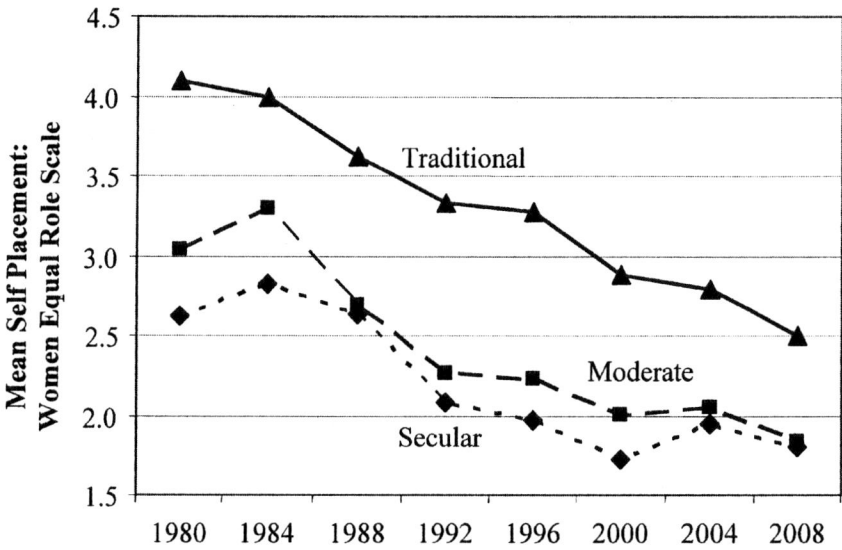

Figure 3.5. Mean Scores on ANES Seven-Point Women's Equal Role Scale by Religiosity

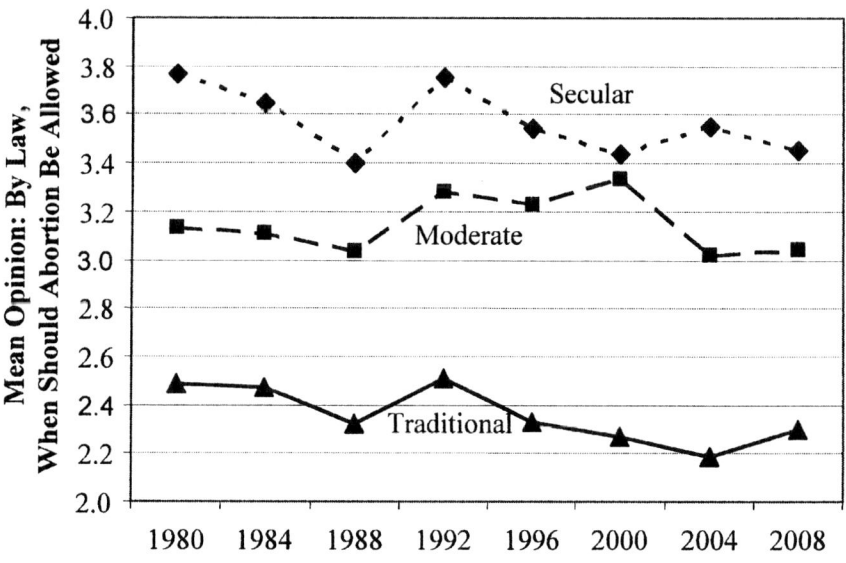

Figure 3.6. Mean Scores on ANES Index of Abortion Opinions by Religiosity

only under some restricted circumstances. Although support for abortion rights among traditionalists has declined since 1980, as of 2008 only about a quarter of them agreed with the most restrictive position ("By law, abortion should never be permitted").

The 2008 ANES included a number of new questions on abortion. Respondents in half the sample were asked whether they would support or oppose abortion under a variety of conditions: rape, incest, birth defects, fatal or nonfatal maternal health conditions, sex selection, or financial pressures. As table 3.4 shows, seculars would support abortion under each of these conditions except for sex selection, but their degree of support ranged from 86 percent in case of a fatal health risk to only 44 percent in case of financial pressures. Traditionalists also showed considerable variation, with a majority (63 percent) willing to support abortion in the case of a fatal health risk to the mother. But traditionalists were more likely than seculars or moderates to hold strong opinions on these questions concerning abortion, or to consider abortion to be an important issue.[16]

Finally, consider how seculars, moderates, and traditionalists view the major religious groups in American society. Table 3.5 shows the mean thermometer scores for Protestants, Catholics, and Jews, averaged over ANES surveys since 1980 since the questions were not asked about every religious group in every survey. The mean scores shown exclude those of people who identified with each of those groups, since they tended to rate their own group much more positively. All scores are in the positive range (over 50), suggesting a considerable degree of tolerance of religious diversity. However, seculars are less positive than moderates or traditionalists about all these mainstream religions. Additional analysis (not shown) found no clear trend over time in scores for any group.[17]

Beginning in 1988 the ANES included thermometer scores for "Christian fundamentalists," and here we see far more polarized responses across the three religious categories. In 2008 four other groups (Muslims, Hindus, Christians, and atheists) were also added to the ANES thermometer questions. Seculars viewed atheists more positively than did

Table 3.4　Opinions on Abortion Conditions by Religiosity, 2008

| Percent in favor of abortion if: | Seculars | Moderates | Traditionalists |
|---|---|---|---|
| Fatal health risk to mother | 86 | 74 | 63 |
| Rape | 86 | 69 | 43 |
| Serious birth defect | 71 | 74 | 31 |
| Nonfatal health risk to mother | 55 | 40 | 25 |
| Incest | 52 | 35 | 20 |
| Financial constraints | 44 | 26 | 12 |
| Child is wrong sex | 15 | 6 | 4 |

Source: ANES

Table 3.5  Thermometer Scale Scores for Religious Groups by Religiosity

|  | Years | Seculars | Moderates | Traditionalists |
|---|---|---|---|---|
| Catholics | 1980–2008 | 58 | 66 | 68 |
| Protestants | 1980–2008 | 58 | 73 | 71 |
| Jews | 1980–2008 | 61 | 63 | 68 |
| Christian fundamentalists | 1988–2008 | 39 | 52 | 67 |
| Muslims | 2008 | 51 | 53 | 50 |
| Hindus | 2008 | 56 | 55 | 55 |
| Atheists | 2008 | 52 | 39 | 34 |
| Christians | 2008 | 63 | 80 | 86 |

Source: ANES

moderates or traditionalists, but still gave them lower mean scores than they gave Catholics, Protestants, or Jews. Secular thermometer scores for "Christians," while positive, are considerably lower than those for moderates or traditionalists. However, these three groups differ little in their views of Muslims or Hindus, whose mean scores are lower than those for Protestants, Catholics, or Jews. But it is striking that seculars hold even more negative views of Christian fundamentalists than they do of atheists, Muslims, or Hindus.

One likely explanation is that attitudes toward Christian fundamentalists have been conflated with attitudes toward the Religious Right. Although the media do not always point out such distinctions, not everyone identified with the Religious Right is fundamentalist—or even Christian. Since the Religious Right has become more closely identified with the Republican Party, secular Democratic partisans or voters are more likely to view it negatively. As recent voting studies have found, evaluations of groups identified with either the Democratic or Republican parties have a considerably stronger impact on vote choice than perceptions of party differences on issues.[18] Also, both Christian fundamentalists and the Religious Right pose a much greater threat to seculars' values and public-policy preferences than do the much smaller numbers of Americans who can be classified as Muslims or Hindus.

## TRENDS IN POLITICAL MOBILIZATION, 1980–2008

Although Americans have considerably more positive views of gays or lesbians and of women's rights since 1980, seculars, moderates, and traditionalists have very different views on these hot-button social issues. Seculars are much more supportive of abortion, gay rights, and equal roles for women. And seculars are considerably more liberal and Democratic in political orientation than more religious Americans. But are these viewpoints likely to have much political impact? As Schattschneider famously observed, "Some opinions are organized into politics while others are organized out."[19]

Ample evidence suggests that the opinions of religious traditionalists have been more effectively "organized into" politics in recent years. Church attendance has emerged as a powerful predictor of voter turnout as well as Republican voting patterns. Organizations affiliated with the Religious Right have made use of churches and church membership lists to mobilize their sympathizers; priests and some pastors have directed their congregants to "vote their values," or to support a particular party or candidate.[20] Religious media networks (including Christian radio, televangelists, and more recently the Internet) have successfully raised millions of dollars to support candidates sympathetic to their causes, to educate voters, and to generate letter-writing or e-mail campaigns to lobby Congress or state legislatures. Further, political leaders have made successful use of hot-button issues to mobilize conservative voters. George Bush's reelection in 2004 was widely credited to successful efforts by political strategists such as Karl Rove to keep the focus on moral issues, including state referenda on gay-marriage bans, in order to turn out the base.[21] Mormons spent millions of dollars in 2008 to help pass Proposition 8 (a constitutional ban on gay marriage) in California, a generally liberal state (an issue to be analyzed in more detail in chapter 6).[22]

As chapter 5 will show, seculars have developed an organizational base as well, but in terms of membership and fund-raising they still lag far behind the Religious Right. Unchurched seculars are still less likely than religious traditionalists or moderates to be involved in other community or social organizations, or to be contacted during political campaigns.[23] Figure 3.3 showed seculars to be considerably less partisan than traditionalists or moderates, and partisanship is a powerful predictor of political awareness and involvement. For all of these reasons, the conventional wisdom has been that secular perspectives are less likely to be articulated in mass political behavior.

The conventional wisdom has certainly had some validity, according to most measures of political involvement; as of 1980, traditionalists were more politically interested and active than seculars. But the gaps in political mobilization have narrowed considerably since then. To illustrate these trends, table 3.6 compares seculars, moderates, and traditionalists on a number of indicators of political activism in 1980, 2004, and 2008, although comparable measures are not available in every survey. Seculars lagged behind traditionalists in their degree of interest in the election in 1980, but exceeded them by 2004, when all three groups claimed greater interest. ANES interviewers have consistently ranked seculars as higher in level of political information than either traditionalists or moderates. By more objective measures (correctly stating which party controlled the House or Senate), seculars likewise usually performed better than traditionalists. It is interesting to note that although the ANES interviewers rated all three groups higher in political information in 2008 than in 1980, accurate knowledge of party control of the House actually declined across the board.[24]

Table 3.6 Political Activism by Seculars, Moderates, and Traditionalists, 1980, 2004, and 2008

|  | Seculars | | | Moderates | | | Traditionalists | | |
|---|---|---|---|---|---|---|---|---|---|
|  | 1980 | 2004 | 2008 | 1980 | 2004 | 2008 | 1980 | 2004 | 2008 |
| Interest in election | | | | | | | | | |
| % "Very much interested" | 31 | 44 | 36 | 26 | 40 | 37 | 37 | 42 | 39 |
| Political information | | | | | | | | | |
| Interviewer rating: % High | 45 | 58 | 41 | 33 | 52 | 43 | 31 | 45 | 38 |
| % correct answers | | | | | | | | | |
| Party control of House | 81 | 51 | 53 | 72 | 56 | 51 | 66 | 55 | 54 |
| Party control of Senate |  | 55 | 51 |  | 50 | 48 |  | 51 | 58 |
| Reported voting | 69 | 81 | 73 | 69 | 78 | 74 | 76 | 78 | 86 |
| Registered to vote | 74 | 91 | 79 | 78 | 89 | 86 | 82 | 91 | 89 |
| Voted in presidential primary | 36 |  | 31 | 34 |  | 39 | 43 |  | 54 |
| Influenced others' votes | 38 | 51 | 60 | 37 | 49 | 57 | 34 | 46 | 55 |
| Membership in other organizations | | | | | | | | | |
| None |  | 63 | 63 |  | 57 | 64 |  | 55 | 48 |
| One |  | 18 | 17 |  | 20 | 18 |  | 17 | 19 |
| Two or more |  | 19 | 20 |  | 23 | 18 |  | 28 | 33 |
| Donated to political party/candidate | 7 | 15 | 12 | 7 | 15 | 12 | 7 | 14 | 10 |
| Donated to charity |  |  | 46 |  |  | 67 |  |  | 91 |
| Volunteer work |  | 30 | 27 |  | 40 | 32 |  | 56 | 56 |
| Contacted by major party | 18 | 46 | 38 | 39 | 54 | 39 | 31 | 53 | 42 |
| Contacted by other group |  | 19 | 15 |  | 15 | 16 |  | 22 | 23 |
| Media use | 24 | 14 | 14 | 16 | 15 | 19 | 15 | 13 | 18 |
| Campaign activism scale (mean score) | 1.55 | 1.93 | 1.81 | 1.64 | 1.95 | 1.90 | 1.60 | 1.93 | 2.00 |

Source: ANES

In terms of voter turnout, we see a striking change since 1980, when traditionalists were the most likely voters. As of 2004 seculars were just as likely as moderates or traditionalists to be registered to vote, and even more likely to claim they had voted (of course, self-reports of voting or registration are notoriously overstated in surveys; actual turnout in 2008 was closer to 60 percent).[25] However, table 3.6 shows that turnout in primary elections in both 1980 and 2008 was much higher among religious traditionalists. And since seculars are more likely to be independents, they are ineligible to vote in states with closed or semi-closed primaries.

The overall percentages of ANES respondents donating to political campaigns have apparently increased since 1980, but with no differences across the three groups in either year. Seculars were more likely to report that they tried to convince others how to vote, and such political proselytizing also increased for all three groups in 2004 and 2008. Analyses of social networks have found that political proselytizing does appear to influence people to change their votes.[26] If seculars are now more likely to engage in this activity, they have the potential to have a greater impact than by simply voting.

The ANES scale of campaign activism includes attendance at speeches or rallies, displaying a yard sign or bumper sticker, contributing to a party or candidate, or belonging to a political organization. Such activism increased for all groups in 2008 compared with 1980, but in 2008 was considerably higher among both seculars and moderates than traditionalists. As figure 3.7 shows, seculars and moderates ranked below traditionalists until 2004, when activism by all three groups spiked. Campaign activism by traditionalists even fell off a bit in 2008, when many on the Religious Right questioned John McCain's evangelical credentials.

We do see striking differences in reports of contacts by the major political parties or (in 2004) by other "religious or moral" groups. Such grassroots efforts were apparently much more frequent in 2004 than in 1980, but in both years seculars were less likely to report such contacts.[27] As of 2004 they were considerably less likely than either moderates or traditionalists to belong to other organizations, donate to churches or charities, or engage in volunteer work. Seculars made use of a greater range of media sources for campaign coverage in 1980, but by 2004 the groups differed little in overall media exposure. As of 2008, however, seculars (who tend to be considerably younger than moderates or traditionalists) made much more use of the Internet. According to the 2008 ANES, 66 percent of seculars, compared with only 46 percent of traditionalists, had Internet access, and seculars were also more likely to follow campaign news on the Internet. The Internet and social networking may become a functional substitute for door-to-door personal contacts during campaigns.[28]

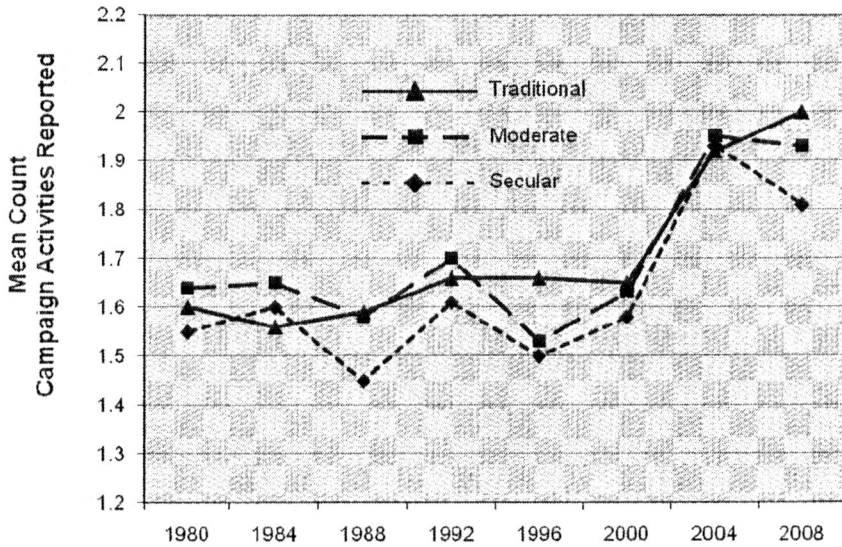

Figure 3.7. Mean Level of Campaign Participation by Religiosity (ANES)

Republicans and conservatives have consistently higher voter turnout than Democrats, while seculars are more likely to be younger and politically independent—both factors that tend to discourage political activism. But are differences among these groups due only to demographics and party ties? Multivariate analysis will be used to test whether religious involvement (specifically church attendance) has a significant independent effect on campaign involvement, based on the campaign-activism scale displayed in table 3.6. As table 3.7 shows, based on ANES data for presidential elections from 1980 to 2008, contacts by political parties strongly encourage political involvement, and such contacts have been far more likely to be reported by moderates and traditionalists than by seculars. Once these other factors are controlled, however, African Americans and Hispanics are actually more rather than less likely to be active in campaigns. Over this time period church attendance has indeed had a significant impact on both campaign activism and voter turnout, even with controls for party identification, strength of partisanship, and demographic factors (age, education, income, sex). However, additional regression analysis (not shown) revealed that the impact of church attendance since 2000 was considerably less than in earlier years with respect to vote choice as well as campaign activism.[29]

As table 3.5 demonstrated, white seculars exhibit considerable antipathy toward Christian fundamentalists. Such antipathy is higher among the young, the better educated, Democrats, and political liberals. But has

Table 3.7  Multivariate Prediction of Campaign Activism and Voter Turnout, 1980–2008

| | Campaign Activism Scale (OLS) | | | Voter Turnout (logit) | | |
|---|---|---|---|---|---|---|
| | b | SE | t | b | SE | Wald |
| Age | -0.002 | 0.00 | -0.070 | 0.031 | 0.00 | **767** |
| Sex | -0.113 | 0.01 | **-8.638** | -0.066 | 0.04 | 4 |
| Partisanship | 0.154 | 0.01 | **23.180** | 0.408 | 0.02 | **886** |
| Party ID | 0.006 | 0.00 | 1.740 | -0.006 | 0.01 | 1 |
| Education | 0.093 | 0.00 | **21.670** | 0.362 | 0.01 | **885** |
| Income | 0.040 | 0.01 | **6.320** | 0.266 | 0.02 | **243** |
| Contact by party | 0.447 | 0.02 | **30.610** | 0.954 | 0.04 | **530** |
| Hispanic | 0.033 | 0.03 | 1.290 | -0.085 | 0.06 | 2 |
| African American | 0.043 | 0.02 | **2.100** | 0.094 | 0.05 | 3 |
| Frequency of church attendance | 0.018 | 0.00 | **4.220** | 0.170 | 0.01 | **218** |
| Constant | 0.772 | 0.05 | **17.130** | -3.510 | 0.13 | 687 |
| $R^2$ | 0.13 | | | 0.3 | | |
| F | 303.75 | | | 4870 | | |
| N | 19790 | | | 19825 | | |

Source: ANES
Statistically significant t-values (p < .05) in bold

it affected political mobilization? We would expect that seculars with particularly negative views of Christian fundamentalists would be more active in political campaigns in order to counter the threats to their values posed by candidates supportive of the policy goals of the Religious Right. By contrast, negative views of atheists could be mobilizing factors for traditionalists who feel threatened by "secular humanism."[30]

In order to test these conjectures, separate regressions were calculated to predict levels of campaign activism by seculars, traditionalists, and moderates, using pooled ANES surveys 1988–2008. The results (table 3.8) show that some standard predictors of political activism (male sex, strength of partisanship, education, income) applied to all three groups. Younger seculars, but also older traditionalists, were more likely to be active in campaigns. Democratic Party identification encouraged activism by seculars, while Republican identification led to more campaign involvement by both moderates and traditionalists. African American traditionalists (who tend to have highly positive views of Christian fundamentalists) were also more active, as were Hispanic moderates, but neither race nor ethnicity influenced campaign activism by seculars. Contacts by political parties were highly significant for all three groups, but as shown earlier, were much more common among church attendees, and exerted greater influence on campaign activism by traditionalists and moderates than by seculars.

Table 3.8  Multivariate Prediction of Campaign Activism by Religiosity

|  | Seculars | | | Moderates | | | Traditionalists | | |
| --- | --- | --- | --- | --- | --- | --- | --- | --- | --- |
|  | b | SE | t | b | SE | t | b | SE | t |
| Age | -0.002 | 0.00 | -1.34 | 0.000 | 0.00 | -0.2 | 0.004 | 0.00 | **3.29** |
| Sex | -0.072 | 0.05 | -1.55 | -0.095 | 0.03 | **-3.53** | -0.155 | 0.04 | **-4.24** |
| Partisanship | 0.172 | 0.02 | **7.18** | 0.163 | 0.01 | **11.57** | 0.141 | 0.02 | **7.94** |
| Party ID | -0.020 | 0.01 | -1.55 | 0.010 | 0.01 | 1.37 | 0.034 | 0.01 | **3.76** |
| Education | 0.100 | 0.02 | **7.18** | 0.087 | 0.10 | **9.22** | 0.087 | 0.01 | **7.34** |
| Income | 0.024 | 0.02 | 1.05 | 0.058 | 0.01 | **4.34** | 0.057 | 0.02 | **3.16** |
| Contact by party | 0.465 | 0.05 | **8.78** | 0.470 | 0.03 | **15.88** | 0.420 | 0.04 | **11.04** |
| Hispanic | -0.077 | 0.09 | -0.83 | 0.166 | 0.05 | **3.29** | 0.071 | 0.06 | 1.11 |
| African American | 0.140 | 0.11 | 1.23 | 0.059 | 0.05 | 1.32 | 0.192 | 0.05 | **3.92** |
| Thermometer: Christian fundamentalists | -0.004 | 0.00 | **-3.20** | -0.003 | 0.00 | **-4.23** | 0.003 | 0.00 | **3.53** |
| Constant | 0.878 | 0.14 | **6.09** | 0.822 | 0.09 | **8.75** | 0.525 | 0.13 | **3.98** |
| $R^2$ | 0.17 | | | 0.13 | | | 0.13 | | |
| F | 30.54 | | | 78.5 | | | 45.27 | | |
| N | 1548 | | | 5134 | | | 3071 | | |

Source: ANES
Statistically significant t-values (p < .05) in bold

Yet even with controls for such factors, antipathy toward Christian fundamentalists (as indicated by low scores on the ANES thermometer) indeed encouraged campaign involvement among seculars. Surprisingly, the effect of such antipathy was equally strong and statistically significant for religious moderates. Among religious traditionalists, however, *positive* attitudes toward Christian fundamentalists were significantly related to greater campaign activism. However, separate regressions showed that antipathy toward atheists (based on a thermometer score question asked only in 2008) had no apparent independent impact on campaign activism by any of these groups.

As table 3.8 shows, African American traditionalists were considerably more involved in campaigns relative to white traditionalists, but presumably on behalf of the Democrats. In 2008 the ANES survey found exactly one African American traditionalist (out of 250 in the sample) who voted for John McCain, compared with 77 percent of white traditionalists. Although many on the Religious Right had doubts about John McCain in 2008, table 3.3 showed that white traditionalists still gave the Republican candidate a higher proportion of their votes than in any election since 1980, but they may not have turned out in as large numbers as in 2004. Any analysis of the political impact of values must consider rates of mobilization and demobilization as well as partisan choice (including votes for third parties).[31]

## CONCLUSION

This chapter has found seculars, religious traditionalists, and religious moderates to be quite diverse in terms of demographics: race, ethnicity, gender, age, and marital and social status. And all three groups have been affected by ongoing trends in American society, including changes in the role of women, rising divorce rates, and growth in minority populations. The sharpest contrasts among these groups, however, emerge in their opinions on controversial social issues. Even though religious traditionalists now show greater support for equal roles for women, or positive affect toward gays and lesbians, than they did in the 1980s, they still hold very different views on these issues than seculars do. And divisions between these two groups in terms of opinions (especially on abortion), ideology, and party ties have increased over time.

Whether such increased divergence constitutes polarization is debatable. Traditionalists are somewhat more Republican, but moderates and seculars tend to be moderate or independent in their political views. Sizable proportions of Americans are neither ardently religious nor militantly secular. Religious moderates are divided between the parties and hold centrist positions on most social issues, although in both 2004 and 2008 white moderates were more likely to vote Republican than in previous elections. A further challenge to the culture-wars thesis is that religious moderates still predominate in the electorate (although a smaller proportion than in 1980). Polarization thus applies more to political and party elites than to the general public, and more Americans perceive divisions on the basis of race, class, or party than on the basis of religion.[32]

The diversity within each of these groups also points up the difficulties that both major parties now face in pulling together winning coalitions. Some religious traditionalists have become disillusioned with Republican policies and politicians, and were less involved in campaigns in 2008 than in 2004. Even traditionalists have become more supportive of gay marriage and abortion under at least some circumstances. The Tea Party movement that emerged in 2009 tried to keep its focus away from these divisive issues and on the economy and budget deficits, in order to appeal to younger voters, independents, and religious moderates.[33]

The Democratic Party still includes a sizable number of religious traditionalists, especially among African Americans and Hispanics, but many of these are apparently voting on the basis of racial, ethnic, or economic concerns rather than social issues. The Democrats have also faced defections by Catholics (over reproductive rights and gay marriage) and Jews (over support, or lack thereof, for Israel). Seculars may constitute a larger percentage of the Democratic electoral coalition than in 1980, but they have much weaker partisan ties. This will constrain their participation in party primaries, and may also predispose them to support third-party candidates.

In the 1980s and 1990s, according to most conventional measures of political activism, religious moderates and traditionalists were more interested than seculars in elections, more likely to register and vote, and more active in campaigns. Since they were more involved in both religious and social organizations, traditionalists were considerably more likely to be contacted by political parties or other groups trying to sway their votes, and such contacts are strong predictors of campaign activism and voter turnout. In part because of their higher levels of education, seculars appeared to be somewhat better informed about politics, based on both objective measures and ANES interviewer ratings, but they were considerably less likely to be strong partisans and more likely to support third-party candidates. Thus secular perspectives on politics and social issues were unlikely to carry much political weight, either within the major parties or at the polls.

However, this portrait of apolitical seculars must be updated based on the evidence presented in this chapter. Seculars' levels of voter turnout and campaign activism now differ little from those of religious traditionalists. And as of 2004 they were even more interested in the campaign, and more likely to try to convince others how to vote, than moderates or traditionalists, and equally likely to donate to parties or candidates. One recent analysis estimated that as of 2004, seculars constituted one-sixth of the population and "have become increasingly important in deciding the outcome of American elections." In 2008 Barack Obama's largest support base came from those who never attend church; 75 percent of them voted for him compared with the 67 percent who voted for John Kerry in 2004.[34]

Furthermore, seculars' voting behavior has become considerably more Democratic, especially for president. Not only has their proportion of the population increased from 12 percent in 1980 to 18 percent as of 2008, but based on ANES data, the secular proportion of the total Democratic presidential vote also increased from 16 to 34 percent over this same period. Religious traditionalists provided a sizable 39 percent of Republican presidential votes in 2008, but this represented only a slight increase from 37 percent in 1980.

What accounts for this notable growth in secular political involvement? Not an increase in partisanship, because seculars (despite their increasingly Democratic voting patterns) have weaker ties to the parties than either moderates or conservatives. And not organizational involvement; as analyses of social capital have shown, people who are involved in organizations (especially churches) are more politically involved and aware, more likely to contribute to charities as well as churches, more likely to engage in volunteer work, and more likely to be contacted by political parties or other groups.[35] Seculars still lag considerably behind religious moderates and traditionalists in all of these dimensions (although greater secular use of the Internet could potentially offset their lack of organizational ties).

Based on the results reported in this chapter, the morality-politics cycle provides a plausible alternative theoretical explanation for increased secular political involvement: antipathy to the Religious Right. A multivariate analysis showed that campaign activism among seculars, traditionalists, or moderates was based on similar factors: income, higher levels of education, strength of partisanship, contacts by political parties. Republican Party identification was associated with greater campaign activism by traditionalists, while Democratic seculars were more involved. Even when these factors are taken into account, however, antipathy to Christian fundamentalists (based on ANES thermometer scores) emerged as a significant predictor of political involvement by both seculars and religious moderates. This is suggestive evidence that recent political gains by the Religious Right, and their close ties with the Republican Party, were perceived as deeply threatening to those with secular or religiously progressive views.

However, additional evidence is needed to document how positions on issues, and perceptions of party differences on those issues, affect political involvement. A considerable proportion of Americans in all three religious groupings still perceive no significant differences between the Democratic and Republican parties or presidential candidates. In 2008, 27 percent of seculars, 22 percent of moderates, and 24 percent of traditionalists saw "no significant differences" between the parties (ANES data); slightly higher proportions had perceived significant differences in 2004. In 2004, 49 percent of people who never attended church agreed that "The parties don't offer real policy choices" (GSS data), compared with 44 percent of church attendees. Since people who are unaware of party or candidate differences are less likely to vote, a major purpose of political campaigns is to highlight such differences. Political elites thus have a vested interest in promoting polarization. Chapter 4 will consider in more detail the individual and contextual factors that influence perceptions (or misperceptions) of party differences.

# 4

## Party Differences, Religious "Threat," and Voter Mobilization

Chapter 3 showed that seculars and religious traditionalists in the United States have very different voting patterns and policy preferences. Is this evidence of a society deeply divided by religion, as Hunter's culture-war thesis argues? At the elite level, greater political polarization and ideological coherence have been evident since the 1970s in policy voting in Congress. The Democratic and Republican parties are sharply split over questions of religion, family values, and the role of government. Religious traditionalists constitute the largest single group in the Republican Party's base, and seculars are an increasingly visible portion of the Democratic Party's activists and convention delegates. But at the mass level, the culture-war thesis has much less empirical support. Instead of the Red state/Blue state divide so often emphasized by the mass media, most Americans remain close to the middle on both religious and political questions.[1]

Data on trends since the 1970s show that Americans (especially partisans) are increasingly aware of differences between the Democratic and Republican parties. But despite media and campaign efforts to persuade them otherwise, many others still claim to see *no* significant differences between the parties, or between the presidential candidates, on major issues. This represents an intriguing puzzle for political scientists; in a media-saturated society, why do so many people remain unaware of partisan differences, or even attribute liberal policy stands to conservative politicians (or vice versa)? These misperceptions are a dilemma for politicians as well, because people who see no party or candidate differences are much less likely to vote. In order to mobilize people to vote, or work on a campaign, or contribute to a cause, politicians must somehow convince them that the alternatives *do* matter.

This chapter will consider the impact of church attendance, organizational involvement, and the state political and religious environment on perceptions of party differences. Personal resources clearly influence political behavior; younger people, minorities, political independents, and those with less education or income are less attuned to political cues and less likely to vote. But recent research on social capital has found that organizational involvement is crucial to understanding political awareness and participation. People who are group or union members, or frequent church attendees, have lower information costs and are far easier to mobilize. They are more aware of cues from political elites, and thus more tuned in to party and candidate differences on issues. And people in more competitive and diverse states receive very different political messages than those in solid Red or Blue states, or states where one religion is predominant.

The next sections of this chapter will examine trends in awareness of party differences, and demonstrate the importance of this factor for political participation. I will then consider how personal resources, organizational involvement, and the social context affect awareness of party differences. As I will show, the state's religious environment and degree of electoral competition significantly enhanced awareness of party and candidate positions on the highly salient issue of abortion in 2004, but had little effect on awareness of other issues. Frequent worshippers in more secular states, and non-Catholics in heavily Catholic states, were most aware of candidate differences on abortion, suggesting the impact of the threat to core values posed by competing groups. But on other issues, party differences were significantly more apparent to seculars than to weekly church attendees—despite their weaker partisanship and lack of organizational ties.

## PERCEPTIONS OF PARTY DIFFERENCES, 1980–2008

Democratic and Republican party platforms show increasing divergence in positions on managing the economy, abortion, taxation, and foreign policy. Party-line voting in Congress has increased considerably since the 1970s.[2] But how salient are partisan differences at the elite level to the mass public? Cues from political elites are an important source of public opinion, at least among people who pay attention to politics and the media. As party leaders have polarized, party differences should become more apparent to citizens, especially strong partisans, and especially on issues where the parties diverge.[3]

Figure 4.1 shows that, compared to the 1970s, more ANES respondents now agree that there are "significant differences between what the Democratic and Republican parties stand for." Strong partisans have been consistently more tuned in to party differences, but by 2004, party differences were salient even to independents and weak or leaning partisans. Even so, 17 percent of ANES respondents saw "no difference" between the parties in 2004, compared with 29 percent in 1980, and a similar proportion (10–12 percent) responded "Don't know" to the question in either year. In 2008, policy differences between Obama and McCain were at least as sharp as those between Bush and Kerry, but party differences were a bit less salient to ANES respondents. A possible reason is that the 2008 sample included more African Americans and Hispanics, who tend to be less politically knowledgeable.

The ANES surveys also ask respondents where they would position the parties and the presidential and congressional candidates on a range of issues. The abortion options offered in 2004 were the same as those used in figure 3.6 for respondents' own views, ranging from "Never allowed" to "Abortion as a woman's choice." Yet despite the parties' official platforms and the considerable Bush/Kerry differences on abortion, ANES data show that 24 percent of respondents in 2004 were unable to identify where one or both parties or presidential candidates stood on the issue of abortion; over half were unable to place their congressional candidates (table 4.1). An additional 15–20 percent either attributed identical posi-

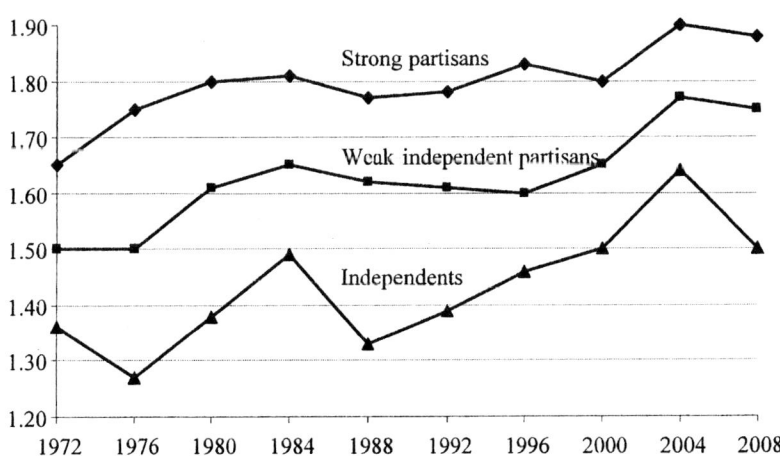

**Y-axis: 1 = no differences; 2 = significant differences

**Figure 4.1. Mean Perception of Party Differences by Partisan Strength (ANES)**

Table 4.1  Perceptions of Policy Differences on Abortion and Seven-Point Issue Scales, 2004

|  | Party Difference | Candidate Differences | | | | | | | |
|---|---|---|---|---|---|---|---|---|---|
|  | Abortion* | Abortion* | Defense | Spending | Women | Blacks | Jobs | Environment | Force/Diplomacy |
| Unable to respond | 27 | 23 | 11 | 14 | 20 | 23 | 16 | 24 | 18 |
| No difference | 13 | 14 | 9 | 12 | 34 | 20 | 14 | 17 | 3 |
| 1 or 2 | 47 | 45 | 34 | 33 | 26 | 29 | 29 | 29 | 21 |
| 3 or more | 13 | 18 | 46 | 41 | 20 | 28 | 41 | 30 | 58 |

Source: ANES
*Four-point index

tions to both parties and candidates or judged the Republican Party or George Bush to be more pro-choice than the Democrats or John Kerry.[4]

Similar patterns are apparent where respondents were asked about their perceptions of candidates' positions on other issues, including government spending on social services or defense, the environment, jobs/income policy, and equal roles for women (table 4.1).[5] Clearly, even during the heated 2004 election campaign some Americans remained unaware of the party and issue conflicts so salient to strong partisans, political elites, and the media.

## PARTY/CANDIDATE DIFFERENCES AND VOTER TURNOUT

Furthermore, people unaware of party or candidate differences are significantly less likely to vote. Rational-choice models of voting behavior posit that if the alternatives offered on the ballot do not appear to differ, the outcome of an election will not matter much, so why bother voting? The costs of voting (in time, information, or opportunity) will far outweigh any potential benefit to an individual voter.[6] Table 4.2 contrasts self-reports of voter turnout in 2004 and 2008 among ANES respondents, based on perceptions of overall differences between the parties (and in 2008, between Obama and McCain). The reported voting rate is also shown for respondents with varying perceptions of party or candidate positions on abortion (actual turnout rates are considerably lower; survey respondents are prone to exaggerate socially desirable behaviors such as voting and church attendance).

In 2004 reported voter turnout was 87 percent among the 80 percent of respondents who perceived "significant" differences between the parties, but only 58 percent among those who saw no differences. In 2008 a slightly smaller proportion of respondents (76 percent) saw significant party differences, but 82 percent of them voted. The 2008 ANES survey also asked whether there were major, minor, or no differences between Barack Obama and John McCain. Voter turnout was far higher (81 percent among the 71 percent of respondents who saw "major" differences) compared with the other groups (67 and 62 percent turnout respectively). Of course, people vote for many reasons other than issues: sense of citizen duty, assessment of candidates' personal qualities, other competitive state/local races. But table 4.2 shows that those who do see issue or candidate differences are significantly more likely to vote.

In both 2004 and 2008, turnout also varied considerably with respect to perceptions of party differences on the abortion issue, with the highest turnout among those who considered Democrats and Republicans to be far apart and the lowest turnout among respondents unable to place the parties at all. Given the effects on turnout, parties and organizations have powerful incentives to deviate from the median-voter position and to take strong stands on this and other issues. The same pattern is evident for the presidential candidates; people who placed Bush and Kerry farther apart on the ANES abortion index were considerably more likely to vote than those who could not place them at all or attributed identical positions to them (table 4.2). Actual candidate positions were considerably more nu-

Table 4.2 Perceived Party, Candidate, and Abortion Differences and Voter Turnout, 2004 and 2008

|  |  | 2004 | | 2008 | |
|  |  | % of sample | % of those who voted | % of sample | % of those who voted |
|---|---|---|---|---|---|
| Significant party difference | No | 20 | 59 | 24 | 61 |
|  | Yes | 80 | 87 | 76 | 82 |
| Candidate differences | None |  |  | 4 | 62 |
|  | Minor |  |  | 25 | 67 |
|  | Major |  |  | 71 | 81 |
| Perceived party differences on abortion | DK | 17 | 56 | 15 | 66 |
|  | None | 14 | 68 | 18 | 64 |
|  | 1 | 25 | 79 | 22 | 79 |
|  | 2 | 30 | 90 | 29 | 88 |
|  | 3 | 14 | 90 | 17 | 88 |
| Perceived candidate differences on abortion | DK | 13 | 50 | 15 | 60 |
|  | None | 16 | 70 | 19 | 66 |
|  | 1 | 19 | 79 | 24 | 82 |
|  | 2 | 32 | 89 | 29 | 86 |
|  | 3 | 20 | 89 | 14 | 81 |

anced than the starkly different response options offered by the ANES surveys; in 2004 Kerry was personally opposed to most abortions, while Bush was willing to allow them in cases of rape or incest. In 2008 Obama and the Democratic Party platform stressed the need to prevent abortion. Still, as table 4.2 shows, despite the best efforts of campaign managers, about a third of the electorate was either not aware of candidate or party stands at all or failed to see any differences on the abortion issue.

Of course several factors other than perceived issue differences affect turnout. Strong partisans and people with more resources (income, education) are more likely to vote, as are frequent church attendees and members of more organizations. Turnout should also be higher in the more competitive states, where one's vote has a greater likelihood of making a difference. Table 4.3 displays the results of a multivariate analysis of voter turnout based on the 2004 and 2008 ANES.[7] As is almost always the case in analyses of voting, in both years the degree of partisanship emerged as the strongest predictor of voter turnout, but the closeness of the election in a respondent's state had only a marginal impact. Higher levels of education and family income likewise significantly increased turnout, but only in 2008 did frequency of church attendance have a strong impact. Involvement in other organizations did not matter much in 2004 but was highly significant in 2008. In both years respondents who reported being contacted by parties or other organizations were considerably more likely to vote (and as we have seen, involvement in churches or other organizations increases the likelihood of such contacts). However, even when these factors are taken

Table 4.3 Models Predicting Voter Turnout, 2004 and 2008

|  | 2004 | | | 2008 | | |
| --- | --- | --- | --- | --- | --- | --- |
|  | b | SE | Wald Sig. | b | SE | Wald Sig. |
| Education | 0.270 | 0.07 | 13.98** | 0.197 | 0.05 | 13.99** |
| Family income | 0.044 | 0.02 | 6.87* | 0.177 | 0.07 | 7.13* |
| Strength of partisanship | 0.635 | 1.12 | 27.13** | 0.779 | 0.08 | 88.26** |
| Parties differ | 1.010 | 0.21 | 24.20** | 0.447 | 0.18 | 6.54* |
| Election contract | -0.234 | 0.05 | 18.72** | 1.051 | 0.17 | 38.73** |
| Closeness of state race | -0.001 | 0.02 | 0.01 | 0.006 | 0.00 | 2.41 |
| Frequency of church attendance | -0.077 | 0.06 | 1.89 | 0.142 | 0.05 | 7.48* |
| Number of organizations | 0.446 | 0.13 | 9.69* | 0.532 | 0.13 | 17.98** |
| Constant | -1.175 | 0.48 | 6.12* | -4.210 | 0.15 | 68.88** |
| Nagelkirke $R^2$ | 0.31 | | | 0.36 | | |
| Log likelihood | 722.3 | | | 1017 | | |
| % correctly classified | 83 | | | 81 | | |

* Significant at p<.05   **Significant at p<.01

into account, perception of party differences still had a strong and statistically significant impact on voter turnout, especially in 2004.

## ORGANIZATIONS, POLITICAL STRATEGY, AND PARTY DIFFERENCES

Parties and candidates not only have to mobilize the strong partisans who constitute their base, they must also somehow convince those closer to the political center that their electoral choices differ enough to justify the costs of voting. Most explanations for differences in political awareness have stressed levels of individual resources. Citizens who are well educated, earn a higher income, or work in professional or managerial occupations are much more likely to be aware of issues and candidates. Partisanship is also a powerful predictor of political involvement, and party identification is a useful heuristic for reducing information costs and for making educated guesses about a candidate's positions.[8]

Beyond individual resources, awareness of political issues is likely to depend on a person's social ties and the political context. In recent years social scientists have emphasized the role of social capital: "the features of social organization that facilitate working and cooperating together for mutual benefit."[9] People who are involved in organizations or social networks, including churches and labor unions, acquire useful political and social skills, higher levels of trust in others, and stronger commitment to democratic norms. Contacts with leaders and other group members help to reduce information costs and to encourage political activism. Since churches are by far the most common organization in American society, it is not surprising that they also contribute to social capital formation. Frequency of church attendance emerged in the 1980s as a powerful factor predicting the vote.

To a considerable extent, organizational involvement reinforces the class bias in participation, since people with higher education and incomes are more likely to be joiners (and as we have seen, frequent church attendees). But some organizations (labor unions, African American churches) provide social capital that offsets their members' lack of personal resources.[10] Labor union leaders and church pastors can provide cues to their members about their personal stake in an upcoming election, and stress differences in the candidates' issue positions. They thus encourage political involvement by the poor or the working class, although the decline in union membership since the 1970s has probably augmented the social-class bias in participation.[11] However, as shown in chapter 3, seculars do not attend church, are less likely to be members of other organizations, and receive fewer campaign contacts. Because of their relative lack of social capital, their perspectives are less likely to be articulated, and we would expect them to be less aware of candidate and issue differences.

Organizations can also be helpful to efforts by political elites to educate voters about the issues, convince them that elections matter, and get them to the polls. Since candidates and parties have limited campaign resources, it is far more efficient for them to work through organizations than to try to reach out to isolated individuals. However, politicians must offer some incentives to persuade leaders of organizations (including churches) to provide an endorsement, contribution, speaking venue, or mailing list. Personal contacts and grassroots door knocking have proven to be effective in turning out the vote, but to convince group members to engage in these time-intensive activities, they must be persuaded that they will gain something significant if that politician is elected (or lose something of value if he or she is defeated).

One tactic to gain organizational support is for politicians to emphasize issues or take positions that reflect the priorities of an electorally important group. Democrats have long been solicitous of organized labor, whose phone banks and workplace efforts can boost turnout of union members and supporters. Republicans have stressed issues such as gay-marriage bans, school choice, or abortion restrictions in order to persuade conservatives to mobilize on their behalf. In 2004 the national Republican organization supported efforts in several states to qualify gay-marriage bans for the November ballot.[12] And in order to encourage Catholic defections from the Democratic Party, the Bush campaign stressed his opposition to abortion, especially in swing states such as Ohio. Parish-level organizing efforts offered even stronger criticism of John Kerry's pro-choice voting record than the U.S. Conference of Catholic Bishops was willing to make.[13]

In theory, parties and candidates should focus their issue stands on the middle of the opinion distribution, where most voters are to be found on most issues. Candidates too far to the right of center (Goldwater in 1964) or left of center (McGovern in 1972) are likely to lose. But if both parties converge on the center, voters have less incentive to bother voting at all. Bringing organizations into the picture helps to explain why it can be rational for politicians to diverge from the median voter in order to gain votes. In recent years the parties (especially the Republicans) have moved further from the political center in order to solidify their strong base among evangelicals (and hopefully to attract some socially conservative Democrats as well).[14] The greater the divergence between parties or candidates on an issue important to that group, the easier it will be for a group's leaders to persuade its members that their votes and opinions do matter.[15] Grassroots organizing and personal contacts have proven effective in boosting turnout, and group members are more likely to engage in such intensive politicking to support a politician who shares their values.[16]

## CONTEXT, THREAT, AND PERCEPTION OF PARTY DIFFERENCES

The broader social context can also affect voters' awareness of differences among parties and candidates. Conflicts over race and immigration are more salient to citizens in racially or ethnically diverse states or communities. Likewise, religious diversity should enhance awareness of party or candidate differences on religious issues. The states vary considerably in religious composition, party dominance, and levels of political competition. Citizens in Bible-Belt Alabama, for example, are likely to receive very different cues from elites than citizens of New York or Minnesota. Candidates and parties lavish far more attention (television ads, grassroots mobilization, visits by the presidential candidates) on the "swing" states than on states considered solidly Red or Blue. Information costs for voters (particularly low-income voters) in "battleground" states should therefore be lower, further increasing the salience of issue differences.[17]

Religious interest groups in the states have gained in political influence since the 1980s. Galvanized by controversy over abortion and gay rights, religious organizations increasingly take public stands on issues and even candidates. Groups opposed to the Religious Right, such as People for the American Way and Americans United for the Separation of Church and State, have also become more active at the state and local level.[18] We would therefore expect some impact from the state's religious environment on awareness of party differences.

Two alternative scenarios are plausible. The first corresponds to Zaller's "one-message" model of political communication. If a particular religious tradition is *predominant* in a state (fundamentalist Protestants in the Bible Belt, Roman Catholics in Rhode Island or Louisiana, Mormons in Utah), the viewpoint of that religious tradition will be widely disseminated and consensus in public opinion is more likely: "Clergy in religiously homogenous areas can afford to be much more pointed in their communications . . . strongly worded socializing messages will not meet resistance or opposition."[19] Thus Roman Catholics in heavily Catholic states, or evangelicals in the Bible Belt, should be more aware of party positions, especially on "values" issues (such as abortion) salient to those traditions. However, clergy differ considerably in their willingness to deliver political messages from the pulpit, and the people in the pews may not welcome such messages. Religiously homogenous communities could also become complacent, leading to lower levels of political efficacy, knowledge, or discussion.[20]

By contrast, greater religious *diversity* in a state may lead to greater public discussion of policies such as abortion or gay marriage, and thus greater awareness of party differences on those issues. Zaller's "two-message" model implies heightened dissensus and debate. While individual voters can control exposure to competing messages to some degree, in a more diverse political or workplace environment, selective exposure or perception may be more difficult to maintain.[21] Religious diversity may thus heighten awareness of issues and of candidates' stands, but it could also be very threatening to the faithful whose views are being challenged.

Issue-oriented seculars have become more numerous and increasingly influential in Democratic Party politics since the 1980s. The more seculars in a state, the more likely the challenges to traditional religious views. One study found evidence of such secular "threat" in the 1996 and 2000 presidential elections; the larger the proportion of seculars in their state or community (county), the more likely white evangelical Christians were to vote for the Republican presidential candidate. That analysis found no evidence in 1996 or 2000 that seculars reacted in parallel fashion to the presence of evangelicals in their environment.[22] But seculars' strong antipathy to Christian fundamentalists may have been heightened since 2000 by the evangelical views and faith-based policies of the Bush administration. So "religious threat" could influence the votes of seculars in conservative religious environments.

In addition to a state's religious profile, the competitiveness of the presidential election in a given state could also affect perceptions of party differences. In more diverse or competitive states, political elites invest more campaign resources, and are motivated to stake out stronger positions on controversial issues in order to gain support from sympathetic organizations. Thus the mass public receives more salient cues, and heightened awareness of party or candidate differences. In 2008, 95 percent of the $495 million spent on campaign ads went to the fifteen battleground states, and voter turnout averaged seven points higher than in the less competitive states, suggesting a greater stake in the outcome for individual voters in those states.[23] And the more competitive the state, the greater the incentive for candidates to commit campaign resources and to emphasize party differences on issues in order to solicit endorsements and group mobilization efforts. Further, the emphasis should be on "wedge" issues with the greatest potential to attract adherents from the opposite party. Hillygus and Shields claim that the Religious Right's focus on cultural issues, such as abortion and gay rights, in 2004 was highly rational, since voters cross-pressured on these issues were more likely to vote across party lines. But they found economic issues to be much less effective as wedge issues.[24]

## TEST CASE—ABORTION AND OTHER ISSUES IN 2004

Figure 4.1 shows party differences to be more salient in 2004 compared with earlier years or with 2008. The hard-fought and very close 2004 election thus provides an ideal case for comparing the impact of individual resources, organizational ties, and the state context on awareness of party and candidate differences. Specific hypotheses to be evaluated include:

- H1. *Impact of social capital*: Frequent church attendees and members of unions or other organizations should be more aware of party or candidate differences.
- H2. *Social capital as compensation*: The impact of religious involvement on awareness of party or candidate differences should be greater for individuals with less education.
- H3. *Secular threat*: The impact of religious involvement on awareness of party or candidate differences should be stronger in states with higher proportions of seculars and thus greater religious diversity.
- H4. *Religious dominance*: The impact of religious involvement on awareness of party or candidate differences by Roman Catholics or evangelicals should be stronger in states with higher proportions of members of those denominations.
- H5. *Issue emphasis*: The impact of religious involvement or state religious composition on awareness of party differences should be greater on the values issue of abortion than on other political or economic issues where churches have not taken stands.

To support any of these hypotheses, religious involvement and the state context should have a sizable or significant impact even with controls for demographics, membership in other organizations, and political factors. Political parties are the preeminent mobilizing institutions in American politics. Partisanship and the level of party competition in a state may therefore dominate the organizational context—even for group members and churchgoers.

### Data and Measures

The 2004 American National Election Studies (ANES) asked questions about party and candidate differences on several issues as well as on church involvement, religious affiliation, and the demographic or partisan factors that could influence awareness of issue differences. The 2004 survey also provides data, not included in previous ANES studies, on organizational involvement and on perceived party and candidate stands on the abortion issue.

These ANES data do not provide detailed information about leadership strategies or organizational processes within churches that might link members with politics and partisan viewpoints. Other studies using different data on local congregations or communities provide some insights into these dynamics.[25] However, none of these address the perceptions of party differences that are crucial to these hypotheses. Further, the ANES national survey can assess the impact of a broader range of contextual variables, such as a state's religious profile and degree of party competition, on awareness of party differences.[26]

**Dependent Variables**

Perceptions of overall party differences will be assessed based on the question about "important differences in what the Democrats and Republican parties stand for" used in figure 4.1. Perceptions of candidate differences on specific issues will be based on the seven-point issue scales used in table 4.1, on which respondents were asked to place George Bush and John Kerry. The specific indicator is the absolute difference between the respondent's placements of the presidential candidates on these scales; these scores range from 0 to 6.[27]

In 2004 respondents were also asked to place themselves, the parties, the presidential candidates, and the congressional candidates in their district on the four-point abortion index described earlier, ranging from 1 ("By law, abortion should never be permitted") to 4 ("Abortion is a woman's choice"). The specific indicator to be used is the difference between the Democratic and Republican party/candidate placements on abortion, which ranges from 0 to 3. As noted earlier, given the limits of the ANES question wording we make no claim that respondents have correctly identified either party or candidate positions. However, clearly "incorrect" responses, by the 8 percent of respondents who perceived Republicans (or Bush) as more liberal or more pro-choice on abortion than Democrats (or Kerry), are excluded from the analysis.

**Independent Variables**

*Organizational involvement*: Number of organizations to which ANES respondents say they belong. In 2004, 58 percent belonged to none, 19 percent to one, and 23 percent to two or more.

*Frequency of church attendance*: A five-point scale ranging from 1 (never attends) to 5 (attends worship services weekly).

*Denomination*: Evangelicals and Roman Catholics are expected to be particularly sensitive to party/candidate differences on abortion, because of strong pro-life signals from leaders of these denominations. Indicator variables will be included for self-identified Roman Catholics and for evangelicals.[28]

*Opinion on abortion*: The respondent's self-placement on the four-point index. Since the abortion issue has been found to be especially salient to people who are pro-life,[29] those individuals are expected to perceive sharper party or candidate differences.

Control variables include several individual factors expected to affect perceptions of party differences. First is strength of partisanship, ranging from 1 (independents) to 2 (leaners), 3 (weak Democrat or Republican), or 4 (strong Democrat or Republican). Standard demographics include education, household income, race (non-Hispanic white/others), and age. We would expect candidate and party differences to be more salient to whites and to those with higher levels of education or income. Older people should also be less aware of issue differences; they may also remember the years before 1980 when the parties did not differ much on abortion.[30]

### Contextual (state-level) Variables

*Religious composition*: Data for the proportion of seculars, Roman Catholics (including Hispanic Catholics), and evangelicals by state are from Green.[31] In the 2004 ANES sample of twenty-eight states, Washington, with 25 percent, had the highest percent of seculars, while Bible-Belt Alabama had the lowest; the median was 15 percent. (See figure 4.2.)

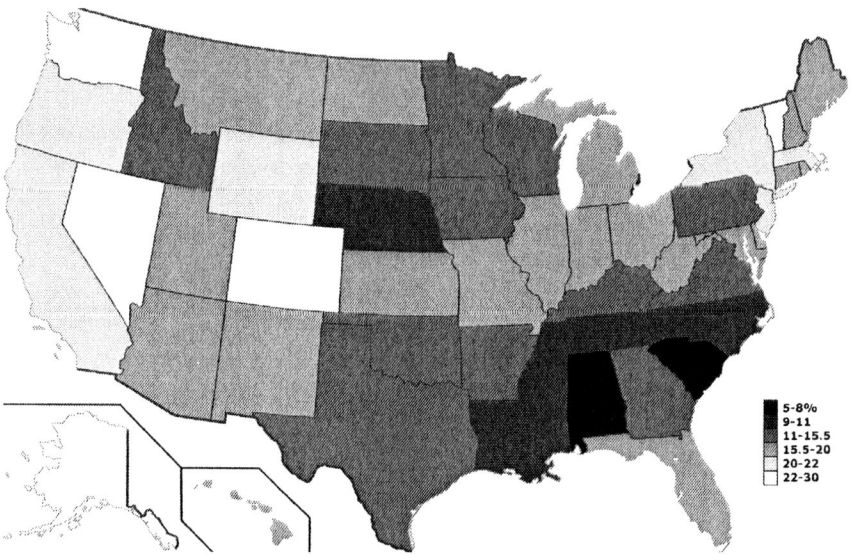

Figure 4.2. Proportion of Seculars by State (created by author from data in Green [2007])

*State electoral competition*: The absolute difference between 50 and the Republican proportion of the state's 2004 two-party vote, inverted so that higher values indicate more competition.

**Interaction Terms**

To test H2 (whether religious involvement had more impact on those with less education, the education variable was multiplied by frequency of church attendance (INTED). To test H4 (whether the state religious environment had more impact on regular church attendees), the frequency of church attendance was multiplied by the proportion of seculars in a state (INTSEC). And to test whether the proportion of evangelicals or Roman Catholics in a state had any impact on the perceptions of their church members, dummy variables for individual evangelical and Roman Catholic affiliation were multiplied by the proportions of evangelicals and Roman Catholics, respectively, in a state (INTEVANG, INTCATH).

## RESULTS FOR PERCEPTIONS OF ABORTION DIFFERENCES

Multivariate analysis was used to assess the independent effects of group involvement and the social/political context on perceptions of party or candidate differences.[32] Table 4.4 shows the prediction equations for perceptions of overall party differences (logit) and party or candidate differences on the abortion issue (ordered logit). As might be expected, the better-educated, non-Hispanic whites, and strong partisans perceived significantly greater differences; household income has no impact. Also as expected, younger people were more aware of party or candidate differences overall and on abortion. However, the positive coefficients for the respondent's opinion on abortion indicate that (contrary to expectations and to previous research) candidate and party differences were more salient to those with pro-choice views.

Self-identified Roman Catholics perceived significantly greater candidate differences on abortion, as expected, but respondents classified as evangelicals perceived fewer differences. Once these factors are controlled, however, frequency of church attendance had little independent impact; neither did involvement in other organizations.[33] Even after taking all of these individual characteristics into account, the state religious and electoral environment affected views of party differences. Greater electoral competition in a state (based on presidential vote) was not related to perception of overall party differences, but was positively associated with perceptions of differences on the abortion issue. Greater candidate and party differences on abortion were also perceived among respondents in

Table 4.4 Perception of Party and Candidate Differences, 2004

| | Perception of Differences on Abortion (ordered logit) | | | Dem/Rep Difference | | | Perception of Overall Party Differences | | |
|---|---|---|---|---|---|---|---|---|---|
| | Bush/Kerry Difference | | | | | | | | |
| Predictor Variables | b | SE** | z | b | SE** | z | b | SE** | z |
| Electoral competition | 0.035 | 0.01 | 3.93* | 0.048 | 0.01 | 3.22* | 0.001 | 0.01 | 0.10 |
| State % seculars | -0.511 | 0.22 | -2.32* | -0.319 | 0.17 | -1.90* | 0.039 | 0.27 | 0.15 |
| INTSEC | 0.139 | 0.06 | 2.41* | 0.106 | 0.05 | 2.08* | 0.060 | 0.07 | 0.86 |
| State % Catholics | 2.050 | 0.50 | 4.12* | 0.672 | 0.47 | 1.43 | 0.750 | 0.57 | 1.32 |
| Catholic | 1.672 | 0.42 | 3.99* | 0.820 | 0.44 | 1.85+ | 1.270 | 0.65 | 1.72 |
| INTCATH | -0.932 | 0.27 | -3.41 | -0.347 | 0.32 | -1.07 | -0.667 | 0.37 | -1.85 |
| State % Evangelicals | 0.118 | 0.20 | 0.58 | -0.352 | 0.21 | -1.71+ | 0.361 | 0.32 | 1.11 |
| Evangelical | -0.184 | 0.16 | -1.13 | -0.348 | 0.15 | -2.26* | 0.361 | 0.32 | 1.11 |
| INTEVANG | 0.098 | 0.07 | 1.29 | 0.171 | 0.06 | 2.96* | -0.069 | 0.10 | -0.72 |
| Church attendance | 0.061 | 0.18 | 0.50 | -0.048 | 0.13 | -0.36 | -0.154 | 0.25 | -0.61 |
| Pro-choice on abortion | 0.106 | 0.09 | 1.24 | 0.212 | 0.08 | 2.61* | 0.131 | 0.09 | 1.52 |
| Strength of partisanship | 0.101 | 0.14 | 0.74 | 0.214 | 0.07 | 3.24* | 0.608 | 0.12 | 5.17 |
| Member of organizations | 0.081 | 0.09 | 1.04 | 0.034 | 0.09 | 0.38 | 0.121 | 0.10 | 1.22 |
| Age | -0.004 | 0.00 | -1.04 | -0.009 | 0.00 | -2.34* | -0.123 | 0.01 | -1.63 |
| Race | -0.722 | 0.16 | -4.54 | -0.725 | 0.16 | -4.64- | -0.672 | 0.21 | -3.24 |
| Income | 0.004 | 0.01 | 0.48 | -0.001 | 0.01 | -0.10 | 0.020 | 0.01 | 1.37 |
| Education | 0.462 | 0.09 | 4.98* | 0.341 | 0.09 | 3.55* | 0.178 | 0.13 | 1.40 |
| INTED | -0.084 | 0.03 | -2.96* | -0.021 | 0.03 | -0.94 | 0.024 | 0.04 | 0.64 |

**Table 4.4** Perception of Party and Candidate Differences, 2004 *(continued)*

| | Perception of Differences on Abortion (ordered logit) | | | | Perception of Overall Party Differences |
|---|---|---|---|---|---|
| | Bush/Kerry Difference | | Dem/Rep Difference | | |
| Cut 1 | -2.15 | 0.73 | -1.38 | 0.74 | |
| Cut 2 | -0.88 | 0.74 | 0.08 | 0.70 | |
| Cut 3 | 1.08 | 0.71 | 20.40 | 0.72 | |
| Constant | | | | | 0.737 0.85 0.86 |
| Wald $x^2$ | 290.89* | | | | 219.26* |
| Pseudo $R^2$ | 0.05 | | | | 0.11 |
| N | 721 | | | | 912 |

\*\* Standard errors corrected for data clustered by state   \*Significant at $p < .05$   +Significant at $p < .10$

states with a higher proportion of Catholics. The significant coefficients in the candidate equation for Catholics and for heavily Catholic states are not surprising given the church and media focus on abortion during the 2004 campaign, and the public debate over whether John Kerry should be denied communion because of his pro-choice positions. Although the party platforms also differed strongly on this issue, Bush/Kerry differences were probably more salient to voters.

By contrast, fewer party and candidate differences on abortion were perceived by respondents in states with a higher proportion of seculars; these coefficients reach statistical significance in the candidate-difference equation. But the strongly positive interaction term INTSEC in the candidate equation indicates that the most frequent church attendees in the more secular states perceived sharper Bush/Kerry differences. The effect is also positive but more modest for the party-difference equation, suggesting that secular "threat" helped to mobilize the Religious Right in 2004 as it had in 2000.[34] As predicted by H4, evangelicals were significantly more aware of party differences on abortion in states with a high proportion of evangelicals.[35] But in states with a high proportion of Catholics, the negative coefficients for INTCATH indicate that sharper candidate differences on abortion were apparent to non-Catholics.

In the candidate equation in table 4.4, the significant negative interaction term INTED for education and church attendance provides some support for H2. Thus the less educated who attend church frequently perceived sharper Bush/Kerry differences on abortion. But this pattern is not evident in the party-difference equations. Neither electoral competition, church attendance, state religious composition, nor the interaction terms combining these significantly affected perceptions of overall party differences; partisanship, race, and education were more important. Once other factors were taken into account, partisanship had little impact on perceived Bush/Kerry differences on abortion.

States with high proportions of seculars also tend to be more religiously diverse. Does religious diversity, rather than the more specific threat posed by a high proportion of seculars, contribute to perceptions of party differences? An index of religious diversity in a state was computed to test this possibility.[36] The results showed positive but much weaker relationships with perceptions of party differences than did the state's proportion of seculars. It thus appears that secular threat, rather than overall religious diversity, has a greater impact on perceptions of party or candidate differences by regular church attendees.

The results shown in tables 4.4 provide inferential evidence that the state religious environment affects perceptions of issue differences. But what is the actual impact of church attendance or the proportion of seculars in a state? To estimate this impact, expected values for perceived candidate abortion differences were calculated for those who attended church weekly or never in states ranking low/medium versus high on the proportion of seculars.[37]

As figure 4.3a shows, both weekly attendees and nonattendees in the most secular states had the highest predicted probabilities of perceiving candidate differences of two or more points on the abortion index, and the corresponding lowest predicted probability of seeing no differences or being unaware of candidates' stands. In the less secular states, by contrast, neither weekly attendees nor nonattendees perceived much difference between Bush and Kerry.

Levels of perceived candidate abortion differences for Catholics and non-Catholics were also estimated for states above and below the median

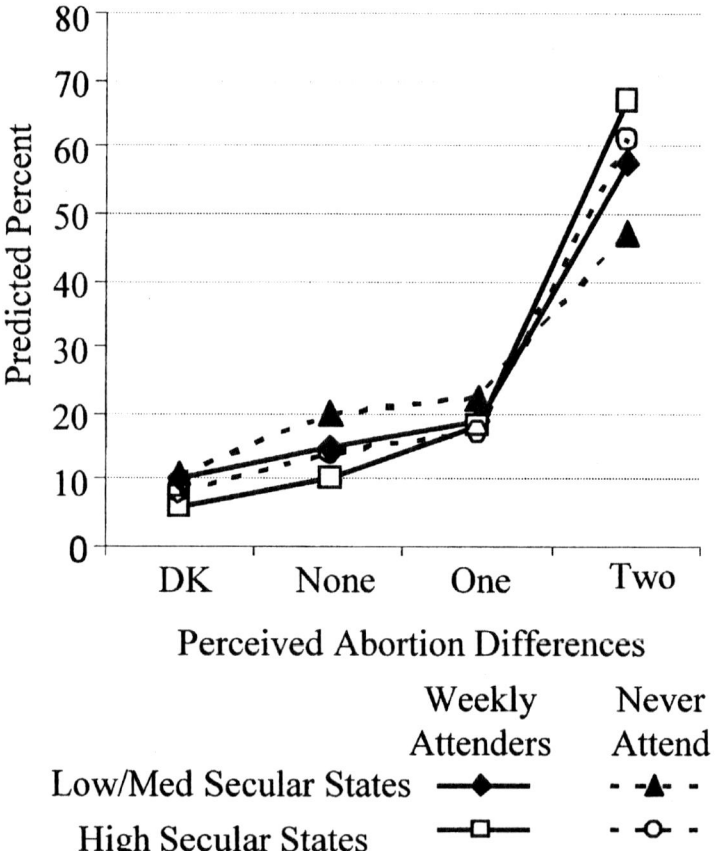

Figure 4.3a. Predicted Candidate Differences on Abortion, by Religiosity and State Percent Seculars (estimates using CLARIFY software and ANES data)

proportion of Roman Catholics. As figure 4.3b shows, non-Catholics in states with fewer Catholic adherents perceived fewer candidate differences on abortion. Catholics tended to perceive greater differences regardless of the state environment, but candidate differences were considerably more apparent to non-Catholics in the more Catholic states. This evidence for Catholic threat may be a response by non-Catholics to concerted lobbying by Catholic interest groups in those states with sizable Catholic populations.[38]

## PERCEPTIONS OF CANDIDATE DIFFERENCES ON OTHER ISSUES

Hypothesis H5 predicted that organizations would have less influence on issues not central to their mission or membership. To test this claim,

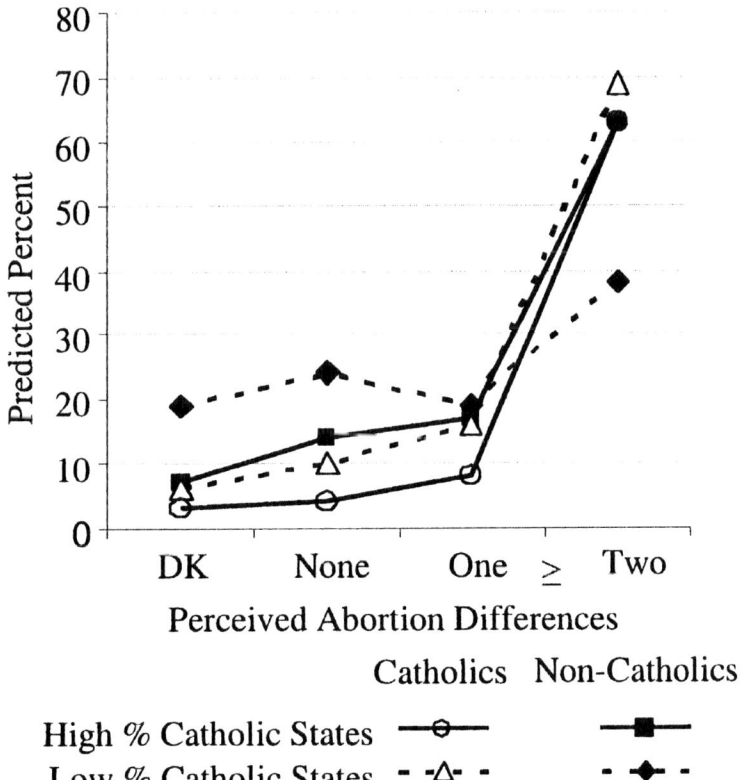

Figure 4.3b. Predicted Candidate Differences on Abortion, Catholics and Non-Catholics (estimates using CLARIFY software and ANES data)

table 4.5 compares the impact of religiosity, partisanship, education, other demographic factors, and the state contextual variables on perceptions of candidate differences on issues other than abortion. Views of candidate differences on these issues varied considerably, as table 4.1 shows; "no difference" responses ranged from 34 percent for women's roles to 3 percent for military force versus diplomacy.

As expected, education and strength of partisanship were significantly related to perceptions of differences across all these issues; income had little effect. Pro-choice respondents were more aware of candidate differences on other issues as well as the abortion issue. Minorities were significantly more likely than non-Hispanic whites to perceive candidate differences on government spending, jobs/incomes, and aid to blacks. But (contrary to H2) all coefficients for the education/religiosity interaction INTED were positive, indicating more polarized views of candidate stands on jobs/incomes and aid to blacks among *more* rather than less educated churchgoers.

Frequency of church attendance was strongly related to perceptions of differences on all issues except the status of women. But the coefficients are uniformly negative, indicating that people who never attend religious services perceived sharper differences between Bush and Kerry on issues across the board. However, membership in other organizations showed no relationship to perceived candidate differences on any issue. Whatever other contributions group membership makes to individuals' stores of social capital, awareness of candidate issue stands is apparently not one of them.

Nor do any of the state contextual variables (not even, surprisingly, electoral competition) show any significant relationships with perceptions of candidate differences on other issues. Yet the coefficients for the state proportion of seculars are uniformly positive, suggesting somewhat more polarized perceptions of candidate differences in these states. But we again see some evidence of secular threat in the positive coefficients for the interaction term INTSEC: frequent churchgoers in states with the highest proportions of seculars perceived significantly greater candidate differences on government spending, force versus diplomacy, and the environment. Strong support for an expansive military has been identified as an important segment of the ideology of religious conservatives,[39] and the environment is emerging as a salient issue for the Religious Right as well. Weekly attendees perceived greater candidate differences on aid to blacks in more secular states as well; the strongly positive coefficient for race suggests that many of these were attending African American churches.

Table 4.5 also shows that neither individual Catholic or evangelical affiliation nor the state proportions of these denominations affected percep-

Table 4.5  Candidate Differences on Issue Scales

| | Women | Spending | Defense | Jobs/Incomes | Blacks | Environment | Diplomacy |
|---|---|---|---|---|---|---|---|
| Electoral competition | 0.002 (.01) | 0.013 (.01) | 0.002 (.01) | 0.008 (.01) | 0.009 (.01) | 0.003 (.01) | 0.003 (.01) |
| State % seculars | 0.015 (.15) | 0.188 (.15) | 0.193 (.15) | 0.050 (.15) | 0.062 (.15) | 0.158 (.15) | 0.105 (.15) |
| INTSEC | 0.026 (.03) | 0.082 (.03)* | 0.057 (.03) | 0.032 (.03) | 0.056 (.03)+ | 0.063 (.03)* | 0.070 (.03)* |
| State % Catholics | -0.464 (.40) | -0.425 (.39) | 0.216 (.39) | -0.285 (.39) | -0.082 (.39) | -0.323 (.39) | 0.200 (.40) |
| Catholic | -0.050 (.22) | -0.019 (.21) | 0.115 (.21) | -0.140 (.21) | 0.027 (.21) | -0.182 (.21) | 0.314 (.47) |
| INCATH | 0.108 (.29) | 0.150 (.28) | -0.160 (.27) | -0.009 (.28) | -0.106 (.28) | 0.013 (.28) | -0.253 (.28) |
| State % Evangelicals | -0.420 (.28) | -0.067 (.28) | -0.088 (.27) | -0.147 (.27) | -0.456 (.28) | -0.126 (.27) | -0.235 (.29) |
| Evangelical | 0.061 (.39) | 0.423 (.39) | 0.145 (.37) | 0.050 (.39) | 0.080 (.39) | 0.110 (.38) | 0.118 (.60) |
| INTEVANG | 0.020 (.18) | -0.204 (.18) | 0.018 (.18) | -0.054 (.18) | 0.068 (.18) | -0.114 (.18) | -0.078 (.19) |
| Church attendance | -0.050 (.12) | -0.306 (.11)* | -0.246 (.11)* | -0.194 (.11)+ | -0.286 (.11)* | -0.233 (.12)* | -0.266 (.12)* |
| Pro-choice on abortion | 0.170 (.06)* | 0.007 (.06) | -0.103 (.06) | 0.140 (.06)* | 0.071 (.06) | 0.056 (.06) | 0.079 (.06) |
| Strength of partisanship | 0.206 (.07)* | 0.408 (.07)* | 0.350 (.07)* | 0.340 (.07)* | 0.313 (.07)* | 0.256 (.07)* | 0.228 (.07)* |
| Member of organizations | 0.095 (.08) | 0.091 (.07) | 0.031 (.07) | 0.010 (.07) | 0.056 (.08) | 0.084 (.08) | 0.088 (.07) |
| Age | -0.005 (.00) | 0.007 (.00) | -0.005 (.00) | 0.004 (.00) | 0.004 (.00) | 0.002 (.00) | -0.007 (.003)* |
| Race | 0.198 (.14) | 0.477 (.14)* | -0.090 (.14) | 0.500 (.14)* | 0.693 (.14)* | 0.209 (.14) | -0.456 (.15)* |
| Income | -0.010 (.01) | 0.003 (.01) | 0.002 (.01) | 0.014 (.01) | 0.019 (.01)+ | -0.002 (.01) | 0.013 (.01) |
| Education | 0.146 (.07)* | 0.218 (.07)* | 0.176 (.07)* | 0.237 (.07)* | 0.293 (.07)* | 0.189 (.07)* | 0.176 (.07)* |
| INTED | 0.001 (.02) | 0.017 (.02) | 0.016 (.02) | 0.029 (.02) | 0.033 (.02)* | 0.002 (.02) | 0.020 (.02) |
| Wald $x^2$ | 55.9* | 97.4* | 50.4 | 81.8* | 108.2* | 68.6* | 78.27* |
| Pseudo $R^2$ | 0.016 | 0.026 | 0.013 | 0.022 | 0.030 | 0.019 | 0.026 |
| N | | | | | | | 899 |

\* Significant at p < .05    + Significant at p < .10

tions of greater candidate differences on any of these issues. These results thus lend support to H5; organizations are more likely to have an impact on issues more central to their members and mission, as is the case with abortion for Roman Catholics and the Religious Right.

**CONCLUSION**

Election campaigns try to heighten the salience of party differences on significant issues, and thus convince the public that their vote will make a difference. But even in the closely contested 2004 election, considerable numbers of Americans still saw no significant differences between the parties or candidates, including differences on the hot-button issue of abortion. This chapter considered several reasons why the general public does not always pick up on the party polarization increasingly evident among political elites. Clearly perception of candidate or party differences is a function of individual characteristics, particularly partisanship, education, age, and race. Organizational involvement was hypothesized to provide important cues about issue stands from leaders and other group members, but once individual-level factors were taken into account, neither frequency of church attendance nor other group memberships had much independent impact. In fact, table 4.5 showed that it was the people who never darken the door of a church who consistently perceived more candidate differences on issues. Further, weekly church attendance had no independent effect on perceptions of abortion differences, even among devout Roman Catholics or evangelicals.

However, the impact of individual characteristics and organizational involvement is mediated by the state political and religious context. Perceptions of party and candidate differences on abortion were significantly greater in the more competitive states in 2004; the investment of campaign resources in these battleground states may well have had some impact. Roman Catholics and residents of heavily Catholic states were also more likely to perceive party and (especially) candidate differences on abortion, perhaps reflecting intense efforts by the Catholic Church, the Religious Right, and the Republican Party to mobilize voters in those states. But a more secular environment may pose a threat to people strongly committed to religious values. Thus frequent church attendees had much more polarized perceptions of candidate positions on abortion in the more secular states.

Campbell found no evidence that the "threat" of the presence of active evangelical church members in one's environment affected the voting behavior of seculars in 2000.[40] But in 2004, the negative coefficient for INTCATH in table 4.4 indicated that non-Catholics in heavily Catholic states perceived greater party or candidate differences on abortion. In the early 1990s abortion was especially salient to people who were pro-life,[41] but in 2004 pro-choice respondents perceived greater party and candidate differences on abortion (and on other issues as well). They may feel increasingly threatened by the Religious Right's views on reproductive rights and the 2007 Supreme Court *Gonzales v. Carhart* decision upholding a ban on partial-birth abortion.

The argument that religious dominance enhances political awareness (H4) receives some support, with sharper perceptions of party and candidate differences on abortion (but not other issues) in the most heavily Catholic states. But perceptions of issue differences, even including abortion, were consistently lower in states with higher proportions of evangelicals (mostly Southern Bible-Belt states) even with controls for level of education. Still, the positive coefficients for INTEVANG in table 4.4 suggest that evangelicals in those states were somewhat more aware of candidates' abortion stands and overall party differences.

Only on the abortion issue (table 4.4) did greater religious involvement affect perceptions of candidate stands among the less educated. In table 4.5, all of the coefficients for the education/religiosity interaction INTED are positive, indicating that church attendance affected perceptions of candidate issue differences among the well educated rather than among those lacking in personal resources. Yet none of the coefficients for membership in other organizations were significant. These findings thus lend credence to critics of social capital, who argue that groups benefit from the interests, resources, and skills their members bring to the group, and do not have an independent causal effect on political behavior.[42] But when a group's political stance is quite explicit, as it is for the Roman Catholic Church on reproductive rights, we can expect both the individual and contextual effects shown in the candidate-difference equation in table 4.1.

One outcome of this analysis is puzzling: people who never attend church tend to be less partisan, belong to fewer other organizations, and are less likely to be contacted during campaigns. Nonattendees are somewhat better educated, but even when all of these factors are considered, nonattendees in 2004 were significantly *more* aware than weekly attendees of candidate and party differences across the range of issues shown in table 4.4. One possible reason, as suggested in chapter 3, is antipathy to Christian fundamentalism. But regardless of the reasons, this evidence of heightened awareness of issue differences by nonattendees could account for their recent increases in voter turnout and campaign activism.

An increasingly well-educated and partisan electorate may be less subject to the individual-level influence of group membership. However, even if organizational involvement today does not have much independent impact on members' views of party or candidate differences, groups still can have a political impact. Organization members and frequent church attendees are better informed, more likely to vote, and easier to mobilize than the nonaffiliated. In 2004, 56 percent of weekly church attendees, but only 42 percent of nonattendees, reported they were contacted by parties or other groups about the election, and people so contacted were more likely to vote. Group leaders, parties, and candidates can capitalize on these factors even if group involvement does not necessarily contribute to them. But the impact of religious involvement (or lack thereof) on perceptions of issue differences clearly depends on the state religious context.

# 5

# Secular and Religious Right Organizations
## *Challenges and Alliances*

> Atheists are nonjoiners by nature. Getting them to cooperate even in a loose way is the miracle of the century.
>
> —Madalyn Murray O'Hair, founder of American Atheists

This chapter moves from the individual to the social and organizational level to consider the costs and challenges of mobilizing both seculars and the Religious Right. As interest-group theories predict, it is far more difficult to organize people who never attend religious services, and who are less likely than regular church attendees to be involved in other organizations. However, secular viewpoints and opposition to the Religious Right are represented by a number of national organizations. Although most of these do not have a sizable membership base, they have other resources: funding, legal talent, experienced lobbyists, access to political elites, media and Internet skills, influence within the Democratic Party.

Chapter 1 described two contrasting theories of organization, one based on cost/benefit analysis and the other on the morality-policy cycle. Both of these approaches have been used to explain the historic development of the Religious Right. The first section of this chapter will consider the current status of the Religious Right. Despite the considerable organizational advantages of a base in churches and an extensive network of religious broadcasting, many of the mass-membership groups composing the Religious Right have faced serious challenges in recent years involving theological differences, scandal, leadership rivalries, and conflicts over issue priorities. Alliances with the Republican Party, and more recently with the emerging Tea Party movement, have had costs as well as benefits. One response has been to specialize; traditional Christians and their conservative and business supporters have set up parallel legal and scientific organizations to try to counter the influence of secular groups such as the American Civil Liberties Union (ACLU) or the National Academies of Science (NAS).

The second section of this chapter will document the organizational basis of secularism, including atheist, agnostic, and civil-libertarian organizations. Alliances with the Jewish community, feminists, gay-rights groups, and the scientific establishment have also been forged to combat specific policy or legal initiatives that threaten secular values or the separation of church and state. The third section will consider the contribution to secular perspectives by mainstream media and the Internet, and the fourth section will examine the uneasy alliance of seculars with the Democratic Party. The final section will explore relationships between seculars and the Religious Left. As the case studies in chapter 6 will show, secular organizations, strategies, and alliances have on many occasions been able to offset the grassroots strength and organizational advantages of the Religious Right.

## ORGANIZING THE RELIGIOUS RIGHT

The rise of the Religious Right since the 1960s can be explained by both organizational theory and the morality-politics cycle. First of all, churches had memberships and communication networks (mailing lists, sermons, newsletters, study groups) already in place, thus reducing the costs of organization. Second, technological advances made it possible to reduce the costs of information and organization. In the 1960s Richard Viguerie pioneered the use of direct mail, using church mailing lists to reach out to the many small, scattered, and rural congregations then typical of evangelical and fundamentalist churches. Televangelism also drew in people (especially many older people) sympathetic to conservative Christian viewpoints.[1] Viewers could thus be informed, solicited for contributions, and persuaded to support policies or candidates favorable to traditional religious views.

The major television networks had long-standing relationships with mainline Protestants and Roman Catholics, but they were fearful of controversy and provided little access for the more doctrinal and emotional religious expression favored by fundamentalists and evangelicals. However, televangelism proved to be a highly successful tool for fund-raising, so religious broadcasters were able to raise millions of dollars to support on-air ministries based on local television stations or the new cable channels.[2] Talk radio also emerged as a popular medium and was dominated by conservative broadcasters and listeners.[3] The Christian Broadcasting Network and the National Religious Broadcasters organizations were founded to provide resources and technical assistance, and also to lobby Congress and the Federal Communications Commission (FCC) for policies favorable to religious broadcasting. FCC policies to encourage local broadcasting competition helped fuel the growth of Christian radio, which in 2002 included 20 percent of all radio stations.[4] Televangelism and the flourishing new megachurches also produced entrepreneurial leaders with formidable fund-raising, institution-building, and communications skills.[5]

The Religious Right could use these organizational and technological advantages to respond to perceived threats, such as the 1963 *Engel v. Vitale* decision on school prayer, *Roe v. Wade*, or the Equal Rights Amendment after it passed Congress in 1972. Religious elites and their conservative and business allies could play on these threats to persuade people to become politically involved to protect traditional religious values. During the 1970s and 1980s millions of previously quiescent evangelicals and fundamentalists registered to vote, turned out in both national and local elections, and became involved in Republican Party politics. Churches provided membership lists, venues for meetings, office staff, and buses for travel to state capitals or Washington, D.C., for lobbying or massive rallies, such as the annual protest of the *Roe v. Wade* decision on January 23. Protestant televangelists, talk-radio hosts, Republican Party strategists, and Roman Catholic bishops encouraged such activism by the faithful.[6]

These resources could also be used to build national organizations, many with state and/or local affiliates. The development of these organizations, their leadership, and the evolution of their strategies and purpose, have been described in detail elsewhere.[7] The major ones are listed in table 5.1 in five categories: mass membership, media, lobbyists, scientific, and legal. The largest (Focus on the Family) overlaps several categories; it includes numerous publications, a sizable television audience, and legal and science foundations. The Religious Right and the Roman Catholic Church have developed a major lobbying presence in many state capitals as well as in Washington, D.C.[8] The Church of Latter-day Saints (Mormons) is not only a major presence in Utah, but has provided funding, expert advice, and grassroots volunteers when issues arise in other states (such as Proposition 8 to ban gay marriage in California).

The Religious Right has faced organizational difficulties as well. The Moral Majority collapsed in 1989, and other groups have had to deal with scandals, leadership rivalries, declining contributions, and intense disputes over theology as well as political strategy. The Christian Coalition and Focus on the Family suffered major losses of funding and members

**Table 5.1  Major Religious Right Organizations**

*Mass membership*
Moral Majority—1978–1989
Christian Coalition—1988
Faith and Freedom Coalition—2009
Concerned Women of America—1979
Eagle Forum—1972

*Media*
Focus on the Family—1982
National Religious Broadcasters—1944
Christian Broadcasting Network—1961

*Lobbying*
U.S. Conference of Catholic Bishops—1966
National Association of Evangelicals—1942
National Organization for Marriage—2007
Traditional Values Coalition—1980
Orthodox Union Institute for Public Affairs—1898

*Scientific/Think Tanks*
Discovery Institute—1989
Elliot Institute—1988
Breast Cancer Prevention Institute—1999
Medical Institute for Sexual Health—1992
Family Research Council—1991
Answers in Genesis—1994
Heritage Foundation Devos Center for Religion and Civil Society—2004
Ethics and Public Policy Center—1976

*Legal*
Alliance Defense Fund—1994
Home School Legal Defense Association—1983
Rutherford Institute—1982
Thomas More Law Center—1989
Justice Foundation—1993
Christian Legal Society—1961
Federalist Society—1982
Education & Legal Institute of the Traditional Values Coalition—1980

when their founders (Pat Robertson and James Dobson, respectively) stepped down, and the National Association of Evangelicals had to deal with the resignation of its president, Ted Haggard, over his involvement in a gay relationship. The ongoing pedophilia scandals facing the Roman Catholic Church have cost millions and constrained its ability to be more outspoken on moral issues in 2004 and 2008.[9]

One solution to problems with existing organizations is to create new ones. Ralph Reed, formerly executive director of the Christian Coalition, emerged from scandals involving the lobbyist Jack Abramoff to establish a new grassroots organization in 2009, the Faith and Freedom Coalition. Its goal for 2012 is to "register an estimated one million new faith-based voters and make tens of millions of voter contacts in what may be the largest conservative get-out-the-vote effort in modern political history." Potential Republican presidential candidates in 2012 (Newt Gingrich, Rick Santorum) have worked with think tanks to help refine and disseminate their messages to religious as well as political conservatives.[10]

Another strategy is for the Religious Right to join the broad shift in the United States from membership-based groups to more specialized lobbying organizations relying on checks from donors. The Christian Coalition and Focus on the Family have both been pursuing this course since the 1990s. Narrowly focused organizations, such as the Home School Legal Defense Association, have retained strong popular support and have won major legal battles in several states. Two types of Religious Right organizations, the legal and science-focused groups, merit further discussion in this chapter because they parallel secular organizations and legal strategies. Other mobilizing options for the Religious Right will be explored more fully in the conclusion.

## Science Groups Supporting the Religious Right

The positions of the Religious Right on issues such as evolution, AIDS, abstinence education, teen pregnancy, and homosexuality have long been challenged by mainstream scientists and medical professionals. The quasi-scientific organizations listed in table 5.1 were established to counter the alleged "liberal bias" in academia and mainstream science, and to provide empirical support for conservative moral views on human sexuality. These organizations foster research on topics such as intelligent design (the Discovery Institute) or the health consequences of abortion (Elliot Institute, Breast Cancer Prevention Institute). The risks of condoms and sex education are stressed by the Medical Institute for Sexual Health, and the Family Research Council touts the advantages of adult versus embryonic stem-cell research.[11] In legal or congressional testimony, spokespersons for these groups claim to justify their policy positions on the basis of science rather than religion or ideology. They produce academic experts and cite statistical evidence to back their claims.

Education is another major function of these groups. Websites, newsletters, congressional testimony, and conferences disseminate the results of their research. The Justice Foundation's website boasts that its amicus curiae brief on the health risks of abortion was cited in the Supreme Court's 2007 *Gonzales v. Carhart* decision.[12] The Creation Museum in Petersburg, Kentucky, is a large-scale "outreach ministry" by the evangelical ministry Answers in Genesis, and attracts busloads of church members and students (and a few skeptical journalists) to learn about "young-earth" science.[13] These groups also provide detailed study guides for use in churches and schools, so as to educate the faithful about topics such as intelligent design or the risks of embryonic stem-cell research. The Discovery Institute produces a steady stream of books and articles touting "intelligent design" as science and criticizing evolution.[14]

A major tactic of the quasi-science organizations is to challenge any mainstream scientific findings that question their economic, theological, or ideological worldviews. Thus their publications and congressional testimony highlight the range of views among climate scientists about the pace or consequences of global warming, or emphasize disagreements among physicians about the costs and benefits of stem-cell research. Such "uncertainty" is touted as grounds for indefinite postponement of any new regulations or policies, or approval of drugs affecting reproduction, until additional "sound science" is performed to weigh costs and benefits, or until "absolute certainty" is obtained about costs or benefits (a standard of proof few scientists would accept). Such "sound science" is also supported by many of the business groups funding these organizations; it is in their financial interest to deflect or delay any further regulations affecting tobacco use, climate change, or endangered species.[15]

The quasi-science organizations also screen potential candidates for elective office or federal appointments for views compatible with conservatives or the Religious Right. During the Bush administration, scientists who did not have the "right" views on abortion, embryonic stem cells, capital punishment, climate change, or drug laws were unlikely to receive appointments to executive positions or advisory boards. But scientists backed by right-wing think tanks (such as the Heritage Foundation) were easily approved, and the founder of the Medical Institute for Sexual Health was appointed by President Bush to two federal boards.[16] Only one out of twenty Republican candidates for the Senate in 2010 was willing to accept evidence for climate change, despite the overwhelming scientific consensus that global warming was occurring and was attributable to human actions. The priority of the incoming Republican House majority elected in 2010 was not to reduce carbon emissions or address climate change, but to hold hearings to harass climate scientists and the staff of the Environmental Protection Agency.[17]

These quasi-scientific groups may claim some policy successes, but a major consequence of their advocacy (to be considered later in this chapter) has been furious countermobilization by mainstream scientists and their allies. They insist that ideological or religiously motivated "research" is not science; it is not replicable or falsifiable, does not appear in peer-reviewed journals, and its challenges to established scientific findings are seriously flawed. Thus the Elliot Institute claims strong links between abortion and breast cancer or depression, based on reports by women who regret having abortions. But mainstream scientists, social scientists, and physicians discount such "evidence by anecdote" as not meeting the standards of experimentation, statistical controls, or clinical trials that could establish stronger claims for causality. They also challenge the credentials of scientists affiliated with these organizations, or reveal their active membership in right-wing or pro-life groups. Some scientists have even questioned the credentials of otherwise-qualified nominees for federal posts who are evangelical Christians, such as President Obama's choice of Francis Collins to head the National Institutes of Health.[18]

## Legal Organizations and Advocacy

Groups in this category, such as the Alliance Defense Fund and the Federalist Society, arose in response to perceived secular gains in the courts (particularly those litigated by the ACLU). The Federalist Society favors "individual liberty, traditional values, and the rule of law." Many on the Religious Right were concerned that the results of successful grassroots mobilization, or the election of even the most sympathetic presidents, could be countermanded by "activist judges." The solution was not only to defend against lawsuits brought by the ACLU, but to mount legal challenges, seek sympathetic venues for such suits, train law students—and elect more conservative judges. These legal organizations vary considerably in size and strategy. The largest, the Alliance Defense Fund (ADF), has a large staff and generous funding from Pat Robertson's Christian Coalition. Some (like the Thomas More Law Center) are active litigators; others (the Justice Foundation, the Christian Legal Society) provide research and other legal resources to groups or individuals involved in active litigation. In addition, a number of smaller legal nonprofits have arisen to defend Christian groups or individuals.[19]

Conservative legal groups have been involved in a number of recent high-profile decisions. Lawyer and activist Michael Farris established the Home School Legal Defense Association (HSLDA) to "defend and advance the constitutional right of parents to direct the education of their children and to protect family freedoms," and HSLDA has successfully challenged laws in many states that restricted home schooling.[20] And as will be discussed in chapter 6, the Thomas More Foundation and Rutherford Institute defended the Dover, Pennsylvania, school board's efforts to introduce intelligent design, and the ADF spearheaded the defense of California's Proposition 8 (banning gay marriage) when it was challenged in federal court. An especially effective tactic has been to use freedom of speech to justify religious expression in schools or the workplace. Arguably, access to public-school facilities or student activity funding by religious groups does not constitute "establishment" if they simply ask to be treated like other, secular groups. The downside of this strategy, however, is that avowedly secular or antireligious groups (and recently, gay or lesbian groups) can claim "free speech" rights as well.[21]

Organizations on the Religious Right have also tried to elect or appoint judges more likely to uphold traditional religious values.[22] Recent court decisions have encouraged the flow of money into judicial campaigns, and since the 2010 *Citizens United* decision, these can be made anonymously by groups at least nominally separate from candidate or party organizations. Groups such as Focus on the Family have weighed in on appointments to federal courts and on judicial elections in the states. They sponsored a series of Justice Sunday events in 2005–2006 to mobilize churchgoers to urge an end to Democratic filibusters of conservative nominees to federal courts.[23] The Religious Right also supports the election of state judges opposed to abortion and same-sex marriage. Due largely to mobilization by conservative Christians, in November 2010 three Iowa Supreme Court justices lost their retention elections because of their decision to uphold gay marriage.[24]

Although efforts have been made to restructure the mass-membership Christian Coalition, specialization rather than broad-based membership is likely to represent the future organizational base of the Religious Right. As the case studies in the next chapter will illustrate, however, specialized legal and scientific advocacy groups based in the Religious Right have not always prevailed in court against their secular counterparts.

## THE ORGANIZATIONAL BASIS OF SECULARISM

Based on organizational theory, seculars, who never attended religious services, have usually been considerably less politically involved than people holding traditional religious views. As chapter 3 showed, although seculars in 1980 were somewhat more knowledgeable about politics because of their educational and occupational advantages, they were less likely to vote or contribute, and much less likely to be contacted during campaigns. Thus by the 1990s church attendance had emerged as a powerful predictor of voting and campaign activism, and organizations on the Religious Right made effective use of churches as bases for political mobilization.

However, the morality-politics cycle can explain why, despite these organizational disadvantages, many hitherto quiescent seculars have recently become more politically active. Policy gains by the Religious Right (especially during the second Bush administration) included restrictions on reproductive rights, bans on gay marriage, funding for faith-based programs and abstinence education, and religious litmus tests for scientific and policy positions. Such actions seriously threatened those who preferred a strong separation between church and state and valued scientific objectivity as the basis for policy. And as chapter 3 showed, negative perceptions of Christian fundamentalists have emerged as a mobilizing factor for both seculars and religious moderates. Such perceptions may be wildly exaggerated; Putnam and Campbell calculate that uncompromising "true believers" constitute only about 10 percent of Americans, and most evangelicals are in fact quite moderate and tolerant in their political views.[25] But for many seculars, having "true believers" in positions of power was an altogether different matter, and a potent spur to political activism.

Threats to fundamental values can also encourage people to run for political office. In the 1960s many parents from traditional Christian backgrounds were enraged by the Supreme Court's decision on school prayer and by the introduction of sex education, "moral relativism," multicultural values, and "pornographic" books into the public-school curriculum. Several leaders of local protests against these measures decided to run for school-board seats, often with strong encouragement from their churches. A national organization, Citizens for Excellence in Education, emerged in 1983 to encourage such candidacies. But the success of religious conservatives in school-board elections has also led to countercandidacies by seculars and religious liberals.[26]

A number of secular organizations, many long-standing, do exist. They may receive less attention from scholars or the media than the Christian Coalition, and have far fewer members than the fast-growing evangelical and fundamentalist churches. But threats from the Religious Right have boosted their memberships and contributions, and even produced newer organizations such as People for the American Way and the Student Secular Alliance.

Groups opposed to the Religious Right can be described in four major categories: nonbelievers, civil libertarians, minorities, and scientific. Major groups in each of these categories are shown in table 5.2. They vary considerably in funding, membership, and leadership, and there is a broad range of viewpoints between the most militant atheist groups listed in table 5.2 and those representing civil liberties or the Religious

**Table 5.2  Secular Organizations and Allies Opposed to the Religious Right**

*Atheist/Agnostic*
American Atheists—1963
Atheist Alliance International—1991
American Humanist Association—1941
Ethical Culture Society
Freedom from Religion Foundation—1978
Secular Coalition for America—2002
Student Secular Alliance—2000

*Civil Libertarian*
American Civil Liberties Union/Foundation—1920
Americans United for Separation of Church and State—1947
People for the American Way—1981

*Jewish*
Anti-Defamation League—1913
Jewish Council for Public Affairs—1944
Jews on First [Amendment]—2005
Jewish Social Policy Action Network

*Feminist*
Feminist Majority Foundation—1987
NARAL Pro-Choice America—1977
National Organization for Women—1966
Planned Parenthood—1923

*African American*
NAACP Legal Defense Fund—1957
Southern Poverty Law Center—1971

*Gay/Lesbian*
Freedom to Marry—2003
Human Rights Campaign—1980
Lambda Foundation—1983
National Gay and Lesbian Task Force—1973
Stonewall Democrats—1999

*Scientific*
American College of Obstetrics and Gynecology—1951
Federation of American Scientists—1945
National Center for Science Education—1981
National Academies of Science—1863
Richard Dawkins Foundation for Reason and Science—2006
Union of Concerned Scientists—1969

Table 5.2  Secular Organizations and Allies Opposed to the Religious Right

*Religious Left*
Bread for the World—1974
Interfaith Alliance—1994
J Street—2008
National Council of Churches—1950
Progressive Religious Partnership—2001
Sojourners—1971
Tikkun—1994

Left. What unites these disparate groups, however, is opposition to the Religious Right. As holders of conservative religious viewpoints have gained positions of power in recent years, they have threatened core secular and liberal values such as separation of church and state, tolerance of religious diversity, the rights of women and gays, or the scientific basis of education and public policy. Many of these secular groups have forged coalitions on specific issues to challenge the Religious Right at the polls, in the courts, in Congress, in the states, and in local schools.

## Nonbelievers

For the general public, avowedly atheist groups are the most problematic of the secular organizations. Especially during the Cold War, atheism was linked to the threat of "godless communism," and atheists are still highly unpopular. Because of the perceived social cost of atheism, many people who doubt the existence of God have been hesitant to admit it publicly. Public perceptions are somewhat more accepting today than in the 1960s, and even "nonbelievers" are now considered to be good Americans. However, even recent polls show that an atheist is highly unlikely to be elected president, and in 2008 atheists received the lowest scores of any group on the ANES feeling-thermometer scales.

Atheists, who tend to reject earthly as well as divine authority, are also not easy to organize, but some avowedly atheist groups have appeared. The oldest is American Atheists, the successor to the Freethought Society of America founded by Madalyn Murray O'Hair (1919–1995). This outspoken and highly controversial woman was termed "the most hated woman in America" by *Life* magazine in 1964 after her legal organization Other Americans, Inc., brought several successful lawsuits challenging school prayer and tax exemptions for church-owned property. O'Hair's organizations faced internal divisions and financial problems. She and her sons disappeared in 1995 and were eventually found to have been murdered by a former associate.[27] American Atheists has only about twenty-two hundred members, but as of 2010 claimed to be "liked" by twenty-one thousand people on Facebook. The group engages in political and legal action to defend the rights of atheists and strict separation of church and state. Its educational efforts include a magazine, *The American Atheist*, a website, and provision of speakers to schools and colleges. In 2010 it financed ads on Fort Worth, Texas, public buses proclaiming "Millions of Americans are good without God," and a billboard by the Lincoln Tunnel claiming the Christmas story was a myth.[28]

Atheist Alliance International (AAI), founded in 1991, is an umbrella organization linking state and local atheist organizations across the United States and around the world. Its stated goal is to "work in coalition with like-minded groups to advance rational thinking through educational processes." The organization sponsors an annual convention, publishes *Secular World* magazine, and supports legal or public-relations efforts to challenge religious influence over schools, charitable giving, or the U.S. military. Several "humanist" associations also promote secular values. The largest of these is the American Humanist Association (AHA). Local chapters of AHA and the Ethical Culture Society espouse ethics based on rationality or human rights. They provide social and intellectual support for those skeptical of religion. They also try to combat the belief, widespread especially among traditional Christians, that atheists or agnostics lack morality.[29]

The Freedom from Religion Foundation currently reports a membership of fourteen thousand, which would make it the largest organization in the country advocating for atheists and agnostics. It initiated lawsuits against the Bush administration's faith-based initiatives, and scored a major victory in 2010 when it won a lawsuit that declared the National Day of Prayer, a fixture since the Truman administration, to be a violation of the First Amendment. The law had called on the president to sign an annual proclamation in observance of the National Day of Prayer, but the judge ruled that constituted establishment of religion.[30]

A newcomer to secular organization is Student Secular Alliance (SSA), founded in 2000. It was established to provide social and organizational support to a new generation of seculars, and currently has chapters at colleges and universities. Another recent addition is the Secular Coalition for America (SCA), also founded in 2000. It is a Washington, D.C.–based lobbying organization comprising ten secular, atheist, or humanist organizations, including AHA and SSA. Its mission is to "amplify the diverse and growing voice of the non-theistic community in the United States," but SCA has also joined with religious organizations in support of freedom of conscience and separation of church and state.[31]

Just as most people do not join churches primarily for political reasons, many people who become involved with atheist or humanist groups are seeking more information or social support from like-minded individuals. The Ethical Culture Society even performs weddings. According to interviews with members of the Student Secular Alliance at the University of Pittsburgh, some were seeking opportunities for philosophical discussion of religion or atheism; others were looking for a refuge from the religious activism and evangelism that were highly visible on campus. But a few did mention political or legal concerns beyond the campus setting, especially gay, lesbian, bisexual, and transgender (GLBT) issues.[32] Yet even if joiners of religious or nonreligious groups are not initially politically motivated, their involvement exposes them to information and cues from leaders, and the national offices of these organizations have a base of members and/or donors to build on.

**Civil-Libertarian Groups**

One of the oldest and best-established organizations is the American Civil Liberties Union. The ACLU is by no means antireligion, and in fact has defended the free-expression rights of religious minorities such as the Amish, Jehovah's Witnesses, and more recently Muslims. But the ACLU is highly skeptical of any policy that could be construed as an establishment of religion. Its full legal and financial resources have been brought to bear against any such threat, such as the Dover, Pennsylvania, case involving the teaching of intelligent design in public schools and the legal appeals of Proposition 8 in California (both to be discussed in chapter 6).

The ACLU does have a sizable membership base, as well as state and local chapters with legal staff. Its members lobby school districts, state and local governments, and Congress in defense of civil liberties and the rights of minorities, and in opposition to policies such as abstinence education or bans on gay marriage. A related group, the ACLU Foundation, is a tax-exempt nonprofit whose main strategy is litigation. It has won significant legal victories, enjoys widespread support within the legal community, and benefits from pro bono work by many individual lawyers and law firms. But its many legal successes have also encouraged the development of conservative legal foundations to defend traditional religious viewpoints.

Americans United for Separation of Church and State (AU) was founded in 1947 by United Church of Christ minister and lawyer Barry Lynn, and includes clergy and both religious and nonreligious members. Its original purpose was to protest congressional proposals to extend government aid to private religious schools, but its agenda now includes a range of church/state issues such as prayer and intelligent design in the schools, school vouchers, and faith-based policy initiatives. AU publishes *Church & State* magazine and other materials to educate the press and general public, and is involved in lobbying and legal actions.

Another organization strongly opposed to the Religious Right is also not necessarily secular in terms of beliefs or membership. People for the American Way (PAW) was founded in 1983 by ex-Congressman John Buchanan of Alabama, a devout Christian who was defeated in 1982 because his political and social views were not deemed sufficiently conservative. PAW draws support from many groups and individuals of faith, but its main purpose is to prevent the Religious Right from imposing its agenda and enacting its policy preferences into law or public policy. Its website lists "Fighting the Right" as a major issue, and it sponsors the online Right Wing Watch to expose the "Far Right's motives, strategies, tactics and influence in current issue and policy."[33]

## Minority Organizations Opposed to the Religious Right

Groups representing several political minorities in the United States, including feminists, gays, Jews, and African Americans, have challenged attempts by the Religious Right to uphold traditional Christian views of families, women, or gays and lesbians. The major feminist organization is the National Organization for Women (NOW), founded in 1966. Its views on working women, divorce, single parenthood, lesbian rights, sex education, and child care are diametrically opposed to those of Concerned Women for America. NOW also advocates for reproductive rights, but two other major organizations, Planned Parenthood and NARAL, concentrate on this issue and on maintaining the legal status of abortion. The Feminist Majority Foundation focuses mainly on lobbying and on legal challenges; it has been particularly active in the fight for legalization of emergency contraception (Plan B) and of the abortion pill mifeprestone.

With very few exceptions (such as the Log Cabin Republicans), groups supporting the Religious Right are adamantly opposed to gay rights, gay marriage, and the "homosexual lifestyle." As the Human Rights Campaign (HRC) website states, "Several extremist right-wing groups, including the Moral Majority and the National Conservative Political Action Committee, were gaining notoriety [in 1980], and HRCF was created in part to counter their anti-gay tactics."[34] Most other GLBT organizations likewise oppose the Religious Right, but they vary greatly in terms of policy priorities and political strategies. Some (such as Bash Back and the Stonewall Democrats) favor confrontational demonstrations; others (HRC, the Lambda Foundation, the National Gay and Lesbian Task Force) rely on insider lobbying, grassroots organizing, or litigation. Freedom to Marry, founded in 2003, is leading the campaign to win marriage equality nationwide in the United States, but not all GLBT groups support gay marriage. Proposition 8 (banning gay marriage) won at the polls in liberal California in 2008, as the case study in chapter 6 will discuss. Yet gay marriage is now legal in several other states, and GLBT groups have gained some impressive legal victories and increasing public acceptance.[35]

Several Jewish groups also actively oppose the Religious Right. The Jewish community has reason to fear that any establishment of religion in the United States, such as prayer in public schools, would privilege Christianity and threaten religious minorities. The ACLU's national board and legal staff include a significant number of Jews, and people of Jewish background are also prominent in the Ethical Culture Society and many other secular organizations. The Anti-Defamation League of B'nai B'rith (ADL), the oldest of these Jewish organizations, has fought anti-Semitism in the media, in popular culture, and in the law since 1913. Roman Catholics and mainline Protestants have had their own historic battles over anti-Semitism; not until Vatican II, in 1965, did the Catholic Church declare that Jews were not responsible for the crucifixion of Jesus. In recent years, however, some groups or individuals on the Religious Right have taken actions that could be construed as hostile to Judaism. The evangelical group Jews for Jesus actively tries to convert Jews, and some fundamentalists insist that only born-again Christians will be saved. The ADL has regularly joined with the ACLU on establishment cases, and is opposed to several key priorities of the Religious Right: school prayer, teaching creationism, displaying the Ten Commandments in public places, bans on gay marriage.[36]

Jews on First is dedicated to "defending the First Amendment against the Christian Right" and supports reproductive rights, GLBT rights, and stem-cell research. The Jewish Social Policy Action Network and the Jewish Council for Public Affairs share similar goals, and provided amici briefs in the Dover and Proposition 8 court cases. Jews are a small minority in Congress and state legislatures, but have been outspoken in opposition to proposals such as the School Prayer Amendment. Reform, Conservative, and Reconstructionist Jews are strongly supportive of reproductive rights and gay rights. This places them at odds with Orthodox Jews and with the Christian Right on most issues—except for support for Israel. Many conservative Christians regard the establishment of the State of Israel as a step toward the Second Coming of Christ, and strongly back American diplomatic, financial, and military support of Israel.[37]

As chapter 3 noted, African Americans tend to hold conservative views on many social issues, and ANES thermometer scores show that they are favorably disposed toward Christian fundamentalists. But some African American groups do oppose many of the policy priorities of the Religious Right. The NAACP Legal Defense Fund (LDF) has primarily litigated on behalf of African Americans, but it also been a party to other challenges to the Religious Right, such as capital punishment and the teaching of creationism, and views gay marriage as a civil-rights issue under the Fourteenth Amendment. The Southern Poverty Law Project primarily targets hate crimes, including those directed against gays. African Americans are divided over gay marriage, and filed briefs on both sides of the lawsuit challenging California's Proposition 8, but the views of younger African Americans (and President Obama) are changing to stronger support.[38]

## Scientific Organizations

Scientific and medical associations are primarily focused on research and professional development, but can on occasion be drawn into the political fray. The American College of Obstetrics and Gynecology (ACOG), for example, presented expert testimony in the 2005 *Gonzales v. Carhart* case, and issued a public protest when its medical expertise was ignored and a congressional ban on partial-birth abortion was upheld.[39] One hundred bioethicists signed a statement to protest the Bush administration's decision to permit research on only a few limited stem-cell lines, and the National Cancer Institute vigorously criticized claims by pro-life science institutes that abortion "caused" breast cancer.[40] Although these actions by specific groups of scientists or doctors can gain them some attention in the news cycle, broader science organizations with a policy focus and staying power are needed to have a consistent, long-term impact on the policy process. Those listed in table 5.2 represent this strategy for advocates of science, and they actively oppose policies based on politics or ideology. To counter these organizations representing mainstream science, Religious Right groups such as the Discovery Institute hope to develop comparable staying power and policy impact.

The National Academies of Science (NAS) is the most prestigious American scientific organization. Its members are chosen based on stellar achievements in their fields (including a few social scientists as well as natural scientists, engineers, and physicians). It has often been asked by the president or Congress to provide summary reports on controversial issues such as ozone depletion, mercury emissions, or needle-exchange programs for drug addicts. NAS recommendations usually carry considerable weight in the policy process, but their reports have also been quoted selectively by conservative media or think tanks seizing on any evidence of conflicting studies or scientific disagreement. Like the Federation of American Scientists, the NAS usually focuses on improving the role of science in the policy process, but it has on occasion filed friend-of-the-court briefs in creationism lawsuits. In 2005 a letter to members from NAS president Bruce Alberts urged them to take action against any attempts in their own state or locality to introduce creationism or intelligent design into public schools, and in 2010 255 members of NAS signed a statement strongly urging action to combat global warming.[41]

The Federation of American Scientists was founded in 1945 to help improve the capacity for government and scientists to deal with pressing issues, such as control of nuclear weapons, peaceful uses of atomic energy, and monitoring arms sales. It has a broad base of support among scientists (including many Nobel laureates) from many disciplines and from officials from government agencies such as NASA and the National Science Foundation. Its policy recommendations have been more process oriented and thus less overtly political than those of the Union of Concerned Scientists, although it has spoken out against weapons in space and advocated for an enhanced role for science in policymaking. Its 2001 report *Flying Blind* was highly critical of Bush's stem-cell decision, in particular the process that led to it.[42]

A scientific organization with an explicitly political agenda, the Union of Concerned Scientists (UCS) was established at MIT in 1969 to highlight the risks of nuclear war and to try to shift research applications away from military technology and toward pressing environmental and social problems. Its opposition to President Reagan's Star Wars missile defense program and its support for efforts to counter global warming have brought it into conflict with conservatives, and it is described by them as a left-wing, liberal-activist organization. The UCS Scientific Integrity program has challenged dozens of instances of political interference in science, and it supports whistleblower protection and free-speech rights for federal scientists. UCS initiated a major report in 2004, "Scientific Integrity in Policymaking," to document the misuse of science by the second Bush administration, and it gathered a petition with signatures from nearly eleven thousand scientists to support this report.[43] UCS claims of misuse of data, doctoring of reports by scientists and federal agencies, and appointment of unqualified people to scientific and advisory posts brought it into direct conflict with the Religious Right over issues such as embryonic stem cells, abortion, and emergency contraception. In 2007 televangelist Jerry Falwell cautioned evangelical Christians against "falling for . . . global warming hocus-pocus" propagated in the mass media, with the UCS "leading the charge."[44]

Since 1981 the National Center for Science Education (NCSE) has steadfastly opposed efforts to introduce creationism (or any variant thereof) into American public schools. NCSE national staff and its member teachers and scientists monitor local districts and state boards of education to make sure that evolution is included in biology textbooks and taught in class, and to head off threats to cover intelligent design or to "teach the controversy" in public schools. Its mission statement attests that its preferred strategy is education rather than litigation, but NCSE has been a party to numerous lawsuits (including the Dover case to be discussed in the next chapter) and provides experts to testify in such cases. Another educational group is the Richard Dawkins Foundation for Reason and Science, whose mission is "to support scientific education, critical thinking and evidence-based understanding of the natural world in the quest to overcome religious fundamentalism, superstition, intolerance and human suffering."[45]

Major science journals, such as *Scientific American*, *Science*, *Journal of Science and Health Policy*, and *Nature*, have also weighed in with editorials on controversial issues. These were particularly vocal in response to Bush administration appointments to medical and scientific positions and to its policies on stem cells, climate change, and abstinence education. These editorials often gain broader coverage from newspapers or television. However, although the mainstream media might be expected to defer to science, few reporters have much scientific training, and may be vulnerable to "spin" efforts put forward by conservative think tanks. Reporters' efforts to provide "balance" by covering both sides equally can also lend credence to counterclaims by advocates of "sound science" or intelligent design.[46]

A major role for scientists is as expert witnesses in court, either through direct testimony or by filing amici briefs. The courts have usually been deferential to scientific evidence in establishing the central facts of a case. The Federal Rules of Evidence establish specific guidelines for expert testimony: peer review and publication, error rates, acceptance within the scientific community. Science can also be used as an authoritative and value-neutral justification for a decision, especially on controversial issues.[47] However, legal deference to science is more problematic in other cases. Courts may engage in "legislative" fact-finding, where a broader range of evidence is considered beyond the facts of a particular case, and where specific rules of evidence are lacking. Lawyers and judges are not scientists and may misinterpret scientific or statistical evidence. Courts can dismiss scientific evidence altogether, or decide that is does not apply in a particular case, or that contradictory findings are equally valid, or that its proponents lack legal standing. Even credible scientific evidence can be trumped by other factors: freedom of speech, equal protection of the laws, states' rights under the Tenth Amendment, broader social implications.[48]

Litigators such as the ACLU try to recruit prominent scientists with solid research records in order to make their cases. By contrast, think tanks and science organizations backed by the Religious Right have had considerable difficulty producing credible witnesses in support of creationism, intelligent design, or the alleged pathologies of gay or lesbians, as the case studies in the next chapter will show. The Religious Right has had more luck with legislatures in finding expert witnesses willing to support its positions on issues. Sympathetic members of Congress or state legislatures can invite these "experts" to testify at hearings to highlight research controversies and try to cast doubt on the evidence presented by mainstream scientists, as will be seen in the South Dakota abortion debate. And if such a "science court" indicates controversy or the need for more research based on "sound science," legislators have a plausible reason to delay further policy actions, such as a response to climate change or approval of emergency contraception. Further, the Religious Right has been actively recruiting judges (like Justice Clarence Thomas) who are likely to be sympathetic to their policy goals and skeptical of "liberal" scientific counterclaims.[49]

## OLD AND NEW MEDIA

Is the "secular" media biased against religion? Many on the Religious Right certainly think so. The critical media coverage of antievolutionists during the Scopes trial in 1925, and the hit Broadway play and movie *Inherit the Wind* based on that trial, portrayed supporters of traditional Christianity as ignorant backwoods yokels prejudiced against reason and science. Televangelism and Christian radio networks were established in part to counter the misinterpretation or marginalization of religion by mainstream television networks and newspapers. The Catholic League, the Mormon church, and Focus on the Family regularly complain against what they regard as prejudicial portrayals of Christians and their beliefs. Fundamentalist beliefs and charismatic worship styles may be described with bemusement or cynicism by reporters with different (or no) religious backgrounds. In 1988, after the Reverend Pat Robertson came in a surprise second in the Iowa Republican caucus, CBS news coverage included clips of him at a religious revival speaking in tongues and claiming to heal hemorrhoids and heart attacks.[50] No presidential candidate could survive such a portrayal.

Objective social-science analysis of religion in the media presents a more complex picture. Reporters and commentators tend to be considerably more secular than the general population, in part because they have higher levels of education.[51] But the media context and professional norms may be more important than reporters' lack of personal religiosity; mainstream media may actually be deferential to established religions.[52] News coverage tends to focus on conflict and vivid personalities. For both legal and professional reasons reporters are expected to cover "both sides" of an issue, and may thus overemphasize disagreements.[53]

The media takes its watchdog role seriously, so sex scandals or financial improprieties affecting religious institutions receive thorough coverage.

Especially in the post-Watergate era, scandal not only sells newspapers but may also gain a reporter a Pulitzer Prize. The Catholic Church's pedophilia scandal and the sexual or financial escapades of Jimmy Swaggart, Jim and Tammy Bakker, Ted Haggard, and the like were thus big news. Sex, violence, gambling, and pornography are also big business; the news entertainment industries have strenuously fought against any forms of censorship of these by conservative religious groups, and have the legal resources and political clout to do so.

The issue with media coverage of religion may be that of ignorance rather than bias. Most reporters know little about religious history, terminology, or the wide range of beliefs within specific denominations, leading to distorted or inadvertently offensive coverage. However, some evidence does suggest media bias against the Religious Right, particularly fundamentalists. The official *Associated Press Stylebook* warns against using that term at all because of its implication of religious extremism, but the term is routinely applied by reporters to evangelicals, conservative Catholics, and Muslims.[54] Given the negative media coverage of Christian fundamentalists it is hardly surprising that they receive much lower thermometer scores than other religious groups on the ANES.

The mainstream media has given considerable (and often critical) coverage to the Religious Right and its expanding role within the Republican Party. But it has paid less attention to seculars and their increasing influence within the Democratic Party; one reason may be that many in the media share secular values and are thus more likely to perceive the views of religious conservatives as a threat.[55] Thus media coverage of George Bush was far more critical than that of John Kerry in 2004. Reporters paid considerable attention to Bush's religious rhetoric and to GOP efforts to mobilize conservative Christians, but downplayed Kerry's religious rhetoric and overtly partisan appearances in African American churches. Although Kerry insisted that "faith affects everything I do," it was Bush who was castigated for basing policy decisions on faith rather than reason or science.[56] The mainstream media may indeed give more sympathetic coverage to secular rather than traditional religious perspectives, and may help to raise legitimate questions about the use of religion as a reason (or rationale) for policy decisions. But the press may have seriously "misunderestimated" the importance of religion and moral values to American voters in 2004, and reporters' lack of knowledge of religion may distort their coverage of both foreign and domestic affairs.[57]

Since the 1990s the Internet and social media such as Facebook have transformed communications. The Internet has also greatly reduced the costs of organization. Individuals can locate kindred spirits, acquire information, contribute to political campaigns, and be contacted by parties or candidates, without the time and effort required by traditional group or church membership. The political impacts of the new media are still being assessed,[58] but in many respects the new media have been beneficial to secular perspectives. Young people, increasingly secular and detached from formal religious organizations, are far more Internet savvy than their elders. MoveOn.org and Organizing for America (OFA) are credited with helping to mobilize young voters in 2008. The Internet may thus have helped to offset young people's "participatory deficit," although it has not offset the socioeconomic bias in political involvement.[59]

However, many of these gains may be transient. Despite considerable efforts by OFA, young voters who had voted in 2008 stayed home in 2010.[60] Senior citizens, who are far more consistent voters, are increasingly using the Internet and e-mail as well. Established churches and Religious Right organizations now have websites and Facebook pages, and Twitter feeds, and are devoting considerable resources to web design.[61]

## SECULARS AND THE DEMOCRATIC PARTY

Political analysts have explored in detail the relationships between the Religious Right and Republican Party, nationally as well as in many states.[62] As shown in chapter 3, white religious traditionalists in the United States have increasingly been voting Republican. Conservative Christians, including observant (white or non-Hispanic) Catholics as well as evangelical Protestants, now constitute much of the base of the Republican Party. A generation ago the Bible Belt in the South was solidly Democratic; it is now mostly Republican in terms of voting and office holding by whites, although African Americans, regardless of religion or religiosity, remain overwhelmingly Democratic.

But less scholarly and media attention has been paid to the growing influence of seculars within the Democratic Party. One study attributed the origin of the "culture wars" not to the resurgent Religious Right, but to the influence of secularists within the Democratic Party. A third of the 1972 national convention delegates had no religious affiliation or never attended services, and were widely perceived as antagonistic to traditional religious values.[63] In the 1970s only about 5 percent of the population lacked ties to religion, but since then seculars have become an increasing proportion of Democratic voters as well as campaign volunteers and party convention delegates. As chapter 3 suggested, based on ANES data, the secular proportion of Democratic voters has increased from 16 percent in 1980 to 34 percent in 2008. In 2004, the unaffiliated were 17 percent of Democratic campaign volunteers, but only 4 percent of Republican volunteers.[64]

National party convention delegates reveal a similar profile. Table 5.3 summarizes the religious backgrounds of national convention delegates in 2004 and 2008. In both years, observant evangelical (white) Protestants were the largest single religious category among Republican delegates. Their proportion declined somewhat between 2004 and 2008, offset by increases in observant Catholic delegates. Mainline Protestants, regardless of church attendance, were more likely to be found among Republican rather than Democratic delegations. But only a scattering of Jews, African Americans, other Christians (including Mormons), Hispanics, or people of other faiths served as Republican convention delegates.

Democratic convention delegates present a very different picture. As of 2008, the unaffiliated were the largest single religious grouping among Democrats, followed by African American Protestants, less observant mainline Protestants, and less observing or Hispanic Catholics. Further, the unaffiliated proportion of Democratic delegates has increased since 2004 (and even more dramatically since 1972). By contrast, the proportions of Catholics, (white) evangelical Protestants, and other

Table 5.3 Religious Affiliations of Party Convention Delegates, 2004 and 2008

|  | 2004 | | 2008 | |
| --- | --- | --- | --- | --- |
|  | Republicans | Democrats | Republicans | Democrats |
| *Republican Constituencies* | | | | |
| Weekly attending evangelical Protestants | 23.1% | 3.0% | 19.8% | 1.8% |
| Other Christian | 5.0% | 7.4% | 3.0% | 1.3% |
| Less observant evangelical Protestants | 5.6% | 4.8% | 7.0% | 2.0% |
| Weekly attending Catholic | 9.6% | 9.0% | 13.6% | 5.8% |
| Weekly attending mainline Protestants | 11.0% | 4.4% | 11.8% | 4.2% |
| Hispanic Protestants | 0.6% | 1.0% | 3.3% | 1.8% |
| *Swing Constituencies* | | | | |
| Less observant mainline Protestants | 20.1% | 14.6% | 18.4% | 11.5% |
| *Democratic Constituencies* | | | | |
| Hispanic Catholics | 3.0% | 3.0% | 3.7% | 11.8% |
| Unaffiliated | 3.6% | 14.0% | 4.0% | 17.7% |
| Jews | 2.2% | 6.4% | 2.5% | 6.0% |
| Other faiths | 0.4% | 1.8% | 0.5% | 1.8% |
| Black Protestants | 5.0% | 14.4% | 1.5% | 16.2% |
| ALL | 100.0% | 100.0% | 100.0% | 100.0% |

Source: 2004 data from Green, *Faith Factor* (2007), 157; 2008 data provided by Green, personal communication, October 2010

Christians have declined.[65]

Clearly the unaffiliated are a force to be reckoned with in the Democratic Party, at all levels. In part due to secular influence, the Democratic and Republican party platforms still diverge sharply on the hot-button issues. The Republicans since 1980 have pledged to overturn *Roe v. Wade*, and remain adamantly opposed to gay marriage; the 2008 Democratic platform supported gay marriage and ending don't ask–don't tell, and also pledged to end the politicization of science policy. Yet although elites of both parties have become increasingly polarized along religious lines, candidates must still appeal to religiously involved moderate voters.

Stung by John Kerry's loss in 2004, and by the active role played in that campaign by evangelical Christians and Catholics, many Democratic leaders concluded that their party needed to pay more rather than less attention to religion.[66] Much soul-searching ensued, and significant changes were made at the 2008 Democratic convention in Denver. A pro-life Democratic senator, Bob Casey of Pennsylvania, was allowed to speak. The party platform continued to uphold reproductive rights, but (over vociferous objections from pro-choice and women's groups) language was added about the need to prevent abortions and provide alternatives for women facing problem pregnancies. These efforts may have succeeded, since the proportion of Catholics voting Democratic increased between 2004 and 2008. After impolitic statements on race by his former pastor, Reverend Jeremiah Wright, Barack Obama was obliged to resign his long-standing membership in Wright's church and to publicly defend his commitment to Christianity (although a significant proportion of Americans, including 43 percent of Republicans, continue to insist he is in fact Muslim).[67]

## SECULARS AND THE RELIGIOUS LEFT

In many respects people and organizations on the Religious Left should be natural allies of seculars. Both groups tend to be politically and socially liberal; both are strongly committed to separation of church and state. Furthermore, "for all of the diversity one can find among [religious] progressives, one of the central catalysts of solidarity over the years has been their hostility to the leaders, organizations, ideology, and agenda of the Christian Right."[68] The Christian Left rejects a literal reading of the Bible and the emphasis of the Christian Right on personal piety, traditional family structures, and strict sexual morality. Its liberal theology and progressive political views include strong support for the "social gospel" and help for the disadvantaged. Some have claimed that Christianity has been "hijacked" by the Christian Right and turned away from Jesus's emphasis on help for the poor and downtrodden. However, the Religious Left is a diverse group, with a broad range of values and priorities not necessarily shared with seculars. And in part because of this diversity, the Religious Left has serious organizational weaknesses of its own, hindering its ability to mobilize on behalf of either secular or religiously liberal views.

The Religious Left comprises three basic groups. First, there are members of historically liberal Protestant denominations (Unitarian Universalists, United Church of Christ) and the "peace" churches (Society of Friends, Church of the Brethren, Mennonites), although not all members of such churches consider themselves to be religious liberals. Second, there are liberal members of other denominations, including mainline Protestants, some evangelicals, and Roman Catholics who have been active on behalf of peace and social justice. And third, there are religiously liberal non-Christians, including Reform and Reconstructionist Jews and some Buddhists and Muslims. But even under the broadest definition, the Religious Left is a small segment of the American religious landscape; the historic liberal and peace churches constitute only 1.3 percent of the U.S. population. A 2000 Princeton survey found 21 percent of the public willing to classify themselves as religious liberals, and the GSS data reviewed in chapter 2 showed that this proportion has increased since the 1970s. But only 7 percent of respondents in a 2004 Religious Values survey were willing to identify with the "religious left political movement."[69]

The constituent groups of the Religious Left are not only small but most are also declining in number, especially in comparison to the rapid growth of congregations on the Religious Right, including evangelicals, Pentecostals, fundamentalists, and Mormons. Many on the Religious Left are committed to using political means to bring their values into fruition, but the lower rate of church attendance among religious liberals, coupled with declining congregation size, constitutes a political as well as a religious liability.[70] Most supporters of the Religious Left are Democratic in terms of voting and party preference. But since they lack the extensive social networks and organizational depth of the Religious Right, it is not easy for parties or candidates to contact them. However, new organizations have been established to give a stronger voice to the Religious Left; these include the Interfaith Alliance (founded 1994, with assistance from Democratic donors and activists), Sojourners (founded by Jim Wallis in 1971), and the Progressive Religious Partnership. Rabbi Michael Lerner's Tikkun movement (founded 1994) has attempted to unite liberal Jews and liberals from several faith traditions under the banner of "spiritual progressives."[71]

The Religious Left, like the Religious Right, has produced several notable leaders and spokespersons whose writings, public appearances, and fund-raising skills have helped build their organizations and attract media attention. They can usually be counted on for a quotable rejoinder to policy initiatives or public statements from the Religious Right, and join with the historic peace churches to speak out against war and military spending. In addition to Jim Wallis and Michael Lerner, this group includes the outspoken Roman Catholic nun Joan Chittester, who has advocated for peace, social justice, and the ordination of women. Bill Clinton's spiritual adviser, Tony Campolo, argued for a stronger political focus on poverty. James Forbes, senior minister at the liberal interdenominational Riverside Church in New York City, endorsed John Kerry in 2004. Dr. Bob Edgar, former six-term member of Congress and president of the National Council of Churches, spoke out against the war in Iraq.[72]

Those on the Religious Left share many political and social views with seculars, including support for the rights of women and gays, opposition to school vouchers, and concern for the environment. But three characteristics of the Religious Left render them uncertain allies of seculars. First, many of these groups share deep religious commitments, and argue that social change depends on expansion of moral and social policies inspired by religion. As progressive evangelical Jim Wallis said, only *spiritual* values "can provide the moral direction and energy required to renew our impoverished political process."[73] And some identified with the Religious Left are conservative on social issues, particularly abortion and gay marriage. Most seculars, however, vigorously question the supposed link between religion and morality; they would prefer to base morality and ethics on human reason. Critics of religion have argued that, historically, religion has led to intolerance, oppression of minorities, conflict, and war.[74]

Second, many religious liberals find themselves at odds with other members of their churches or organizations. Liberal Jews such as Michael Lerner, who support universal human rights and a two-state solution for Palestinians, face strong opposition from the superior funding and organization of the ardently pro-Israel AIPAC. Liberal clergy in mainline Christian denominations and their national Washington-based lobbying organizations have long worked for peace, civil rights, and social justice. But since progressive clergy provide a range of interpretations of scripture, their views are not always viewed as authoritative. Members of liberal churches are less likely than evangelicals to approve of political activism by clergy. Many of the lay people in the pews do not share the passions or priorities of their leaders, and will withhold money or membership if leaders stray too far afield. In part because of these internal conflicts, activists on the Religious Left have increasingly focused on local issues like homelessness or hunger.[75]

And third, many of those identified as religious liberals in a 2000 survey expressed considerable satisfactions with the status quo. In part, this was because some historic concerns of the Religious Left (racism, status of women, conflicts in Viet Nam or Central America) had already been addressed. In part, those on the Religious Left tended to have high social status in terms of education, income, or occupation. And political mobilization is difficult without the "fire in the belly" fueled by profound dissatisfaction with current policies or social trends.[76] However, as the morality-politics cycle would predict, George Bush's 2000 and 2004 elections and his support for many policies favored by the Religious Right led to much more discontent on the Religious Left and to a corresponding increase in political involvement and voting for Democrats.

Seculars and the Religious Left share an ironic dilemma. Because of their support for strict separation of church and state, they have been reluctant to use religious language to justify their positions on issues such as human rights, world peace, or assistance to the poor. Thus public discourse has been dominated by the fervently expressed theological or moral viewpoints of those on the Religious Right.[77] But the majority of the American public responds favorably to arguments couched in moral or religious terms, and they have considerable respect for politicians who stick with their convictions (hence the scorn of John Kerry as a "flip-flopper" in 2004). Over strong objections from many seculars, Democrats in 2008 used the party platform and Barack Obama's campaign rhetoric to make explicit appeals to religious values—and perhaps as a result Obama attracted many more votes from religious groups than John Kerry had in 2004.[78]

## CONCLUSION

This chapter has used two different perspectives on political organization, the cost/benefit model and the morality-politics cycle, to describe both the Religious Right and groups supportive of secular views. Since the 1960s organizations identified with the Religious Right made effective use of new technologies and entrepreneurial leadership to mobilize church members and clergy, and were thereby able to mount a strong challenge to threats to traditional moral views. They were not always successful; the complex American political system, with its many veto points, has frustrated many initiatives, and public opinion on a number of issues has been moving in a more secular direction. But regardless of any initial advantages, organizational maintenance is difficult, especially when clouded by scandal or leadership challenges.

The Religious Right achieved some significant victories with the election of an evangelical president, George W. Bush, with strongly moral perspectives on both foreign and domestic policy. But the ensuing policy gains (conservative appointments to the courts and federal agencies, funding for abstinence education and faith-based programs, bans on stem-cell research and partial-birth abortion) came at a cost, as the morality-policy cycle would predict: media skepticism, legal challenges, and furious countermobilization in Washington, D.C., as well as in the states. The Religious Right has expended considerable resources to set up legal and quasi-scientific organizations to counter effective use of the courts and mainstream science by seculars and their allies. Conservative religious groups have also established parallel communications networks and educational institutions to counter secular influence in the schools, the news media, and the entertainment industry.

Secular interests have been defended by a number of long-standing organizations, including the ACLU, Jewish groups such as ADL, and Americans United. Jews (both religious and secular) and mainline Protestants (many sympathetic to the Religious Left) have high social standing and personal ties to those in power, thus augmenting their lobbying impact.[79] Despite their small size and narrow geographic focus, these groups have nevertheless won some significant legal victories, especially under the Warren court. Gay-rights groups once had negligible visibility or influence, but have now become major players, winning many legal cases and changing public opinion (but almost always losing out under direct democracy). But there have been failures for secular groups as well; lack of effective grassroots organizing in many states doomed the ERA, and abortion is increasingly restricted by both state and federal laws. Despite concerted efforts by scientists and educators, Americans' understanding of science remains abysmal, with nearly half the population still rejecting evolution, and widespread skepticism concerning climate change.

New secular organizations have emerged, including umbrella organizations designed to focus lobbying efforts. Seculars may never be able to match grassroots mobilization of church members on behalf of values issues or conservative candidates. But their political activism has increased nevertheless, and they have a strong presence within the Democratic Party. Coalition formation is a crucial element. Despite their organizational weaknesses, seculars have a number of sympathizers within the media, entertainment industry, scientific community, Religious Left, and among minorities. The challenge is to forge effective coalitions, often at the state or local level, to combat policy initiatives by the Religious Right.

In one view, the expansion of religious interest groups has helped to democratize the pressure-group system and to articulate the concerns of less influential citizens.[80] However, in order to maintain their organizations, mobilize supporters, or turn out the vote, leaders of both secular and religious interest groups have strong incentives to emphasize the "threat" posed by their opponents. Inflammatory rhetoric about the "American Taliban" or "baby-killing abortionists" may raise more money, but it can also lead to polarized politics and mutual misperceptions. In the process views of the "moderate middle" are likely to be drowned out.[81]

On the other hand, competition among groups representing diverse interests may prevent any one group (even one representing the majority) from dominating. The Religious Right, despite its considerable organizational advantages, must now confront countervailing influences from increasingly effective mobilization by seculars, the Religious Left, and their allies. The case studies in the next chapter will show how secular forces have mobilized and made use of coalition formation, the courts, and political strategy to help overcome their organizational deficits at the grass roots.

# 6

✛

# Case Studies in Countervailing Power

This chapter will examine three controversial policy issues where forces aligned with the Religious Right came into direct conflict with more secular viewpoints: a ban on gay marriage (Proposition 8) in California, two abortion referenda in South Dakota, and attempts to introduce intelligent design into the schools in Dover, Pennsylvania. All three cases illustrate distinct stages of the morality-politics cycle and highlight both elite strategies and the public's response. Furthermore, these cases take place in three very different states. Since so many morality-policy struggles take place in the states, it is crucial to understand how state institutions, political elites, and interest-group environments can influence policy outcomes. While an argument can certainly be made that morality policies *should* reflect differences in public preferences across states and communities, both secular and religious forces are making strenuous efforts to shift those preferences toward their own values.

In each instance, the outcome (at least in the short term) reflected the organizational strengths, legal tactics, and political strategies of each side. The issues at stake, gay marriage, reproductive rights, and the teaching of evolution, have by no means been decided definitively, and these struggles over morality policy are likely to continue in different venues in the future. But an analysis of these three cases will illustrate the ongoing challenges faced by both seculars and the Religious Right in their attempts to influence public opinion and enact policies reflecting their values.

## PROPOSITION 8 IN CALIFORNIA

### Gay-Marriage Policy "Shocks," 1993–2006

Gay marriage is a relative newcomer on the morality-politics playing field. Less than twenty years ago it was not even a political priority for gays and lesbians in their struggle for social acceptance and legal equality, and it was an unthinkably radical concept for most Americans.[1] Political elites and the mass public shared these values, as is the usual case at the initial stage of the morality-politics cycle. The Supreme Court's 1986 *Bowers v. Hardwick* decision, upholding state laws against sodomy, exemplified such broad consensus on fundamental values.

In 1993 a shock to the status quo catapulted gay marriage into the political limelight. The Hawaii Supreme Court ruled that their state's constitutional provisions concerning equal protection of the law did not preclude marriage between same-sex individuals. That decision was a shock even within Hawaii; citizens in the Aloha state voted overwhelmingly in 1998 to amend the state's constitution to permit the state legislature to forbid gay marriage, and it promptly did so. Traditional religious groups and advocates of "family values" feared that other states might follow the Hawaiian court's example.

The shock waves extended to Washington, D.C., as well. Most interpretations of the Full Faith and Credit clause of the U.S. Constitution required states to recognize each other's laws concerning marriage and divorce.[2] Members of Congress quickly introduced legislation to change that. The Defense of Marriage Act (DOMA) passed decisively in both houses in 1996. Under DOMA neither the federal government nor other states were obliged to recognize the legalization of gay marriage by any state. Gay spouses would not be eligible for federal benefits such as Social Security, immigration status, or veterans' pensions that were extended to heterosexual couples. President Bill Clinton's signing statement reaffirmed his personal opposition to governmental recognition of same-gender marriages, but also noted that the federal DOMA would not preclude the rights of any state to enact antidiscrimination laws or even to permit gay marriage.[3] Surveys at the time indicated that this was not a very tough political decision, since Americans overwhelmingly rejected the idea of gay marriage. As of 1993, only about 20 percent of the public would support it, and gay marriage had few proponents among political leaders of either party.[4]

After the Hawaii decision, public support for gay marriage continued its slow but steady upward trend. Passage of the federal DOMA may have temporarily reassured opponents of gay marriage that their values were not at risk. But in some states, courts and legislatures began to debate demands for civil unions or gay marriage in light of their own constitutions and in response to cases brought by gay-rights advocates and civil libertarians. In 1999 the Vermont Supreme Court ruled that exclusion of same-sex couples from the benefits and protections of marriage under state law violated the common-benefits clause of the Vermont Constitution. By 2010 five states (Vermont, Massachusetts, Connecticut, Iowa, and New Hampshire) and Washington, D.C., permitted gay marriage; such marriages were recognized but not performed in New York, Maryland, and New Hampshire. In New Jersey the state legislature created legal unions that, while not called marriages, are explicitly defined as offering all the rights and responsibilities of marriage under state (though not federal) law to same-sex couples. Ten other states have created legal or civil unions for same-sex couples that offer varying subsets of the rights and responsibilities of marriage.[5]

Concerned with these trends, opponents of gay marriage also mobilized to counter any further expansion of gay marriage by legislation or by judicial interpretation of state constitutions. Efforts quickly emerged to enact state-level DOMAs. Maine's legislature enacted a gay-marriage law, but it was overturned by referendum in 2009. As of 2010, nineteen states ban any type of same-sex unions that would be equivalent to civil marriage. Thirty states now have constitutional amendments explicitly barring the recognition of same-sex marriage by defining civil marriage as a legal union between a man and a woman. Such bans passed in every state where they were subject to popular vote on an initiative, referendum, or constitutional amendment.[6] Considerable evidence further suggests that Republican political elites helped to instigate referenda on gay marriage in order to boost turnout in the 2004 election. While this interpretation has been challenged by some political scientists, opinion polls continued to show widespread opposition to gay marriage. So elected officials and party elites were arguably responding to popular sentiment.[7]

### Proposition 8 in California, 2008

California is one of thirty states where the constitution can be amended by popular initiative. A provision of the state's Civil Code enacted in 1977 described marriage as a "civil contract between a man and a woman." To further strengthen this definition, a voter initiative (Proposition 22) was introduced in 2000, which would amend the California Family Code to specify that only marriage between a man and a woman is valid or recognized by California law. This passed by a sizable margin (61 to 39 percent), but was subsequently appealed to the California Supreme Court. The court ruled on May 15, 2008, that Proposition 22 violated the equal protection clause of the California Constitution.[8] Thousands of gay and lesbian couples immediately filed for marriage licenses, and newspapers and television broadcasts featured numerous pictures of the joyous wedding celebrations that ensued.

This profound policy shock quickly led opponents of gay marriage to draft a constitutional amendment (Proposition 8) that would define marriage as legal for heterosexual couples only. In less than three weeks they amassed far more than the requisite number of signatures (694,000 required, or 8 percent of the previous vote for governor; 1,120,000 submitted) to qualify the measure for the November 2008 ballot. A huge political battle then ensued. Since the state was widely expected to vote for Barack Obama, much of the media attention, fund-raising, interest-group activity, and voter mobilization efforts focused on Proposition 8. The campaigns for and against raised $43 million and $40 million, respectively; this spending surpassed every campaign in the country except for the presidential contest. Contributions came from all fifty states and over twenty foreign countries.[9]

All ten of the states' major newspapers, including the *Los Angeles Times*, the *Sacramento Bee*, and the *San Jose Mercury News*, came out against Proposition 8. As the *San Francisco Chronicle* editorialized,

> Constitutions are revered, at the state and federal levels, because they so plainly and adamantly guarantee individual rights. The idea of using a ballot measure to single out a certain group of Californians for denial of individual rights—based on their sexual orientation—would represent an ugly distortion of the very purpose of a constitution.[10]

Several political-action committees were formed specifically to challenge Prop. 8, and numerous celebrities and entertainers (including Governor Arnold Schwarzenegger) spoke out against it.[11] The largest national gay, lesbian, bisexual, and transgender (GLBT) organization, Human Rights Campaign, joined with California Faith for Equality to coordinate efforts by several liberal church groups (Unitarians, Society of Friends, Metropolitan Church) with those of gay-rights activists. Although they were outspent, opponents of Proposition 8 expected it to fail; the California Field Poll in September showed Prop. 8 losing, 55 to 38 percent. Even the final poll before the election showed Prop. 8 trailing by 49 to 44 percent, although with 7 percent still undecided. On Election Day, Obama carried the state as expected, 61 to 39 percent. But Proposition 8 passed 52 to 48 percent, in an election with the highest turnout (79 percent) since Proposition 13 was on the ballot in 1978.

Shocked opponents wondered what had gone wrong; how had their lead evaporated? Opponents of Prop. 8 had not been outspent by a large margin, and had had sufficient funds to saturate the airwaves with ads opposing Prop. 8. The director of the California Field Poll attributed the discrepancy between the preelection polls and ballot results to "regular church-goers" who "were more prone than other voters to be influenced by last-minute appeals to conform to orthodox church positions when voting on a progressive social issue like same-sex marriage."[12] Some evidence also suggests that voters may have been confused by the question's wording; support for gay marriage required a no vote on Prop. 8.[13]

Because they had expected to win, opponents had not put sufficient energy into grassroots mobilization, especially during the last crucial days before the election. Opponents were also criticized for not making sufficient effort to reach out to African Americans or Hispanics; these minorities constitute a significant proportion of the population of California, and their turnout surged in 2008. Although they usually vote for Democratic candidates, African Americans and Hispanics tend to be conservative in their religious beliefs and opinions on social issues. While Prop. 8 opponents had leafleted in minority neighborhoods, they had not involved minority political or religious leaders in their strategizing. A few African Americans church leaders did urge their congregations to vote against Prop. 8 because of its implications for civil rights, and the NAACP Legal Defense Fund opposed Prop. 8 as well.[14]

By contrast, grassroots mobilization efforts by opponents of gay marriage started much earlier and were far more effective, aided considerably by their links to well-organized religious groups. Prominent among these was the Latter-day Saints (LDS; Mormon) church. LDS leaders (bishops) saw gay marriage as a direct assault on their religious beliefs and their concept of family. The LDS church teaches that God meant marriage to be eternal, and that humans enter Heaven as families consisting of fathers, mothers, and their children (including "spirit children" that faithful couples might conceive in the afterlife).

Mormons constitute only 2 percent of the population in California (compared with 57 percent in Utah, 20 percent in Idaho, and 10 percent in Wyoming).[15] But Mormons from other states sent millions of dollars (an estimated 40 percent of the $40 million campaign chest of Prop. 8 backers); about 45 percent of out-of-state contributions to ProtectMarriage.com came from Utah, over three times more than any other state.[16] The LDS also sent thousands of volunteers to California to combat this perceived threat to their values. ProtectMarriage, the official proponents of Proposition 8, estimated that "eighty to ninety percent" of the early volunteers going door-to-door were LDS.[17] The LDS church produced and broadcast to its California congregations a video program depicting the threat posed by gay marriage and proposed a timeline for grassroots efforts to support the proposition.[18] Backers of Prop. 8 also made effective use of new media (Google, YouTube, Twitter) on the Internet. One analysis found that such messages by proponents outnumbered those by opponents before the vote.[19]

Backers of Prop. 8, including LDS and the Roman Catholic Church, also made a special effort to reach out to African Americans and Hispanics, visiting their churches and knocking on their doors. African American turnout was also expected to be high because of Obama's presence on the ticket. And Obama himself (like all other Democratic presidential candidates in 2008) was personally opposed to gay marriage on religious grounds, although he did support civil unions. Were African Americans therefore to blame for the passage of Proposition 8? A solid majority of them indeed voted for it. But according to Egan and Sherrill's analysis, the yes vote was due primarily to African Americans heavily involved in churches, and religious voters overall were the strongest supporters of Prop. 8.[20] This again illustrates the importance of organizational ties for political mobilization.

**After the Vote**

Proponents of gay marriage were stunned by their loss, the end of legal gay marriages in California, and the threat to their values posed by the popular and religious support of Proposition 8. A backlash started shortly after the 2008 vote. TV ads portrayed Mormon missionaries invading the home of a lesbian couple and stealing their wedding rings. Mormon businesses were boycotted; Mormon churches were picketed or vandalized; individual Mormons (some of whom had actually voted no on Prop. 8) were assaulted. A successful lawsuit led the California Fair Political Practices Commission to fine the LDS church $5,538 for not disclosing nonmonetary contributions in the two weeks before the election.[21] Although mainstream media coverage of the issue fell off sharply after the vote, opponents made use of the new media to express their outrage and frustration, some of it directed against their own supporters.[22]

Under California law, provisions of a successful initiative take effect immediately after the election. Although it was too late to change the election results, supporters of gay marriage turned to the courts. The first legal challenge to Proposition 8 went against them: the state Supreme Court ruled on May 25, 2009, that Proposition 8 was a valid amendment to the California Constitution, not a "revision," which would have required approval by two-thirds of the state legislature as well as a popular vote. The court also found that the voter-approved ban on gay marriage was a "limited and allowable exception" to the equal protection clause of the California Constitution.[23] Opponents of gay marriage also appealed to the courts to invalidate same-sex marriages already in effect, but California's Attorney General Jerry Brown maintained that these would remain valid.

Gay-marriage supporters had better luck in federal court. Chief Judge Vaughn Walker of the federal district court ruled in August 2010 that

Proposition 8 did violate the state's constitution. His opinion rejected two major arguments made by opponents of gay marriage: that courts should not overturn the popular will expressed in a vote, and that gay marriage would cause direct harm to children and to heterosexual marriages. The judge noted that many previous court rulings (such as the one striking down most of Proposition 187, which would have denied public services to illegal immigrants) had gone against popular votes if fundamental rights were judged to be at stake. Judge Walker said Proposition 8 was unconstitutional because it violated both the due process and equal protection clauses of the state constitution.

The judge also ruled that opponents of gay marriage had presented no credible evidence that any traditional marriages would be harmed if Proposition 8 were overturned, stating that "Proposition 8 fails to advance any rational basis in singling out gay men and lesbians for denial of a marriage license." Walker also ruled that the evidence offered by the biologist David Blankenhorn, to justify a ban on gay marriage as harmful to children, was "not supported by reliable evidence or methodology," and that Blankenhorn failed to consider evidence contrary to his view in presenting his testimony. Even the expert witnesses against gay marriage admitted that they could produce no empirical evidence of harm to heterosexual marriages.[24]

**Conclusion**

This case study supports evidence that direct democracy is usually inimical to minority rights.[25] Even in a liberal state, seculars, gay-rights groups, and the Religious Left found it difficult to prevail at the polls against the superior grassroots organization and fund-raising abilities of traditional religious groups. African Americans and Hispanics may vote for Democratic candidates, but are still likely to express their more conservative social viewpoints when presented with an opportunity to do so in an initiative or referendum. However, secular viewpoints have powerful allies in the media, the scientific establishment, and the courts. All of California's major newspapers opposed Proposition 8, as did many people in the state's influential entertainment industry. Judge Walker found empirical analyses of beneficial gay adoptions far more credible than claims to the contrary based on religious grounds. One observer concluded that "what really won out today was science, methodology, and hard work."[26]

The Supreme Court's decision in *Lawrence v. Texas* (2003) overturned its own previous ruling in *Bower* and banned all state antisodomy laws. Justice Antonin Scalia's biting dissent claimed that *Lawrence v. Texas* effectively calls for "the end of all morals legislation" against "bigamy, same-sex marriage, adult incest, prostitution, masturbation, adultery, fornication, bestiality, and obscenity" on constitutional grounds of privacy and equal protection of the laws. The U.S. Supreme Court might yet rule against gay marriage, although their decision in the *Lawrence* case suggests otherwise. Judge Walker's 120-page ruling also cited Justice Anthony Kennedy extensively and strategically. Kennedy is likely to be the swing vote if a state ban on gay marriage is appealed to the Supreme Court, and opposition to gay marriage would require him to reverse many of his own previously stated opinions.[27]

Gay marriages in California are still on hold until additional federal appeals are handed down. Even if it ultimately upholds state or federal DOMAs, the U.S. Supreme Court might still allow gay-marriage laws to stand in states that have enacted them. While every attempt to adopt gay marriage by popular vote has failed, the Religious Right has also successfully placed gay marriage beyond the reach of legislative majorities by passing constitutional bans in thirty states. But time is not on their side; polls in August 2010 reported that for the first time, supporters of gay marriage now outnumber opponents in the general public. This continues a twenty-year trend, which has moved upward even in states that have enacted legislative DOMAs or constitutional bans on gay marriage.[28] Support for gay marriage is widespread among the younger generation of both whites and minorities.[29] As these groups come to dominate in the electorate, the right of gays to marry should eventually prevail—but not without a fight.

## TEACHING INTELLIGENT DESIGN IN DOVER, PENNSYLVANIA

### The Battle against Evolution

The publication of Charles Darwin's *On the Origin of Species* in 1859 was a profound shock to Victorian sensibilities and to religion. Furious debate ensued over his conclusions and their implications for science and society. By the early twentieth century most mainline Protestants and Roman Catholics had accepted the overwhelming geological and paleontological evidence for the evolution of life on earth over four billion years. But to Christian fundamentalists, the story of creation in six days as told in Genesis was not only literally true but also the foundation for a moral view of the universe. If man is created in God's image, human life has a transcendent purpose to worship God and obey his laws. Darwin's theory of evolution, based on random mutations, natural selection, and survival of the fittest, was yet more evidence of scientific materialism, the triumph of atheism, and the breakdown of the social order. A series of pamphlets titled *The Fundamentals*, written between 1910 and 1915, and the World Christian Fundamentals Association (founded in 1919) challenged the liberal theological views of "modernist" mainline Protestants and argued strongly for a literal reading of Genesis.[30]

Evolution emerged as a political issue during the 1920s, especially in the South, because many more students were now attending high schools in that region.[31] The educational professionals who were hired to teach and administer these new schools favored progressive trends in both education and science and assigned biology texts that discussed evolution.[32] Families, churches, and school boards realized that their children were being exposed to ideas directly contradictory to the fundamentalist or evangelical Christian beliefs widely held in the Bible Belt. This very real and immediate threat to core values led to denunciations from the pulpit, protests at school-board meetings, and efforts to pass state or local laws to restrict the teaching of evolution. As early as 1922 William Jennings Bryan, former presidential candidate and now social reformer, began to call for legislation to ban the teaching of "Darwinism" in schools and universities, and gave hundreds of speeches on the topic.

Thus by the time of the Scopes trial in 1925, several states, including North Carolina, Texas, Kentucky, Virginia, and Georgia (even New York), were considering such laws. Oklahoma and Florida had enacted limited laws or resolutions.[33] In Tennessee, after vigorous debate, the state legislature passed a bill that made it a crime to teach evolution at any school within the state. Governor Austin Peay actually favored progressive education and more high schools, but signed off on the bill in order to help pass a large education-reform measure. The president of the University of Tennessee likewise made no public protest of the law against teaching evolution (which applied to universities as well as to high schools) because his school's budget was tied to the education-reform bill (which did soon pass). Some newspapers, educators, and more liberal church leaders protested the bill as an assault on science and free speech, but to no avail.[34]

A high-school science teacher in Dayton, Tennessee, John Scopes, was accused (and eventually convicted) of violating this Butler law in Tennessee, and his trial quickly became a contentious state and national issue. The American Civil Liberties Union (ACLU) took on the case because they saw it as a challenge to freedom of speech and the rights of teachers, as well as to the establishment clause.[35] A high-profile lawyer, Clarence Darrow, offered to defend Scopes for free. The school board hired the well-known politician, former presidential candidate, and flamboyant speaker William Jennings Bryan. Bryan was actually willing to accept Darwin's arguments concerning the geologic history of the earth and the evolution of plants and animals, but he categorically rejected the idea that man was descended from apes or lower animals. He was also opposed because Darwin's arguments concerning the "survival of the fittest" had been widely used to justify eugenics, unchecked capitalism, and social Darwinism. Bryan the populist argued that these policies were detrimental to the poor and the working class. Bryan was also strongly in favor of majoritarian democracy; if voters and taxpayers did not want evolution taught in their community, local school policies should reflect those preferences. Darrow's caustic questioning during the trial highlighted Bryan's lack of scientific knowledge and the contradictions inherent in any literal reading of the scriptures.[36]

Despite Darrow's best efforts, the judge and jury sided with Bryan. Scopes's conviction was overturned on appeal due to a technicality, but the Tennessee Supreme Court upheld the law. Scopes and Clarence Darrow may have lost in court in Dayton, Tennessee, but they triumphed in the court of public opinion. Reporters from all over the United States flocked to Tennessee for the trial, and the media coverage of the creationist perspective (especially that by H. L. Mencken of the *Baltimore Sun*) was scathing. Mencken depicted fundamentalist Christians as "yokels, hillbillies, peasants, gaping primates, morons, and Babbitts," and their ministers as "shamans" and "inquisitors."[37] The hit 1955 Broadway play *Inherit the Wind*, and the 1960 movie and 1980 television drama based on it, were likewise neither flattering nor fair to fundamentalists. Bryan's views on social Darwinism and majority rule were not considered, and the townspeople of fictional "Hillsboro" were portrayed as "far more frenzied, mean-spirited, and ignorant" than were the real citizens of Dayton, Tennessee. The Ku Klux Klan marched only in the movie.[38]

After the fiasco of the Scopes trial and the defeat of Prohibition in 1933, most fundamentalists retreated from politics and mass culture and returned to their historic mission of saving souls. But state and local opposition to teaching evolution continued. In many schools throughout the South the subject was simply avoided, in part because conservative Christians convinced the publishers of science textbooks to omit any reference to evolution. A few other Southern states subsequently enacted laws restricting the teaching of evolution, and these remained on the books because the Supreme Court generally set a high threshold for considering establishment cases. Not until 1968 did the court agree to hear a case brought by an Arkansas public-school teacher who feared criminal prosecution for teaching evolution, and in *Epperson v. Arkansas* it struck down an Arkansas law that forbade the teaching of evolutionary theory. In *Edwards v. Aguillard* (1986) the court ruled that a Louisiana law requiring the teaching of both Darwinism and creationism was unconstitutional, because creationism was religious in nature and therefore violated the establishment clause.[39]

Most conservative Christians were outraged by these decisions, which not only advanced secular viewpoints but limited religious discourse in public schools and eroded the widely cherished principle of local control of schools. Other strategies were attempted to encourage creationism, such as efforts to remove discussion of evolution from approved biology texts, or to insert in these texts a sticker with language drafted by the state legislature discounting evolution as an unproven theory. But none of these could pass legal muster since the court in this "strict separation" era of jurisprudence appeared determined to block any efforts to bring religion into public education.[40] Televangelists and other leaders of the Religious Right attacked *Edwards v. Aguillard* as yet more evidence of the threat posed by secular humanists and activist judges, whom they blamed for many of the problems afflicting American schools (violence, teen pregnancy, juvenile delinquency). They argued that if children were taught that they descended from animals, they would behave like animals.[41] Home schooling or private schools became increasingly popular options for fundamentalist or evangelical parents.

Another strategy soon emerged: introducing "creation science" or "intelligent design" (ID) into the biology curriculum. The basic argument of ID was that some biological features (the human eye, DNA, bacterial flagellum) were so complex that they could only have been introduced in complete form by a "designer." ID proponent William Dembski saw design as a problem in information theory, of empirically detecting the "complex specified information" that we attribute to intelligent causes. The search for extraterrestrial intelligence (SETI) is touted as a counterexample to the claim that detecting "unknown intelligence" is impermissible as a scientific project.[42] Proponents of ID claimed that the identity of the designer was not important for their arguments; it could be an entity from outer space, but it was widely assumed to be the Christian God. Further, if the identity of this designer was left unspecified, the courts would not be able to argue that intelligent design was religious and therefore in violation of the establishment clause.

Wealthy conservatives funded the Discovery Institute in Seattle in 1990 to encourage and publicize research on intelligent design. ID proponents were trying to squeeze through the window the court left open in *Aguillard:* "Teaching a variety of scientific theories to children might be validly done with the clear secular intent of enhancing the effectiveness of science instruction."[43] Major proponents of ID, such as biologist Michael Behe and mathematician and philosopher William Dembski, serve on the board of the Discovery Institute and have published numerous books and articles on ID. However, according to a leaked "wedge" fund-raising memo, the Discovery Institute's main purposes were to influence public opinion, build up a base of support among Christians, integrate "design theory" into public schools, and support any legal challenges that might result. Arguments for ID had been widely circulated within the evangelical community, but they had not been tested in court until the Dover school board tried to introduce ID into the curriculum.

**Dover, Pennsylvania: The School Board's Strategy for Intelligent Design**

The Dover saga began three years before the trial, when two ardently conservative Christians were elected to the school board in this small town near York, Pennsylvania. Both expressed concerns about the lack of morality among Dover students and the need to restore school prayer. At a board retreat in 2002, one said his highest priority for the schools was "creationism." The high school was facing a shortage of biology texts, but these board members were reluctant to approve new ones unless, as they stated at a public board meeting in June 2004, they could "balance the teaching of Darwinism with the teaching of creationism."[44] The negative reaction was immediate; several board members, concerned parents, and a local newspaper reporter called the ACLU chapter in Harrisburg. The ACLU immediately threatened to take legal action if creationism was introduced into the science curriculum. The next public board meeting was packed and the battle was on.[45]

The first step for the critics of evolution was to solidify their majority on the board. Any opposition was shouted down; advocates of teaching evolution were denounced as atheists or communists or un-American. Two board members eventually resigned as a result and were replaced with staunch conservative Christians. The next step was to introduce an intelligent-design textbook, *Of Pandas and People*, as a "supplement or alternative" to a standard biology text. But after the board was advised by its own lawyers that they were risking a lawsuit, a majority voted against setting money aside for this purchase. However, the Dover schools soon received an anonymous donation of sixty copies of the book, which were placed in the school library. The third step was to amend the high-school science curriculum. The board passed a resolution stating that "students will be made aware of gaps/problems in Darwin's theory and of other theories of evolution including, but not limited to, intelligent design." The board's memo of June 4 constituted the "first officially mandated mention of intelligent design in U.S. public schools."[46]

To introduce intelligent design, the board would require teachers to read a four-paragraph statement to all incoming biology students. The high-school science teachers adamantly refused to do so, arguing that reading such a statement would violate the Code of Professional Practice and Conduct for Educators. As their memo to the board stated in capital letters, "INTELLIGENT DESIGN IS NOT SCIENCE." So the board called in school administrators to read the statement, which argued that Darwin's "theory" is not a fact and has gaps; intelligent design is an alternative theory. Students were urged to "keep an open mind" but to consult the reference book *Of Pandas and Peoples* if they wanted to understand what ID actually involves. The statement also noted that students were obliged by Pennsylvania academic standards to learn about Darwin's theory of evolution and to be tested on it.[47] By making no mention of religion, providing student access to a "donated" book on a purely voluntary basis, and noting that the teaching of evolution was still required, the conservative Christians dominating the Dover school board hoped to find a way around the Supreme Court's ruling in *Aguillard*.

## The Trial: Competing Experts and Legal Strategies

The school board's own lawyers had warned that a lawsuit was likely, and eleven parents of Dover students soon brought suit. They would be represented by the ACLU and by Americans United for Separation of Church and State. The bench trial in the federal district court for eastern Pennsylvania was presided over by Judge John Jones III, a conservative Republican appointed by George W. Bush. The stakes were huge; even if ID could be discredited as "science," the defense was claiming that schools should be able to "teach the controversy." Denying this right would constitute both religious and scientific discrimination and would violate their right to freedom of speech.[48] Court sanction of "freedom of speech" concerning ID could thus bring religious perspectives into science classrooms through the back door.

*Aguillard* had officially designated creationism as religion, but intelligent design was advocated as being based on science. *Of Pandas and People* had been recommended to the Dover school board by the conservative Thomas More Law Center, which also offered to defend the school board pro bono against any lawsuits that might result. Dover would thus be the first test case for ID. Several biologists were recruited to provide critiques of Darwin's theory and to publicize any challenges or amendments to it by other scientists. But the Discovery Institute was only a reluctant partner in the process and later withdrew; scientists on its staff refused to testify for the defense. The Discovery Institute felt more time was needed to establish ID as science distinct from creationism, and also realized the many weaknesses in the school board's case. The defense could produce only two "expert witnesses": biologist Michael Behe and sociologist Steve Fuller. Both were skewered by the plaintiffs' attorneys for their lack of peer-reviewed publications on ID and the low esteem in which they were held by their colleagues. All of Michael Behe's biological sciences department colleagues at Lehigh University had signed a statement that "intelligent design has no basis in science."[49]

The ACLU also drew major resources into the debate: an experienced staff attorney, Witold "Vic" Walczak, and the pro bono services of Pepper Hamilton, a prominent Philadelphia law firm. The National Center for Science Education also provided legal and scientific advice. The plaintiffs drew up a "wish list" of the scientific talent they would like as expert witnesses, and every one of their top picks agreed to testify. Many of these witnesses were personally devout, undercutting defense arguments about links between evolution and atheism. Their expert testimony not only challenged any scientific basis for ID but also provided the court with a thorough review of the meaning of "theory" in science and of the geological and biological evidence for evolution.[50]

A key witness for the plaintiffs, Barbara Forrest, was not a scientist but a philosopher. She made effective use of the "wedge" document and other statements by the Discovery Institute itself to show that ID was indeed religious in intent. But her most telling testimony revealed that *Of Pandas and People* had originally been written as a creationist text. During revisions after *Aquillard*, the term "creationism" had simply been replaced (sometimes not completely by the word processor) by "intelligent design." And it was later revealed that the anonymous donor of the book was in fact school-board member Bill Buckingham, who had denied any knowledge thereof during the discovery process. He had actually solicited funds for the purchase in his congregation, then laundered them through a check from a former school board member.[51]

## Judge Jones's Decision and Its Aftermath

Even before Judge Jones issued his decision, these revelations of perjury on the witness stand helped defeat all eight of the conservative school-board members up for election. Lying under oath to a federal judge is seldom a good idea. As one Dover resident stated, "We don't vote for liars."[52]

Judge Jones's sweeping 139-page *Kitzmiller* decision not only vindicated the plaintiffs but also thoroughly discredited any claims of ID as science. He concluded that although ID might be an interesting theological argument, it distorted the paleontological evidence and led to no peer-reviewed publications; it was a "religious view, a mere re-labeling of creationism." He quoted a 1999 report from the National Academy of Science:

> Creationism, intelligent design, and other claims of supernatural intervention in the origin of life or of species are not science because they are not testable by the methods of science. These claims subordinate observed data to statements based on authority, revelation, or religious belief.[53]

Judge Jones also accepted the plaintiffs' argument that a "theory" was not an admission of uncertainty, as the defense claimed, but made testable predictions that led to testable hypotheses to confirm or refute them. The judge further rejected defense arguments that freedom of speech legitimated discussion of "the controversy" over intelligent design versus evolution. But the free-speech argument has in many other instances been a successful legal strategy for the Religious Right. The Discovery Institute soon published *The Truth about the Dover Intelligent Design Trial*, which argued that *Kitzmiller* was in reality a free-speech case, not a test of ID, and the institute is backing the "teach the controversy" approach. It castigated the ACLU for supporting the free speech of John Scopes to teach evolution but denying the same right to ID proponents. The Discovery Institute continues its well-funded efforts to raise questions in the public mind about the "theory" of evolution and "gaps" in evidence supporting it.[54]

Judge Jones's scathing conclusion was that the Dover school board had made a decision of "breathtaking inanity" that "dragged its community into a legal maelstrom with its resulting utter waste of monetary and personal resources." Ironically, the newly elected, pro-evolution school board had to pay the million-dollar settlement Judge Jones imposed. Still, the battle over the teaching of "values" in public schools is far from over. The ruling of a federal district court in Pennsylvania, sweeping as it was, did not set a national precedent. Efforts to introduce intelligent design into public schools continue in this country,[55] as do appeals to "teach the controversy" (endorsed by President George Bush in an August 2005 speech). A 2005 Gallup poll showed that by a margin of 49 to 38 percent, respondents opposed teaching creationism instead of evolution. However, a solid majority (64 percent) of Americans would favor "teaching creationism along with evolution in public schools." U.S. public opinion is therefore at odds with the biology curricula mandated by most of the nation's state governments.[56]

## Lessons Learned by Both Sides

Many decisions concerning the role of religion in public policy are made at the local level, with schools as the primary battleground. While the Christian Right has been accused of running "stealth" candidates to pursue its agenda, that was not the situation in Dover, Pennsylvania, since the conservative Christians elected to the board were quite open about their priorities. They could win in low-turnout elections, with strong support from the congregations of local evangelical churches. But once in office, their efforts to introduce creationism and religious values into the school curriculum galvanized opponents among parents and teachers. Previously sleepy school-board meetings were packed, and turnout soared in both primary and general elections for board members, who were replaced by opponents of ID.

Yet regardless of court rulings, state laws, or school board policies, "It is teachers, rather than court cases that determine what is presented in science class." A national survey of teachers found that 12–16 percent of the nation's biology teachers were creationists, and one in six believed the earth was created within the last ten thousand years.[57] Even a biologist who testified for the plaintiffs in *Kitzmiller*, Kenneth Miller, had inserted language about the "strengths and weaknesses of evolution" in his best-selling biology text in order to placate the conservative Texas State Board of Education, which approves textbooks for the huge Texas market and thus influences publishers nationwide.[58] As with the *Perry* decision on Proposition 8, this case also illustrates the usually favorable view of courts toward scientific evidence. An impressive array of experts testified for the plaintiffs, and amici briefs by seventy-two Nobel prize winners and the National Academy of Sciences also influenced Judge Jones's opinion.

The *Kitzmiller* case further highlights the importance of existing organizations ready and willing to challenge any introduction of religion into public education. The ACLU and its local chapters have long been active in Pennsylvania, and their lawyers have an impressive record of prevailing in church/state and free-speech cases. The Harrisburg chapter responded almost overnight to the initial contacts concerning the school board's intentions. The NCSE likewise has an experienced staff of scientific and legal experts and carefully monitors the media and the Internet for any hints that creationism or ID are being considered in public schools. However, the Discovery Institute and the Thomas More Law Center also poured considerable resources into the trial.

The *Kitzmiller* case attracted considerable media attention, and coverage was largely unfavorable to the school board and to intelligent design. National and international media flocked to Dover, comparisons with the 1925 Scopes trial abounded, and defense attorney Thompson was depicted as speaking William Jennings Bryan's lines. As in Dayton, Tennessee, decades earlier, many Dover residents were appalled at the depiction of their town as an intellectual backwater in the thrall of religious bigots. National media also gave broad coverage to the Reverend Pat Robertson's statement on his 700 Club broadcast that by voting out of office eight members of the Dover school board who had advocated intelligent design, Dover citizens had "rejected God" and shouldn't bother trying to pray in the event of a natural catastrophe because "God wasn't going to listen." Robertson said, "If they have future problems in Dover, I recommend they call on Charles Darwin. Maybe he can help them."[59]

Public television also took on an unprecedented role by sponsoring a two-hour *Nova* special on the Dover case. The program reviewed Darwin's research and theory as well as the scientific evidence for evolution, legal aspects of the trial, and Judge Jones's ruling. It also highlighted perjury committed by some witnesses for the defense, who contradicted their own statements made during the discovery process, and thoroughly discredited ID arguments.[60]

The battle to influence public opinion continues. According to a 2005 Pew report, what Americans actually believe about evolution or creationism depends on the questions asked. The option "God had no part in the process" had little support (13 percent in a 2004 Gallup poll), while 38 percent accepted "evolution guided by God" and 45 percent accepted the Genesis version. Gallup polls using consistent wording showed little change in views since 1982. Polls also show considerable confusion: a quarter of Americans accept both arguments, 17 percent are not familiar with evolution, and 24 percent are unfamiliar with creationism. The newer term "intelligent design" was unfamiliar to a majority of Americans in the 2005 Gallup survey.[61]

A 2007 Gallup poll found that 66 percent of the public thought creationism was "definitely or probably" true, but 53 percent said the same about evolution. Such contradictory opinions are clearly structured by party ties or church attendance. Sixty-eight percent of Republicans do not believe in evolution, compared with only 37 percent of independents and 40 percent of Democrats. Among weekly church attendees 74 percent did not accept evolution, a view shared by 45 percent of occasional attendees and only 26 percent of nonattendees. Over 70 percent of respondents who rejected evolution gave religious reasons for doing so. And three of the eight Republican presidential candidates in 2008 (Mike Huckabee, Tom Tancredo, Sam Brownback) said during a nationally televised debate that they rejected evolution.[62]

Thus public opinion surveys continue to show that a sizable proportion of Americans do not believe in evolution. And large numbers also reject the growing scientific consensus on global warming or climate change caused by human actions. Further, according to the GSS, many also distrust scientists (although Americans still have more confidence in science than in organized religion).[63] Scientists may have solid research on their side, but on values issues their impact on public opinion may be outgunned by cues from party and religious leaders, and by the millions of dollars that underwrite the activities of the Discovery Institute, the Thomas More Law Center, and business opposition to any legislation to address climate change.[64] The best legal strategy for creationists and ID proponents may thus be arguments to "teach the controversy," even if the controversy is one they themselves have created. An article in a prominent medical journal concluded, "As long as the controversy is taught in classes in current affairs, politics, or religion, and not in science classes, neither scientists nor citizens should be concerned."[65] Scientific and secular organizations opposed to ID will exert every effort to keep such discussion out of science classes, if not out of public schools altogether.

However, supporters of teaching evolution face an uphill battle because in the United States decisions about classroom content and textbook purchases are highly decentralized. Ultimately teachers decide what will be taught about evolution, and whether it is to be presented as solid science or an unprovable theory about which students should decide for themselves. A considerable number of high-school biology teachers do not personally accept evolution, or have minimal training in evolutionary science.[66] Even teachers who do understand and accept evolution may give it short shrift because they fear backlash from students or parents. The science teachers in Dover dared to stand up to their administration and to the elected school board, but other teachers may simply decide to avoid the controversy altogether. More emphasis on evolution may be encouraged by development of national standards for teacher training under No Child Left Behind, or by business interests in improving the scientific competency of the labor force. However, "as long as many citizens view acceptance of evolution as a test of their faith in God, public education efforts will have only limited impact."[67]

## RESTRICTING ABORTION IN SOUTH DAKOTA

### South Dakota Politics, Direct Democracy, and Abortion Laws

South Dakota is generally viewed as a solid Red state. Although it has regularly elected Democrats (such as Senators George McGovern and Tom Daschle) to Congress, it gave 60 percent of its votes to George Bush in both 2000 and 2004, and 53 percent to John McCain in 2008. Its governors since 1980 have been Republicans, as have both houses of the state legislature. The Christian Right is considered to have "high influence" within the state Republican Party, compared with only moderate influence in the neighboring states of North Dakota, Iowa, or Minnesota.[68]

South Dakota is also a direct-democracy state. It was the first state in the country to adopt the initiative and referendum in 1898, with support from the Populist, Farmers' Alliance, and Socialist parties. And due in part to direct democracy, and in part to liberal laws concerning ballot access, South Dakota has consistently had one of the highest voter turnout rates in the United States.[69] In terms of religion, South Dakota has similar proportions of evangelical Christians (25 percent), mainline Protestants (29 percent), and Roman Catholics (25 percent). Fifteen percent claim no religion, about the national average. The state has very few Jews, African Americans, or Hispanics, but has a sizable Native American population.[70]

Further, South Dakota has long had strict regulations concerning access to abortion. Only one clinic in Sioux Falls provides abortions, performed by physicians from Minneapolis who are flown in once a week. State law mandates a 24-hour waiting period to receive an abortion, and also requires physicians to inform women that the procedure would "terminate the life of a whole, separate, unique living human being." Physicians are further required to state that abortion increases the risk of "suicide ideation and suicide," despite lack of medical evidence thereof. Medicaid funding only covers abortion if the women's life is at stake, and pharmacists who oppose abortion can refuse to dispense emergency contraception or drugs designed to produce abortions.[71]

Approximately eight hundred abortions per year are performed in the state, and the abortion rate (calculated in relation to the number of women of childbearing age) is 5.1, well below the national average of 19.4. Planned Parenthood, which operates the sole clinic providing abortions, argues that the state's restrictions impose serious hardships on women, especially those living at a distance or on Native American reservations. Pro-life groups in the state counter that help is available for women facing unplanned pregnancies, that abortion should not be used as birth control, and that abstinence education would prevent abortions.[72]

Given South Dakota's background of conservative voting patterns, Christian Right influence, and stringent restrictions on abortion, one would not expect that direct democracy could be used to overturn the state's legislative ban on almost all abortions. But that is exactly what happened in 2006—and again in 2008. This outcome is even more surprising since a constitutional ban on gay marriage was also on the ballot in 2006, and passed, 52–48 percent. So how did pro-choice groups opposed to the Religious Right succeed in a Red state on this issue?

## The Legislative Ban on Almost All Abortions

In early 2005 the South Dakota House established a task force to study abortion. The task force solicited testimony from experts on reproductive health from the Alan Guttmacher Institute, Planned Parenthood, the American Psychological Association, and the American College of Obstetricians and Gynecologists. But it discounted all such testimony and data from the Centers for Disease Control "due to other testimony and materials" from pro-life doctors, psychologists, and crisis-pregnancy centers. The task force also solicited written and oral testimony from over two thousand women who reported that they "regretted" their abortions, and it recommended even stricter requirements than the state's existing laws.[73] A Republican state senator complained that "the report was theologically based [and] has patent untruths and misrepresentations."[74]

On the basis of the task force report, the South Dakota Women's Health and Human Life Protection Act (HB 1215) was introduced into the South Dakota House as a direct challenge to *Roe v. Wade*. This bill would prohibit almost all abortions in the state; the only exception was if the life of the mother was at stake. Any provider of abortion for any other reason would be guilty of a class 4 felony punishable by up to ten years in prison. The bill passed both houses overwhelmingly and was signed into law by Republican governor Mike Rounds on March 6, 2006.

In direct-democracy states, research has generally found legislators to be responsive to public opinion.[75] National polls show that although a majority of Americans oppose overturning *Roe*, restrictions on abortion (limited public funding, parental notification for minors, waiting periods, mandating the reading of a script describing fetal development, bans on late-term abortions) generally have majority support.[76] Little public outcry had arisen over the strict regulations on abortion already adopted in South Dakota, so state elected officials probably assumed that the public would raise few objections to the new law. They also assumed that legal challenges would ensue before the law went into effect.

But in this case the politicians were wrong. Governor Round's popularity dropped by 14 points after he signed the bill.[77] A January 2006 state poll by Survey USA had shown a nearly even split between the number of people in the state who opposed abortion (48 percent) and those who believed in a woman's right to an abortion (47 percent). But after the law was signed, a survey by state polling firm Robinson & Muenster reported 57 percent were opposed to the law, 35 percent supported it, and 8 percent were undecided.[78] However, four of the eight Republican legislators who had voted against the ban lost their primaries in June (the others had no primary opponent) after strong mobilization against them by the Christian Right.[79]

**The Campaign to Overturn the Ban**

Pro-choice groups quickly obtained a court injunction to block implementation of the ban. They considered mounting an appeal because the bill was clearly in violation of *Roe* (and had in fact been intended by its supporters to challenge that decision). Pro-choice groups were also concerned about the implications of the South Dakota bill for reproductive rights in other states since thirty states had already passed measures to outlaw abortion, to be triggered the moment *Roe* was overturned.[80] But litigation was risky as well; an adverse decision by the Supreme Court could eviscerate *Roe*, which had been reaffirmed by only one vote in the 5–4 *Planned Parenthood v. Casey* decision of 1992.

Another option was to overturn the new law by referendum. Under South Dakota law, seventeen thousand signatures (5 percent of the previous vote for governor) are required to place a "legislative veto" measure on the ballot. A referendum might not succeed, but since the courts did not always adhere to majority rule in civil-rights cases, even a loss would risk little if litigation eventually ensued. So a petition drive was mounted to place repeal of the measure on the November ballot as Referred Law 6.

A full-scale mobilization began, not only within the state but from around the country, by organizations supportive of women's reproductive and civil rights: Planned Parenthood, Feminist Majority, NOW, NARAL, and the ACLU. According to Sarah Stoesz, the president of Planned Parenthood for the Dakotas and Minnesota, "The legislators and governor in South Dakota have made a significant political overreach. . . . It has really awakened and stirred the passions of the reproductive rights movement across the country."[81] National pro-choice groups sent money as well as supplying volunteers to cultivate the grass roots. The petition drive gathered more than twice as many signatures (thirty-eight thousand) as required.

Groups opposed to the abortion ban raised almost $4 million to defeat it. The largest contributor was South Dakota Campaign for Healthy Families ($2.5 million), the umbrella organization coordinating the campaign. It was followed by Planned Parenthood ($856,000), Working Assets (liberal for-profit mobile phone business, $120,000), the ACLU ($105,000), and the Feminist Majority Foundation ($85,000). An estimated 80 percent of the funding came from out of state.[82]

Also involved were clergy from the Religious Left: the more liberal denominations in the state, such as Quakers, Unitarian Universalists, some mainline Protestants, and reform Jews. A few such clergy from college towns and more urban areas had support from their congregations, but other liberal clergy serving more conservative or divided congregations had to tread cautiously. Mobilization of pro-choice clergy, Pastors for Moral Choices (P4MC), was led by a retired minister who was no longer responsible to a congregation.[83] At a press conference P4MC acknowledged that "there are people of faith in our congregations who will vote differently. We respect their right to do so, and we speak only for ourselves and not as representatives of our congregations." But P4MC argued that the abortion ban would restrict religious freedom, since many faith traditions did allow for abortions to save the life or health of the woman or for other extenuating circumstances.[84]

Pro-life groups mobilized as well. The lead organization, South Dakotans for 1215/Vote Yes for Life, raised $2,780,000. Much smaller amounts came from the SD Family Policy 2006 Issue Fund, the Catholic Chancery Office, and the National Right to Life Committee. Their total ($2,920,000) was impressive, but considerably less than that raised by groups opposing the ban.[85]

In South Dakota, the secretary of state publishes a Ballot Question Pamphlet before every election. This includes an explanation by the state's attorney general of the legal implications of any proposed initiatives, referenda, or constitutional amendments. Pro and con arguments by each side are also included. The pro text on Referred Law 6, written by its chief legislative sponsor, State Representative Roger Hunt (R-Brandon), summarized the task force conclusions that life began at conception and that women are harmed both physically and mentally by abortions. He also said that the bill "allows an exception for rape and incest"—namely, provision of emergency contraception. The con side disputed this in its campaign literature, since an amendment to the bill specifically permitting abortions in case of rape or incest had been voted down in the legislature.

In the Ballot Question Pamphlet the con side, written by a doctor associated with Planned Parenthood, said that the law was too restrictive, did not provide any exception for women's health, would subject doctors to imprisonment, and offered no real options for rape or incest victims. It also noted that the state already had few abortions and did not need additional government intrusion into a "difficult, private decision."[86] The South Dakota State Medical Association, in an internal memo, noted its "grave concerns" that the abortion ban would intrude into medical decisions but stopped short of direct public opposition to the ban.[87]

The media market in South Dakota is inexpensive compared with more urban areas, so the state was soon saturated with television ads and billboards pro and con: Vote Yes for Life. Abortion Is Murder. No on 6. I'm Pro-Choice and I Pray. Volunteers from both sides staged rallies and went door-to-door. But despite concerted efforts by the Yes for Life groups, statewide polls showed that opponents of the ban were gaining. The impending vote drew national attention and extensive coverage by both national and international media. Some prominent Republicans (Senator John McCain, Governor Charlie Crist) said they would support the ban. President Bush refused to take a stand, considering it a state rather than a federal matter; his statements reaffirmed his pro-life convictions, but also noted he would support abortion in cases of rape or incest.[88]

Newspapers in the state gave the issue extensive coverage, but mostly avoided editorials backing either side. The *Madison Daily Leader* said that abortion and the death penalty were separate issues and should not be linked, but failed to take a stand on either one. The *Aberdeen News* published op-ed pieces by spokespersons for both sides. The *Rapid City Journal* voiced concerns in January 2006 about the legal costs that would result if the abortion-ban bill passed, but in June 2006 said "the people should decide" whether to put HB1215 into effect or not. On October 28, however, the *Journal* did oppose the ban.[89] The state's largest newspaper, the Sioux Falls *Argus Leader*, expressed no opinion; the editor said in an interview that any editorial would upset readers, would not change people's minds, and could cause doubts about the objectivity of their coverage of other issues.[90]

## The Election and Reactions

Turnout on Election Day was high by most states' standards (67 percent) but still a bit lower than the 72 percent in the midterm years of 2002 or 1998. A number of other initiatives and constitutional amendments were on the 2006 ballot, including a constitutional amendment to ban gay marriage. This ban passed as it had in every other direct-democracy state, 52 to 48 percent. But voters in South Dakota also overturned the legislative abortion ban, by the decisive margin of 56 to 44 percent.[91]

What happened? The immediate consensus was that the legislation had gone too far by restricting abortions even in cases of rape or incest and penalizing the doctor. The public may favor most restrictions, but not such a sweeping ban, and many were uncomfortable with the notion of sending ob-gyns or pregnant women to jail. Further, while funding from outside the state had come in for both sides, the larger influx from pro-choice groups was sufficient to finance a vigorous TV ad campaign and to mobilize grassroots supporters. The attention of other groups on the Religious Right was less on South Dakota (a safe Republican state) than on trying to maintain control of Congress and to pass gay-marriage bans in other states; they were outspent and outorganized. They were also criticized for overreaching: "By making the [2006] bill so extreme, they made the right-to-life movement look like a bunch of nuts."[92]

But Yes for Life activists were not ready to give up. Supporters commissioned a poll to ascertain why they had lost, and found that the lack of exemptions for rape, incest, or women's health had hurt them with many South Dakotans.[93] So they introduced a new bill in the legislature to ban abortions that now included these exemptions. But the bill died in a Senate committee, and even pro-life legislators were wary of revisiting the issue. Also, some pro-life supporters opposed the new language; if abortion was indeed the murder of innocent life, no exemptions could be justified.[94]

Direct democracy was again the chosen alternative, but this time for pro-life groups. Yes for Life mounted a successful petition drive to place Initiative Measure 11, which contained language similar to the bill that had died in the legislature, on the 2008 ballot. Another hard-fought campaign ensued. Most of the same groups lined up pro and con, but South Dakota Right to Life broke with the Yes for Life coalition and refused to support any bill that contained exceptions. The South Dakota State Medical Association had not taken a stand in 2006, but in 2008 opposed the initiative (although physicians spoke out in favor of both sides).[95] But even with exceptions allowing abortions in cases of rape, incest, or maternal health risks, the outcome was almost the same: 45 percent in favor of the initiative, 55 percent opposed.

However, there were some crucial differences from the 2006 election. Voter turnout actually *declined* from 67 percent in 2006 to 62 percent in 2008. South Dakota, usually near the top of state rankings for voter turnout, now ranked 26th.[96] A possible explanation is that although John McCain carried the state with 53 percent of the vote, many conservative voters questioned his evangelical credentials and stayed home. But turnout by more liberal groups was buoyed by the Obama candidacy and the worsening economy, and these voters were likely to oppose the ban. Another explanation for the defeat of Initiative 11 is that South Dakota has enacted and enforced numerous restrictions on abortion, so many voters may have concluded that a sweeping ban was unnecessary. A 2005 law mandated that doctors were required to read a script stating that an unborn baby was "a whole, separate, unique living human being." This has been stayed pending appeal, but was upheld by a federal district court in 2008. And in 2007 the state legislature passed a law requiring abortion clinics to offer an ultrasound to any woman seeking an abortion; she was not required to watch it, but did need to sign a statement that she had been offered the option. Planned Parenthood had appealed both these measures on the grounds that they limited the freedom of speech of doctors and thus interfered with good medical practices, but both were upheld in court.[97]

A third possibility is that the "healthy families" theme adopted by opponents of the ban focused public attention on the broader medical and social context in which abortion decisions actually take place. Even people who defined themselves as pro-life in a survey were willing to permit abortion under some circumstances. A 2006 survey had found that women were far more likely than men to oppose a sweeping ban, and this was presumably the case in 2008 as well.[98]

## Conclusion

In recent years, advocates for abortion rights have been on the defensive. As noted in chapter 3, public support for a woman's unrestricted right to choose has declined since the 1990s. The congressional ban on partial-birth abortion (which has strong popular support) was upheld in *Gonzales v. Carhart*, and state legislatures continue to pass additional restrictions on access to abortion. Some argued that the abortion fight was over and that pro-life forces had won.[99]

However, in the first-ever popular vote on *Roe v. Wade*, voters in a conservative state decisively rejected an almost complete ban on abortion and repeated that feat two years later by rejecting a ban with some limited exceptions. These actions in South Dakota are supported by national polls; Americans may support most restrictions on access to abortion, but overwhelmingly reject overturning *Roe*.[100]

This case also shows that campaign spending for direct-democracy measures does not always determine election outcomes.[101] Organization matters also; even in South Dakota, where the Religious Right is strong, opponents of the abortion ban were able to mount an effective grassroots campaign, and to recruit allies among college students, liberal clergy, and the medical profession (although out-of-state volunteers and funding for media buys helped as well). Yes for Life groups overreached when they tried to ban almost all abortions and demonized women choosing this option, regardless of the reason. And they lost some of their own supporters when they allowed for at least some exemptions in the 2008 initiative. But organization also matters in the legislature. The Religious Right has consistently supported Republicans for state office, and has effectively lobbied the South Dakota legislature to pass additional restrictions on abortion access.

In 2008, two other abortion measures on state ballots also failed: California voters overturned a parental-notification law, and Colorado voters rejected a constitutional amendment that would define an embryo as a full person from the moment of conception.[102] In those states as well, a combination of direct democracy, effective grassroots organizing, and ample funding was able to counter efforts by the Religious Right to ban or further limit abortion. In California, opponents of Proposition 8 were able to use the courts to overturn results of a popular referendum. But if the Religious Right is unable to ban or limit abortion by means of direct democracy, courts (and especially the Supreme Court) may also represent a strategic alternative.

## MORALITY POLITICS AND FEDERALISM

These three case studies have explored the politics and institutions of three very different states. Some argue that the states are where controversial moral issues should be decided, so that results will reflect the very different histories and political cultures of different parts of the country.[103] But there are two main objections to this view, one theoretical and one practical. The theoretical argument is that fundamental rights, such as a woman's right to privacy, should *not* be subject to popular vote. As the Supreme Court ruled in its *Lawrence* decision in 2003 that overturned all state sodomy laws, the right to privacy of gays is a "fundamental" right and thus not subject to state interference. Considerable evidence also suggests that direct democracy is inimical to minority rights, as opponents of Proposition 8 experienced in California in 2008.[104]

The second argument is practical: state votes on hot-button issues increasingly attract a great deal of money and attention from outside the state. This is true of candidate and judicial elections as well, where the national parties and donors spend millions of dollars.[105] In the case of Proposition 8, sizable contributions came from other states, particularly Utah. In South Dakota, over 80 percent of the contributions to defeat the abortion ban also came from out of state. Pro-life groups complained bitterly that they were outspent by interests far removed from South Dakota (although 40 percent of their own funding also came from out of state).[106] But if states are supposed to be laboratories of democracy, and to reflect a range of policies and viewpoints, their autonomy may be threatened by the influx of money from elsewhere.[107] The problem may be even more acute since the *Citizens United* decision of 2010, where the Supreme Court ruled 5–4 that the identity of donors to "independent" campaign organizations need not be disclosed.[108]

Recent Supreme Court decisions have represented a range of opinions concerning federalism, sometimes deferring to state Supreme Courts, other times asserting federal authority. The *Lawrence* and *Gonzales* decisions both constrained state discretion, but the substance of those decisions reflected opposing views of traditional religious values. Future Supreme Court appointments may well determine whether the states or the federal government have the final say on morality issues.

These three cases also illustrate a crucial aspect of the morality politics cycle: the battle for public opinion. National polls show that the Religious Right has had some success in gaining overall support for the pro-life perspective, and many Americans remain skeptical of evolution and willing to "teach the controversy" rather than ban creationist perspectives entirely from the classroom. Seculars and GLBT groups have seen dramatic increases since the 1980s in attitudes toward gay rights and, as of 2010, even majority support for legalizing gay marriage. But policy outcomes depend on political institutions and on *mobilized* public opinion. Even in liberal California, opponents of gay marriage persuaded more of their supporters to go to the polls in 2008, while in South Dakota many self-defined "pro-life" supporters either failed to vote (especially in 2008) or were unwilling to approve a sweeping ban on abortion. Yet courts have upheld South Dakota's other restrictions on access to abortion, overturned two popular votes to ban gay marriage in California, and thus far resisted all efforts to teach creationism in public schools.

# 7

✣

# Conclusion: A More Secular Future America?

Since the Religious Right emerged on the political scene in the 1970s, it has captured the attention of the media as well as social scientists and religious scholars. But another trend also began in the 1970s: an increase in secular views and in the proportion of Americans with no ties to organized religion. This book has documented that growing secular trend in religious beliefs and behavior, analyzed its causes, and considered its political impact. I have also argued that these two trends are related. The Religious Right emerged in part to challenge the secular humanism and moral relativism that its adherents feared as the legacy of the 1960s. The Equal Rights Amendment, *Roe v. Wade*, and the limits the Supreme Court placed on religion in schools—all of these served as significant shocks to cultural values that had been widely shared by citizens as well as political elites. But many of the policy successes of the Religious Right, including restrictions on abortion, state bans on gay marriage, abstinence education, and faith-based federal policies, were deeply troubling to seculars. These policies also challenged many religious Americans who did not share the theology or the politics of the Religious Right, as well as Americans of all religious backgrounds who valued separation of church and state. Greater political activism by both individuals and organizations ensued to challenge the Religious Right.

The morality-policy cycle thus helps explain the growth of both the Religious Right and its secular opposition. But this book has also emphasized the role of organization. Demographic trends and social movements are unlikely to have much political impact unless the challenges of organization are addressed. Here the Religious Right has had considerable advantages, since its potential members or supporters were already involved in churches. Due in part to technological changes (direct mail, Christian radio, televangelism), entrepreneurial leaders could build on church-based social networks and mobilize in response to threats such as the legalization of abortion or gay marriage. Furthermore, the Religious Right soon developed close ties with the Republican Party structure and leadership, to their mutual benefit. Although this alliance had its drawbacks as well, considerable political success resulted from these organizational advantages, and by the 1990s church attendance has emerged as a powerful predictor of voting behavior. The reelection of George W. Bush in 2004 was widely attributed to the successful grassroots mobilization of conservative religious voters.[1]

Other scholars have noted increases in the number of seculars, but their political influence was usually considered to be fairly minimal. Seculars were not involved in churches and seldom joined other organizations. Many were political independents, and their lack of party ties contributed to lower levels of political involvement and to enthusiasm for third-party candidates. In the early 1980s their political participation lagged considerably behind that of religious moderates or traditionalists, although a few observers did note their growing influence within the Democratic Party.[2] But as chapters 3 and 4 have shown, the portrait of apolitical seculars needs to be updated. By 2004 and 2008 they were far more politically active than in the 1980s and well aware of party and issue differences. Seculars represented a sizable proportion of the Democratic electoral coalition and convention delegates, and were a major presence in many states. Antipathy to Christian fundamentalists was shown to be a major reason for the increased political involvement of seculars (and of religious moderates as well). Thus political as well as demographic and generational factors have accounted for the growth in secularism.[3]

Chapter 5 analyzed the organizational basis of secularism, as well as the organizational challenges facing the Religious Right. No secular group can match the mass-membership base of the Christian Coalition or Focus on the Family. But a number of organizations have emerged to promote secular values, or to challenge the Religious Right, or to uphold the separation of church and state. Feminist, Jewish, and gay-rights groups have opposed efforts by the Religious Right to uphold traditional families and gender roles. Seculars have also found influential allies in the media, among scientists, and within the Religious Left and the legal community.

The case studies in chapter 6 examined three arenas where secular forces and the Religious Right came into direct conflict: battles over banning gay marriage in California, restricting abortion in South Dakota, and teaching alternatives to evolution in Pennsylvania. In each of these three cases both sides invested heavily to further their cause, but seculars gained at least a temporary victory. However, none of these issues can be regarded as settled. Despite its own organizational challenges, leadership rivalries, and internal debates over issue priorities, the Religious Right remains a formidable political force in American politics. The Republican gains in Congress and in the states in 2010 point to a significant increase in congressional and state legislative support for conservative positions on gay marriage, reproductive rights, family structure, and school vouchers. Is this a temporary setback for seculars, or does it portend a long-term trend? What might an increasingly secular society look like? The rest of this chapter will build on the analysis thus far to consider some scenarios for the future, based on trends in demographics and public opinion, the evolution of organizations, the results of the 2010 elections, and the changing role of the courts.

## DEMOGRAPHIC TRENDS AND SECULAR PERSPECTIVES

Chapter 2 used data from the General Social Survey to document considerable growth since the 1970s in the number of Americans who claim no religious affiliation, seldom pray or attend worship services, are more tolerant of atheists, and express doubts about traditional religious beliefs. Some of these trends can be attributed to higher levels of education. But Americans born in the last few decades are increasingly skeptical of organized religion and unlikely to identify themselves as either believers or belongers. Further, these trends do not simply reflect life-cycle changes, with most people becoming more religious as they grow older. Instead, more recent birth cohorts have become progressively less religious than earlier ones, with secular views more similar to those in other advanced industrial countries and growing skepticism about organized religion. Support for gay rights, reproductive rights, and equality for women has thus increased.

Family structure has also changed considerably in the United States (as in most other industrialized countries), with high rates of divorce, cohabitation, and births to single mothers. The proportion of married people declined from 72 percent of the population in 1960 to 52 percent in 2008. Rates of divorce and out-of-wedlock births are actually more common in the Bible Belt than in such bastions of liberalism as Massachusetts.[4] As the social stigmas concerning homosexuality have lessened, many more gay and lesbian individuals or families have emerged. Traditional families (married heterosexual couples with children) tend to be religiously involved and more conservative in their beliefs about religion and morality. As of 2008, 29 percent of married ANES respondents and 40 percent of those widowed could be classified as religious traditionalists, compared with only 21 percent of divorced and 13 percent of single persons. Seventeen percent of self-identified heterosexuals were seculars, compared with 42 percent of gays or lesbians. But despite higher birth rates among religious conservatives (including Hispanic Catholics, Orthodox Jews, and Mormons), the proportion of such traditional families in the total U.S. population is declining. Rates of intermarriage among religious groups have also increased; people in such mixed marriages (and their children) tend to be less religiously observant. Since single or divorced people, gays, and lesbians have much more liberal or secular views than married couples in traditional families, trends in family structure also point to future increases in secular viewpoints.

The proportion of seculars may increase further because of changing social norms concerning religiosity. Social scientists have long been aware that claims of regular church attendance were exaggerated. In midcentury American society, when people were expected to belong to a church, believe in God, worship every week, and consider "godless atheists" to be communist sympathizers, most survey respondents were reluctant to admit otherwise. But as fewer and fewer Americans attend church or claim any ties to organized religion, it has become socially acceptable to admit to a lack of religiosity. In addition to a sizable number of belongers who do not believe, national surveys have identified a growing number of believers who do not belong, and future increases are likely in seculars willing to admit that they neither believe nor belong. Even views of atheists have become more positive, although they are still unlikely to be elected president. Several books by atheists highly critical of religion appeared on national best-seller lists. And a 2006 Faith Matters survey found that 87 percent of Americans agreed that people without a religious faith could be good Americans.[5]

Other demographic projections suggest that secular trends will continue in the United States. Levels of educational attainment are increasing, and better-educated people are considerably more tolerant of atheistic or agnostic views, as well as of alternative lifestyles and nontraditional families. Also, the numbers of African Americans and Hispanics in the U.S. population are increasing due to higher birth rates as well as high levels of immigration. Both of these minorities tend to be more religiously observant, and to hold more conservative views on religion and social issues, than whites. But since younger African Americans and Hispanics, like younger whites, are much less religiously involved than their elders, these minorities are likely to become more secular or moderate in future years.

Table 7.1 provides evidence for this conclusion based on the 2008 ANES, by comparing the opinions of whites, African Americans, and Hispanics age thirty or under with those of people in the same ethnic groups over age sixty. African Americans and Hispanics under thirty are clearly more religiously oriented than younger whites. Only 6 percent of younger African Americans and 19 percent of Hispanics can be classified as seculars, compared with 33 percent of younger whites. A much larger percentage of younger African Americans or Hispanics regard the Bible as the Word of God, compared with only 22 percent of young whites. A majority of younger Americans, regardless of race or ethnicity, claim that religion is an important part of their lives. Wuthnow describes this generation as religious "tinkerers," seeking meaning for their lives from a variety of accessible sources, including formative personal experiences, non-Western and new age philosophies, their friends, and the media.[6] But

Table 7.1 Religiosity and Policy Preferences by Race, Ethnicity, and Age

|  | Whites | | Blacks | | Hispanics | |
| --- | --- | --- | --- | --- | --- | --- |
|  | Under Thirty | Over Sixty | Under Thirty | Over Sixty | Under Thirty | Over Sixty |
| Seculars | 33% | 16% | 6% | 5% | 19% | 4% |
| Moderates | 53% | 48% | 78% | 46% | 69% | 55% |
| Traditionalists | 14% | 36% | 16% | 49% | 12% | 42% |
| Attend church weekly | 13% | 37% | 15% | 51% | 13% | 44% |
| Never attend | 48% | 32% | 32% | 15% | 38% | 26% |
| Religion is important | 57% | 80% | 87% | 91% | 73% | 92% |
| Bible = Word of God | 22% | 44% | 54% | 71% | 44% | 60% |
| Pro-life | 14% | 19% | 15% | 29% | 23% | 29% |
| Pro-choice | 45% | 28% | 55% | 40% | 35% | 11% |
| Favor gay marriage | 59% | 23% | 44% | 17% | 60% | 23% |
| Favor gay anti-discrimination laws | 84% | 72% | 66% | 63% | 73% | 63% |
| Mean score: jobs scale (1 = govt, 7 = private) | 4.28 | 5.08 | 3.02 | 3.23 | 3.21 | 3.58 |
| Mean score: govt spending (1 = more, 7 = less) | 3.59 | 4.25 | 2.69 | 2.89 | 3.21 | 2.35 |
| Mean score: universal health care (1 = govt, 7 = private) | 3.58 | 4.23 | 2.57 | 3.45 | 2.89 | 3.15 |
| Percent of sample | 18% | 26% | 20% | 20% | 29% | 17% |
| N | 1159 | | 569 | | 509 | |

Source: ANES 2008

since only 13–15 percent of those under thirty attend church on a weekly basis, they have limited exposure to traditional religious precepts.

Table 7.1 also shows striking generational differences among African Americans and Hispanics as well as whites. Only 16 percent of younger African Americans are religious traditionalists, compared with 49 percent of their elders. Church attendance and biblical literalism are also far less common among younger than older minorities. But since most younger African Americans consider religion to be important, even if they seldom attend church, they are more likely to be classified as religious moderates than as seculars. The hot-button social issues of abortion and gay marriage likewise reveal generational differences across all three groups. Hispanics (many of whom are Roman Catholic) tend to be more pro-life on abortion, yet 60 percent of younger Hispanics support gay marriage. African Americans are more skeptical of gay marriage than whites or Hispanics, but a significant generational difference is evident for them as well.[7] While younger whites and African Americans are considerably more tolerant than their elders of others' moral standards, Hispanics tend to be tolerant regardless of age.

In addition, table 7.1 indicates that younger African Americans and Hispanics have more liberal attitudes than whites toward government spending and job/income guarantees. Those under thirty in all three groups are more likely than their elders to agree that "The government should guarantee jobs and incomes" (lower values on the ANES seven-point scale); their elders, especially whites over sixty, are closer to the position that "Each person should get ahead on his own." Respondents under thirty in all three groups favor additional government spending on social services (higher values on the ANES seven-point scale), with minorities much more favorable regardless of age. And younger respondents, regardless of race or ethnicity, are also considerably more in favor of government-sponsored or universal health care (lower values on the ANES seven-point scale).

The proportion of minorities in the United States will continue to expand, due both to immigration and to higher birth rates. The United States is projected to be "majority minority" after about 2040, as states such as California already are. Redistricting after the 2010 Census will produce a net shift of congressional seats to Red states. But this may not lead to more support for Republicans or religious conservatives in those states, since most of the population increase is due to Hispanics, and (except for those of Cuban descent in Florida) most of these have been voting for Democrats. The battle for the Hispanic vote is likely to be a defining issue in future elections. But as table 7.1 shows, younger Hispanics tend to be considerably less religious and more liberal than their elders.

The age profile of minorities also points to greater future influence by people with more secular beliefs; based on table 7.1, people under thirty include only 18 percent of whites, but 20 percent of African Americans and 29 percent of Hispanics. The impact on American politics of the views of younger whites, African Americans, and Hispanics may not be apparent for several more years, since their voting turnout lags that of their elders (especially in midterm elections, as 2010 illustrated). But given the sharp generational, racial, and ethnic differences shown in table 7.1, popular acceptance of traditional perspectives on religion and social issues is likely to decline further, while greater support is likely for activist government and economic liberalism.

## ORGANIZATION AND FUTURE RELIGIOUS TRENDS

Although the French philosopher Auguste Compte once claimed that "demography is destiny," population trends do not automatically lead to changes in election results, the political agenda, or policy outcomes. The latent preferences of emerging demographic groupings must be articulated by interest groups, social movements, or entrepreneurial leaders before they gain attention from politicians, parties, or the media. Thus despite a large population of African Americans with long-standing grievances, leadership by the NAACP and African American clergy was essential to the development of the successful civil-rights movement of the 1960s.[8] A sizable number of evangelical or fundamentalist Americans and their clergy shared traditional views of Christianity, but not until the technological revolution of the 1960s and the emergence of new leadership did these perspectives regain political saliency as the Religious Right. And concern for the decline of the traditional family was actually greater in the 1990s, after the Religious Right made it a major issue, than in the 1980s, when divorce and teen-pregnancy rates were considerably higher.[9]

A major task for any social movement is to develop the leadership and the organizational structures to carry its agenda forward. But building viable organizations is no easy task. A savvy political or religious entrepreneur may get the process under way, but an organization must be able to survive the aging or loss of its initial leaders. Maintaining members or contributors is an ongoing challenge. Rival leaders or competing organizations can divide the movement and siphon off funds. Even success can be risky; the pro-choice movement thought it had won the day after *Roe v. Wade*, but has had to rebuild from the grass roots in order to counter ongoing challenges to that decision from the states as well as Congress. And despite the achievements of the civil-rights movement, discrimination and segregation continue in the United States, even though most white Americans assume that racism ended with the Civil Rights Act of 1964. Current civil-rights leaders (and President Obama) must decide how best to address racial discrimination in today's political environment without antagonizing white voters.

Changing social, economic, or political circumstances may also necessitate a shift in a movement's agenda priorities. The Moral Majority was initially energized by school prayer and the tax status of Christian schools. Abortion became more salient during the 1980s, and certainly remains a concern, but the clinic violence and other actions associated with groups such as Operation Rescue limited the public appeal of an uncompromising right-to-life position. In the early 1990s the leaders of several prominent Religious Right organizations decided that homosexuality was the issue most likely to galvanize their supporters. A concerted campaign was begun to stress the evils of gay sex, the risks of AIDS, and the threat of gay marriage or adoption to children and traditional families. In 1996 all Republican presidential-primary candidates were asked to sign a public statement pledging their opposition to gay marriage, an issue not even mentioned in previous party platforms.[10]

Gay marriage and abortion were crucial issues during the 2004 election campaign, and resonated with the sizable proportion of voters who claimed that "moral values" were their major concern. But many younger evangelicals have been energized by issues such as the environment, hunger, the media emphasis on sex, or genocide in Darfur. Some leaders of the Religious Right fear that a continuing emphasis on abortion or gay marriage may drive away younger evangelicals as well as other young Americans. Since assessments of the values of younger evangelicals have varied, depending on the time period or survey used and the definition of "evangelical," it is not yet clear which issues will be the most effective tools for mobilization.[11]

By 2006 and 2008 new issues (the economy, health care, the deficit) gained priority on the national agenda. The 2008 Republican platform still advocated overturning *Roe* and opposition to gay marriage, but party leaders and most Tea Party activists chose not to emphasize these issues in 2010.[12] The focus shifted to unemployment, government spending, health care reform, and the unpopular federal stimulus package; all of these would prove effective in attracting votes from independents and Democrats.

Shifts in the agenda, or moves closer to the political center, have been greeted with dismay by activists originally energized by uncompromising positions on morality issues. Robertson's adoption of more nuanced positions in 1999–2000 led to many resignations from the Christian Coalition. In 2009 Richard Cizik was forced out as vice president of governmental affairs of the National Association of Evangelicals because he said in an interview on National Public Radio that he had voted for Obama and that his views on same-sex equality were shifting.[13] Fund-raising appeals continue to demonize secular humanists, liberals, and the risks to families of the "radical gay agenda." But as one fund-raiser for the Christian Right noted, appeals using softer language failed to bring in as much money.[14]

In response to these organizational challenges, in recent years the Religious Right has focused less on mass membership and more on special-purpose organizations. Chapter 5 documented the growth in conservative or Christian legal firms, quasi-scientific think tanks, and single-purpose groups such as the Home School Legal Defense Association. Well-funded national groups such as Focus on the Family continue to be active behind the scenes and have provided leadership training and financing to legal and scientific organizations supportive of traditional religious views. Efforts have been made to create grassroots groups to elect sympathizers and influence the agenda in state and local governments or on school boards, but with the "eight-hundred-pound gorilla" (namely, Focus on the Family) kept well in the background. In 2004 the U.S. Conference of Catholic Bishops, fearing an anti-Catholic backlash, resisted pleas to publicly excommunicate pro-choice Catholic candidates, but the Bush campaign encouraged parish-based Catholic groups that were willing to do so.[15]

Alliances with major political parties can also be problematic for interest groups and social movements. Support can help provide funding and elect sympathizers, but at the risk of co-optation, compromise, or being taken for granted. Many on the Religious Right bemoaned the lack of real action on its policy priorities by the candidates it had supported. In 2010 some on the Religious Right spoke out against the "secular libertarians" in the Tea Party who ignored moral issues or even supported gay marriage.[16] Grassroots activists flocked to the Tea Party to share their grievances about the deficit, the economy, or "Obamacare," but its main leadership and funding came from the Republican Party or political professionals. Because of its chronic decentralization and lack of organization (attributes strongly supported by many of the political independents who joined it), the Tea Party movement is considered unlikely to endure.[17]

The organizational challenges facing seculars are likewise daunting. Despite their growing presence within the Democratic Party, seculars' values may be sacrificed to political expediency, as supporters of reproductive rights found during the Democratic Party convention in 2008 and the health care reform debate in 2009. The 2008 Democratic platform continued its "strong and unequivocal" support for *Roe v. Wade,* but after intense internal debate and strong support from Barack Obama, added language advocating affordable family planning services and comprehensive age-appropriate sex education in order to reduce the need for abortions. Seculars, feminists, and pro-choice groups objected strongly to this wording, and were also unhappy with the additional restrictions on abortion funding that were required to ensure passage of the Affordable Health Care Act of 2010.[18]

Constructing permanent mass-membership organizations of the unaffiliated is particularly difficult, but ad hoc grassroots groups can be assembled to deal with an urgent local threat to secular values. The citizens of Dover, Pennsylvania, formed a group called Dover CARES that successfully mobilized to defeat the conservative Christians who had dominated the local school board. Parents' groups in several communities have organized to protest the factual distortions and implicit religious messages in abstinence-education programs, and school boards have responded by cancelling those programs.[19] As described in chapter 5, umbrella organizations (such as the Secular Coalition for America) have been set up to coordinate efforts to influence public policy by several atheist, agnostic, or humanist groups. California Faith for Equality helped to coordinate the statewide campaign by GLBT groups and religious liberals to defeat Proposition 8, and it later submitted an amicus brief on behalf of its constituent groups in the successful legal appeal. Feminists, pro-choice groups, and the Religious Left joined forces in South Dakota to defeat the abortion bans on the ballot.

Wealthy conservatives such as the Koch brothers have donated millions of dollars on behalf of the Religious Right. But secular organizations also have billionaire donors, such as George Soros. A grant of $50,000 was made by a wealthy pro-choice couple to assist the fight against the abortion ban in South Dakota. Biologist and best-selling atheist author Richard Dawkins established the Richard Dawkins Foundation for Reason and Science to promote science education and challenge the misuse of science in public policy.[20]

The lack of a church-based network of members and leaders has led many observers to underestimate the growing political influence of seculars. However, the analysis in chapter 3 showed that church attendance is no longer as significant a predictor of political involvement as it was in the 1980s and 1990s. Seculars have become much more politically involved, in part because of their strong antipathy to Christian fundamentalists. In 2004 and 2008 their rates of voting, contributing, and persuading others to vote were comparable to those of religious traditionalists. As chapter 4 showed, candidate differences on abortion were significantly more salient to weekly church attendees in 2004—especially in strongly secular states. "Secular threat" is apparently more of a factor for the religiously observant than any threat that a high proportion of evangelicals or Catholics in a state might pose for seculars. But seculars tend to be more aware of party or candidate differences across a range of other issues, and perceptions of such differences have a significant independent effect on voter turnout.

Seculars are still less likely to belong to other organizations or to report campaign contacts by parties or other groups. However, as this book has documented, seculars have found alternative forms of organization through which to advocate. As the case studies in chapter 6 demonstrated, secular alliances and strategies have on several occasions proved effective against efforts by the Religious Right to ban abortion, or gay marriage, or introduce intelligent design into public schools. As of 2008 seculars were considerably more likely than religious traditionalists to make use of the Internet for information about the presidential campaign. It remains to be seen whether seculars' lack of church or organizational ties will matter less in the era of the Internet and social networking. Certainly the Religious Right has become far more Internet savvy, and has also established legal and quasi-scientific organizations to try to offset secular successes in those arenas.

## 2010 AND FUTURE ELECTIONS

As shown in chapter 3, seculars tend to be younger and weaker partisans, and are thus less likely to vote in primaries or off-year elections. Midterm election voters are considerably older, wealthier, and whiter than the presidential electorate, and Republican gains in 2010 (as in 1994 and 2002) confirmed these patterns. Religious affiliation continues to have a strong impact on the vote. In 2010, as in previous elections, exit polls showed that white Protestants overwhelmingly voted for Republicans, while the religiously unaffiliated voted for Democrats. The Republican margins for white Protestants, and for white evangelicals or born-again Christians, were larger than in any recent election. White Catholics also swung to the Republicans in 2010, giving them 54 percent of the vote compared with only 49 percent in 2006. Republicans even made gains among the unaffiliated: 30 percent in 2010 compared with 22 percent in 2006.[21]

The biggest differences in 2010, compared with 2008, were in turnout: 2010 saw a surge in turnout by voters over sixty (who are more likely to be religious) and a sharp decline in voters under thirty (the age group most likely to have no religious affiliation).[22] The net impact was thus a midterm electorate heavily weighted toward voters holding traditional religious views, and the Republican gains in Congress and state legislatures reflected this.

The most energized voters in 2010 were the activists identified with the Tea Party. They tended to be older, white, male, Southern, and Republican—all demographic groups inclined toward traditional religious perspectives. According to an American Values survey in October 2010, only 11 percent of Americans identified with the Tea Party movement, and many had no idea what it was. But 47 percent of self-identified Tea Party supporters also considered themselves to be part of the Christian conservative movement. Two-thirds opposed abortion under almost all circumstances, and 58 percent agreed that "minorities get too much government attention." However, only 47 percent opposed gay marriage. In addition to political independents and religious traditionalists, the Tea Party has also attracted a sizable number of libertarians, including the new senator from Kentucky, Rand Paul. Libertarians generally favor individual freedom from any government regulations, including restrictions on marriage.[23]

Most Tea Party activists made a deliberate decision in 2010 to downplay these divisive social issues and to focus on the economy, the budget deficit, and opposition to Obama's health care reform. Some of the more radical candidates endorsed by the Tea Party (Sharron Angle in Nevada, Christine O'Donnell in Delaware) lost in 2010, but a significant number of such candidates were elected to Congress. One estimate was that forty-two of the sixty-three seats gained by Republicans went to candidates linked to the Tea Party.[24] This faction is likely to wield influence within the Republican Party in future years, although its supporters have already expressed dismay about political expediency: committee and subcommittee positions in the new Congress went to more traditional Republicans with seniority, earmarks still enjoy political support, and fund-raising efforts with lobbyists continue as usual.

Abortion opponents gained about forty-five House seats after the 2010 election, and many more pro-life state legislators and governors were elected as well. A strongly pro-life representative, Joe Pitts of Pennsylvania, was chosen to chair the Energy and Commerce Subcommittee on Health, which has jurisdiction over the National Institutes of Health, Medicaid, and Medicare. Enacting additional restrictions on abortion access will be a high priority in the states and for the new Republican-controlled House, and are strongly backed by the new Speaker John Boehner.[25] Also, in 2010 three Iowa Supreme Court justices who had supported gay marriage in a unanimous 2009 ruling lost their retention elections after vigorous grassroots efforts by the Christian Right. An ongoing campaign was announced by the National Organization for Marriage to impeach the remaining four Iowa justices, and similar efforts will be initiated in other states.[26]

Yet long-term options for the Republican Party may be more problematic than the 2010 results suggest. As the 1998 and 2006 elections illustrated, even midterm election results can be affected by pressing issues (Clinton's impeachment and the economy, respectively). Because of trends in race, ethnicity, and non-Christian faiths, by 2020 the United States will no longer be a white Christian nation. By 2040 white Christians will constitute only 35 percent of the population, and conservative white Christians an even smaller proportion. The proportion of unaffiliated Americans is also likely to increase. The Republican Party may find itself in a permanent minority unless it moves closer to the center on immigration, family values, and social issues.[27] But as noted above, such moves may be very difficult given the existing structure of Religious Right organizations and the preferences of major donors or activists.

However, support for more conservative economic policies may also result from increases in some minority groups. The growing population of Asian Americans tends to be more conservative than either Hispanics or African Americans. Sizable numbers of Hispanics are moving away from Roman Catholicism and into evangelical or Pentecostal Protestant denominations, which tend to favor self-reliance rather than dependence on government services. The Prosperity Gospel, with its emphasis on faith as a route to earthly as well as heavenly riches, has strong appeal in many Hispanic and African American communities, and people who expect to become wealthy are unlikely to support redistributive policies.[28] A Republican emphasis on hard work, limited government, and traditional families may thus find support among some fast-growing minority groups. But although the number of Hispanic Republicans in Congress increased in 2010, virulent opposition to illegal immigration by many Republicans certainly cost them Hispanic votes—and perhaps control of the Senate.[29]

At least for the next few years, secular viewpoints will have few overt defenders among elected officials. A Pew Forum analysis reported that the unaffiliated (defined as atheists, agnostics, the unchurched, and the uncommitted) constituted 16 percent of the population, but was the largest religious group in America without representation in Congress. Only Representative Pete Stark, a Unitarian Universalist congressman from California, was willing to express any public doubts about belief in God. Given the expressed religiosity of most Americans, few politicians are willing to follow his example. As *New York Times* columnist Charles Blow stated, politicians are "trapped in the religious closet of American politics where nonbelief is a nonstarter. It's not only seen as unholy, it's also seen as un-American."[30]

## THE FUTURE ROLE OF THE SUPREME COURT

The Supreme Court has been the final arbiter of many of the vexing religious conflicts that have confronted the United States. Since the 1940s secular and civil-libertarian groups have made effective use of the court to limit legal establishment and the expression of traditional religious views in the public square. Many of these opinions, such as the ban on school prayer, the legalization of abortion, or the *Lawrence* decision striking down state sodomy laws, were very much at odds with public opinion when they were originally handed down, although the public has generally become more supportive since then (as the cohort analysis in chapter 2 showed).

The Religious Right has strenuously opposed such legal assaults on traditional values and what they regard as the identity of a Christian nation. Compared with the Warren court, the Rehnquist and Roberts courts have moved toward less church/state separation and greater accommodation. Some types of government support of religion are allowable as long as no favoritism is shown to any particular religion. Thus the court has approved limited assistance to parochial schools, vouchers to be used in religious schools, Christmas symbols as part of larger holiday displays, and religious clubs meeting in public schools on the same basis as other clubs.[31] Several of these cases were successfully litigated by conservative or Christian law firms, which were set up to emulate the earlier successes of the American Civil Liberties Union.

However, the most successful strategy of the Religious Right may well be its focus on transforming the state and federal judiciary. Public opinion may be fickle, and transient election outcomes may bring more Democrats, seculars, or religious moderates to power in the states or in Congress. But Supreme Court justices and many other federal judges have tenure for life. If "activist judges" could not be persuaded to support expression of traditional religious values, they could be replaced. The federal judiciary is currently dominated by appointees by Republican presidents. Presidential appointment does not always predict judicial philosophy: Judge John Jones in the Dover case and Judge Vaughn Walker in the appeal of Proposition 8 were both appointed by Republicans George W. and George H. W. Bush, and Judge Walker was initially opposed by liberals who feared he would not be sympathetic to gay rights.[32] Fearing such outcomes, conservative law firms and groups such as the Federalist Society provide a training ground for such judges, as well as a forum for vetting proposed judicial candidates.

Two recent decisions have been particularly problematic for seculars and mainstream scientists. First was the *Gonzales v. Carhart* decision of 2005 upholding a congressional ban on partial-birth abortion. The five in the majority (all Roman Catholics) ignored the recommendations of the American Medical Association and the College of Obstetricians and Gynecologists that the late-term abortion procedure in question was sometimes a medical necessity, and that such decisions should be made by women and their doctors rather than courts or legislatures. Justice Ruth Bader Ginsburg's stinging dissent also objected to Justice Kennedy's majority opinion that "While we find no reliable data to measure the phenomenon, it seems unexceptionable to conclude some women come to regret their choice to abort the infant life they once created and sustained."[33]

A second problematic decision, overturning a federal law on the use of embryonic stem cells, was handed down in 2010 by a federal district court. The court gave standing to two doctors supported by the Alliance Defense Fund, who opposed use of embryonic stem cells on ethical and religious grounds. The doctors wanted to research adult stem cells instead, and argued successfully that continued research on embryonic stem cells constituted "unfair competition" for federal funding. This decision also ignored mainstream medical opinion and the guidelines issued by the Obama administration and the National Institutes of Health.[34]

Justices are usually careful to avoid overt expression of religious beliefs in their decisions. But acceptance of dubious science can bring in traditional religious values by the back door. The future direction of the court may well determine whether the secular values portended by demographic trends will prevail. The closeness of some recent decisions on abortion has been cause for concern by pro-choice supporters: *Casey* 1992 and *Gonzales* 2005 were both 5–4. There are now six Roman Catholics on the court (although Justice Sonya Sotomayor, appointed by Barack Obama, is unlikely to vote to overturn *Roe*). Could the addition of one more pro-life justice mean that *Roe v. Wade* would be overturned?

Although nearly as many Americans claim to be pro-life as to be pro-choice, a solid majority oppose overturning *Roe* or criminalizing abortion.[35] The case study in chapter 6 of the referenda in South Dakota showed that a majority of voters considered an almost complete ban on abortion far too sweeping even for a conservative state. Most legal scholars think an outright ban on abortion would cause a political firestorm and is highly unlikely. But the Supreme Court could rule that *Roe* was wrongly decided and that abortion should remain an issue for the states, as it had been for the previous two centuries. If that were to happen, about thirty states would immediately ban all abortions. Several other states would probably continue to allow them, including the most populous states (California, New York, Illinois) where most abortions are now performed. Thus the nation's overall abortion rate would not change very much. The increased use of the abortion pill mifeprestone could also mean that abortion would become a private decision no longer requiring a visit to a clinic.[36] But additional onerous restrictions or state bans on abortion could also help to galvanize pro-choice supporters, who have not been as active at the grass roots as pro-life groups in recent years.

The issue of gay marriage is also likely to end up in the Supreme Court, and a federal court ruled in July 2010 that DOMA was unconstitutional. Although the Obama Justice Department decided in February 2011 not to challenge this ruling, other appeals are pending. How are the justices likely to rule? Justice Antonin Scalia feared that the sweeping *Lawrence* decision, based on the right to privacy of consenting adults, would open the door to legalization of gay marriage, and he could well be right. Rejection of "don't ask–don't tell" by another federal judge in 2010 also suggests that the court will be skeptical of any restrictions on equal rights for gays and lesbians, and in 2011 the court rejected an appeal of a District of Columbia law allowing gay marriage.[37] As discussed in chapter 6, Judge Vaughan Walker's decision overturning California's Proposition 8 explicitly noted the lack of any compelling evidence from mainstream scientists that gay marriage would be harmful to children or to heterosexual marriages. However, given their reasoning in *Gonzales*, some Supreme Court justices could be sympathetic to allegations of possible future harm from gay marriage even if no such evidence is presented.

The most likely outcome may well be for Supreme Court to defer to state constitutions and state courts on the gay-marriage issue as well as on the question of abortion. The outcomes will thus depend on the relative strength and organizational capacity of secular and traditional religious views in the states. Unlike the Supreme Court, however, judges in most states are either elected initially or, if appointed, must face the electorate in retention elections. State judges may thus be more attentive to public preferences—or at least to preferences expressed in low-turnout judicial elections. All gay-marriage bans on state ballots in direct-democracy states have passed, and as noted earlier, efforts are under way to impeach or recall any judge who supports gay marriage. Research has already shown that elected judges are more likely than appointed ones to support pro-life positions.[38] Seculars, pro-choice groups, their allies on the Religious Left, and GLBT organizations may face an uphill battle in judicial elections, since pro-life and antigay groups have far stronger grassroots support (much of it based in churches) in most states. But the task is not impossible, as the South Dakota example showed.

## VALUES AND SOCIAL CAPITAL IN A MORE SECULAR SOCIETY

What would a more secular America be like? Many on the Religious Right have predicted disastrous outcomes. Francis Schaeffer's influential 1984 book *Bad News for Modern Man* blamed "secular humanists" for a variety of social ills: divorce, rampant sexuality, teen pregnancy, the AIDS epidemic, crime, violence. Leaders of the Religious Right regularly invoke "family breakdown" and immoral behavior (including homosexuality) in order to mobilize the faithful and to advocate for morally restrictive policies. If God and the promise of an afterlife (or threat of eternal damnation) provide the moral basis of society, further decline in religious faith would result in increased immorality. Atheists are viewed negatively by many Americans because they allegedly are devoid of moral principles and therefore cannot be trusted—certainly not as president.

Social scientists are usually more circumspect, but many have sounded the alarm about the decline of "social capital": the bonds of community and trust built up through interactions with others, and the social skills and democratic principles learned through organizational involvement. While groups such as labor unions, PTAs, and fraternal organizations have been on the decline, millions of Americans still belong to churches, which have been described as major generators of social capital.[39] Churches have also been praised for developing the social and political skills of the poor, the less educated, and minorities, thereby offsetting somewhat the socioeconomic bias in most forms of political participation.[40] Based on this logic, further declines in church attendance could be bad for democracy. Increased secularism would lead to diminished social capital, lower voter turnout, and an even greater class bias in political participation.

Advocates of social capital certainly have a point; seculars are significantly less likely than church members to belong to other organizations, to volunteer, or to contribute to charity.[41] However, as chapter 3 showed, church membership is increasingly common among those with *higher* levels of education and income, and in chapter 4 frequent church attendance was found to raise awareness about issues among those with more rather than less education. Since the 1990s church attendance has become less important as a predictor of political involvement. In 2004 and 2008 rates of voting, political proselytizing, political information, and campaign activism by seculars were comparable to those of religious traditionalists (primary voting is a notable exception). Comparative evidence also suggests that secular trends are not necessarily bad for democracy; most European countries are considerably more secular than the United States but have higher, not lower, voter turnout. Low voter turnout in the United States may be more attributable to weaknesses of parties and labor unions than to increases in secularism. We may be entering a new era of social capital formation (especially among the young) based on the Internet and social media, as recent events in Egypt and Tunisia certainly suggest.[42]

Further, higher levels of voter turnout are linked to perceptions of greater differences between parties and candidates, and as chapter 4 showed, those who never attend church are more, rather than less, aware of such differences across a range of issues. Religious conservatives can be mobilized by threats to core values; frequent church attendees were more aware of party differences on abortion in 2004, and have been mobilized by recent state voter initiatives to ban gay marriage. But seculars and religious progressives can be mobilized to defend their values as well, as shown by the defeat of the Dover, Pennsylvania, school-board conservatives and of bans on abortion in South Dakota.

The Religious Right has also received praise for (re)introducing values into politics. But values have seldom been absent from intense political conflicts over wars, slavery, education, or the rights of women and minorities. The New Deal directly challenged the consequences of unbridled capitalism for American workers and families. The key question, of course, is *whose* values will be upheld. In the culture wars, the family and sexual values of religious conservatives have been challenged by the values of religious progressives and seculars: individual freedom, privacy, self-expression, tolerance of opposing views, separation of church and state. Secular values certainly include sexual freedom, but emphasis on this aspect ignores many of the other differences in values between seculars and traditionalists on political and social issues. Based on recent research in neuroscience, "Instead of viewing the left and right as either inherently correct or wrong, a more scientific approach is to recognize that liberals and conservatives emphasize different moral values."[43]

Despite their strongly Democratic voting patterns, seculars tend to be more moderate than liberal in their opinions on social and political issues; as table 7.2 shows, they strongly support the death penalty. Nevertheless, seculars are significantly more likely than (white) traditionalists to favor government-provided health care, expanded government spending on social services, less spending on defense, stricter gun control, and stricter emissions laws, and more likely to agree that the war in Iraq was not worth the cost. By contrast, white traditionalists are strongly Republican and share politically conservative views about limited government, the virtues of markets, and the need for a strong defense. Religious traditionalists and moderates give stronger support than seculars to the foreign-policy goals of combating world hunger or defending human rights, but are less likely to support health care, social services, or welfare for people in the United States. Church members may well be "better neighbors," especially to people within their own social network.[44] But if more secular views are to prevail in the future, the United States could become a country with fewer weapons, expanded social services, health care for all, cleaner air, and greater tolerance of diversity in moral standards.

Considerable social-science research has shown seculars to be more tolerant of others' moral viewpoints. Evidence provided in this book provides confirmatory evidence of greater secular tolerance of women's rights, homosexuality, and freedom of speech for atheists, although seculars are strongly skeptical of Christian fundamentalists whose values directly challenge theirs. Also, since the 1980s, religious traditionalists have become considerably more accepting of gay rights, reproductive rights, and equality for women. High rates of intermarriage and social interaction among people of different religious backgrounds may also lead to greater tolerance. The views of the general public may thus be considerably more moderate and less polarized than those of elites, perhaps providing grounds for future deliberation and compromise.[45] However,

Table 7.2. Policy Preferences of Seculars, Moderates, and Traditionalists

|  | Seculars | Moderates | Traditionalists |
|---|---|---|---|
| Increase spending on social services | 28% | 25% | 18% |
| Decrease spending on defense | 20% | 13% | 12% |
| War in Iraq was not worth the cost | 83% | 81% | 71% |
| Favor government health insurance | 38% | 34% | 23% |
| Favor citizenship for illegals | 46% | 46% | 53% |
| Favor additional assistance for blacks | 17% | 17% | 15% |
| Favor more spending on schools | 46% | 47% | 47% |
| Favor more spending on welfare | 49% | 45% | 47% |
| Increase gun restrictions | 50% | 46% | 44% |
| Support death penalty | 70% | 65% | 58% |
| Support stricter emissions laws | 45% | 42% | 37% |
| U.S. policy goal: combat world hunger | 55% | 65% | 69% |
| U.S. policy goal: protect human rights | 34% | 39% | 42% |

Source: ANES 2008

strong organizational incentives remain for political and religious elites to demonize the opposition and use inflammatory rhetoric to motivate their followers to engage in political activism.

## CONCLUSION

Trends in demographics, family structure, and the views of younger cohorts all point to declining popular support for conservative religious and policy values. However, judicial decisions can countermand popular majorities and election results, as President Franklin D. Roosevelt learned to his frustration when the Supreme Court struck down many of his New Deal policies. In the appeal of Proposition 8 in California, federal Judge Vaughn Walker's ruling overturned the result of a popular initiative to assert that privacy rights (including gay marriage) were fundamental. But while this ruling pleased seculars and their gay-rights and liberal allies, the growing number of conservative judges and justices could also issue rulings that run counter to increasing popular support for gay marriage and resistance to overturning *Roe v. Wade*.

The proportion of unaffiliated or secular Americans is likely to increase as social norms mandating religious ties are changing. The United States remains a highly diverse society, but one in which religious involvement and religious values are still widely shared. Almost all politicians feel obliged to reaffirm religion in their public speeches; nearly every presidential address must now end with "God bless America." Yet while President Barack Obama mentioned God five times in his inaugural address in 2009, he also said, "We are a nation of Christians and Muslims, Jews and Hindus, and *nonbelievers*"[46] (my emphasis). This unprecedented public statement recognized the increasing prevalence of seculars, not only among Democratic Party activists but also in American society as a whole.

Seculars are a diverse group as well. While some are avowed atheists or agnostics, others report that they pray, believe in God, or anticipate life after death. Although seculars reject organized religion, most would probably support the official position of the American Civil Liberties Union: strong opposition to any suggestion of religious establishment, but equally strong affirmation of the right to free exercise of religion. Of course these provisions of the First Amendment may sometimes come into conflict, leaving the courts to try to sort them out. And defense of religious freedom may place the ACLU in an awkward position; in 2010 its Florida branch defended the right of an evangelical preacher in Florida to burn copies of the Koran, because book burning (despite its connotations of Nazism) is still protected freedom of speech. Unfortunately for the ACLU (and for America's public image and foreign policy), the preacher eventually carried out his threat several months later.[47]

The ACLU and seculars are thus committed to what has been termed the "American model" of a secular state and a religious people.[48] But as this book has shown, seculars have been mobilized by recent efforts of the Religious Right to introduce their traditional religious values into public policy. Once-apolitical seculars have used both individual political activism and effective organization to maintain the boundaries between church and state. As *New York Times* columnist Charles Blow said in 2011, "Whether they are organized, cohesive or disgruntled, the unaffiliated are the fastest-growing religious category in America. Nonaffiliation is not un-American. Increasingly, it is America. Eventually, our politics will have to catch up."[49] Nevertheless the Religious Right (despite its recent difficulties) still has considerable organizational advantages, as the 2010 election outcomes illustrated. State and federal courts are increasingly dominated by conservative judges, and may be slow to respond to shifts in public opinion. "Eventually" could therefore take quite a while, and the culture wars over religion and morality are likely to continue even in an increasingly secular society.

# Notes

### PREFACE

1. Lyman Kellstedt, "Seculars and the American presidency," in *Religion and the American Presidency: George Washington to George W. Bush*, ed. Gaston Espinosa (New York: Columbia University Press, 2011), 99.
2. "Many Americans uneasy with mix of religion and politics," Pew Forum on Religion and Public Life, August 24, 2006, http://people-press.org/report/287.
3. Kellstedt, "Seculars," 97.
4. James A. Davis and Tom W. Smith, *General Social Surveys, 1972–2008* (Chicago: National Opinion Research Center, producer; Storrs, CT: Roper Center for Public Opinion Research, University of Connecticut, distributor). The initial survey in 1972 was supported by grants from the Russell Sage Foundation and the National Science Foundation. NSF has provided support for the 1973–2008 surveys.
5. The American National Election Studies, Time Series Cumulative Date File (dataset); Stanford University and the University of Michigan (producers and distributors), 2010. These materials are based on work supported by the National Science Foundation

### CHAPTER 1

1. James C. McKinley, "For atheist ads on buses, equally mobile reaction," *New York Times*, December 14, 2010, A19.
2. Brian Montopoli, "National day of prayer deemed unconstitutional but Obama will recognize it anyway," www.cbsnews.com/8301-503544_162/4-16-2010; Nick Wing, "Michele Bachmann and allies: "Obama doesn't say 'God' enough," *Huffington Post*, December 8, 2010, www.huffingtonpost.com/2010/12/08/michele-Bachmann.

3. Laurie Goodstein, "In Kentucky, Noah's Ark theme park is planned," *New York Times*, December 5, 2010, A1.

4. Carl Hulse, "Senate repeals ban on gays serving openly in the military," *New York Times*, December 18, 2010.

5. James Davison Hunter, *Culture Wars: The Struggle to Define America* (New York: Basic Books, 1991).

6. On the historical development of the Religious Right, see David Leege and Lyman Kellstedt, *Rediscovering the Religious Factor in American Politics* (Armonk, NY: M.E. Sharpe, 1993), and Clyde Wilcox and Carin Robinson, *Onward Christian Soldiers? The Religious Right in American Politics*, 4th ed. (Boulder, CO: Westview, 2010).

7. John C. Green, Mark J. Rozell, and Clyde Wilcox, in *The Values Campaign? The Christian Right and the 2004 Elections* (Washington, DC: Georgetown University Press, 2006), analyze the role of religious mobilization in the 2004 presidential election.

8. Pippa Norris and Ronald Inglehart, in *Sacred and Secular: Religion and Politics Worldwide* (Cambridge: Cambridge University Press, 2004), compare trends in secularization in the United States and other countries. These secular trends will be analyzed further in chapters 2 and 3.

9. See the critique of secularism in Ralph Reed, *Politically Incorrect: The Emerging Faith Factor in American Politics* (Dallas: Word Pub., 1994).

10. Robert Kuttner, "American Taliban: The marriage between religious fundamentalism and market conservatism is as strong as ever," *The American Prospect*, February 17, 2010; Markos Moulitsas, *American Taliban: How War, Sex, Sin, and Power Bind Jihadists and the Radical Right* (Sausalito, CA: PoliPoint Press, 2010).

11. See John C. Green, *The Faith Factor: How Religion Influences American Elections* (Westport, CT: Praeger, 2007), 25–31, for a summary of core evangelical beliefs. His appendix A lists evangelical and fundamentalist (white) Protestant denominations; African American and Hispanic Protestants are classified separately. Green notes other definitions of "evangelical" in note 13, p. 187.

12. The Association of Religious Data Archives provides a website with links to decades of data on church membership. However, any analysis of trends over time is complicated by changes in definitions and in the denominations included; see www.thearda.org.

13. Pew Forum on Religion and Public Life, "Religious knowledge survey: Executive summary," September 28, 2010, http://pewresearch.org/pubs/1745/religious-knowledge-in-america-survey.

14. Liberal theology summarized by John S. Spong, *A New Christianity for a New World: Why Traditional Faith Is Dying and How a New Faith Is Being Born* (San Francisco: HarperSanFrancisco, 2001); Laura R. Olson, "Clergy and American politics," in *The Oxford Handbook of Religion and American Politics*, ed. Corwin E. Smidt, Lyman A. Kellstedt, and James L. Guth (New York: Oxford University Press, 2009), 371–93.

15. Peter L. Berger, Grace Davie, and Effie Fokas, *Religious America, Secular Europe? A Theme and Variation* (Burlington, VT: Ashgate, 2008).

16. Corwin E. Smidt, Lyman A. Kellstedt, and James L. Guth review changes over time in measures of religiosity and the methods used by social scientists to

analyze the impact of religion on politics. "The role of religion in American politics: Explanatory theories and associated analytical and measurement issues," in *The Oxford Handbook of Religion and American Politics*, 3–43.

17. Stephen T. Mockabee, Kenneth D. Wald, and David C. Leege, "Is there a Religious Left? Evidence from the 2006 and 2008 ANES" (paper presented at the American Political Science Association, Toronto, 2009, http://ssrn.com/abstract=1451098).

18. Recent examples include Norris and Inglehart, *Sacred and Secular*; Andrew Kohut, John C. Green, Scott Keeter, and Robert C. Toth, *The Diminishing Divide* (Washington, DC: Brookings, 2000); Robert D. Putnam and David E. Campbell, *American Grace: How Religion Divides and Unites Us* (New York: Simon & Schuster, 2010).

19. Louis Bolce and Gerald De Maio, "Secularists, antifundamentalists, and the new religious divide in the American electorate," in *From Pews to Polling Places: Faith and Politics in the American Religious Mosaic*, ed. J. Matthew Wilson (Washington DC: Georgetown University Press, 2007), chap. 10; Green, *Faith Factor*, 60.

20. See Green, *Faith Factor*, appendix B, on the distribution of religion across states and page 157 on the religion of Democratic and Republican convention delegates. Those Green classified with no religion include atheists, agnostics, and "respondents with generic affiliations and those with no religious commitment" based on data pooled from GSS surveys and other sources (179, 181).

21. Green, *Faith Factor*, 58.

22. Green, *Faith Factor*, chaps. 2–5.

23. E. E. Schattschneider, *The Semi-Sovereign People* (Hinsdale, IL: Dryden Press, 1960), 35.

24. David Broder, *Democracy Derailed: Initiative Campaigns and the Power of Money* (New York: Harcourt, 2000).

25. "About NPR: Public radio finances," ww.npr.org/about/aboutnpr/publicradiofinances.html (December 13, 2010).

26. Mancur Olson, in *The Logic of Collective Action* (Cambridge, MA: Harvard University Press, 1965), provides an economic perspective on organizational costs and describes how large and small groups cope with the free-rider problem.

27. Susan B. Hansen, in *Globalization and the Politics of Pay* (Washington, DC: Georgetown University Press, 2006), discusses the evolution of right-to-work laws and their impact on unions and labor costs in the American states.

28. Christopher Z. Mooney, *The Public Clash of Private Values: The Politics of Morality Policy* (New York: Chatham House, 2001).

29. Kristin Luker, in *Abortion and the Politics of Motherhood* (Berkeley: University of California Press, 1985), describes the membership and motivations of pro-choice and pro-life activists.

30. Razelle Frankl, *Televangelism: The Marketing of Popular Religion* (Carbondale: Southern Illinois University Press, 1987). Bob Lochte, in *Christian Radio: The Growth of a Mainstream Broadcasting Force* (Jefferson, NC: McFarland, 2005), documents the dramatic surge in Christian radio, which in 2002 included 20 percent of all radio stations.

31. Richard Viguerie and David Franke, *America's Right Turn: How Conservatives Used New and Alternative Media to Take Power* (Chicago: Bonus Books,

2004); Scott Thumma and Dave Travis, *Beyond Megachurch Myths: What We Can Learn from America's Largest Churches* (San Francisco: Jossey-Bass, 2007).

32. Wilcox and Robinson, *Onward Christian Soldiers?*, 422–50.

33. Kimberly H. Conger, *The Christian Right in Republican State Politics* (New York: Palgrave, 2009).

34. Clyde Wilcox and Gregory Fortelny consider the role of political entrepreneurs in "Religion and social movements," in *The Oxford Handbook of Religion and American Politics*, 266–98. The uses of issues for political mobilization are described in Jo Renee Formicola, *The Politics of Values: Games Political Strategists Play* (Lanham, MD: Rowman & Littlefield, 2008).

35. David C. Barker, *Rushed to Judgment: Talk Radio, Persuasion, and American Political Behavior* (New York: Columbia University Press, 2002).

36. Kellstedt, "Seculars and the American presidency," 81–100.

37. Recent critical assessments of the political impact of the Internet include Karen Mossberger, Caroline J. Tolbert, and Ramona S. McNeal, *Digital Citizenship: The Internet, Society, and Participation* (Cambridge, MA: MIT Press, 2008); Matthew S. Hindman, *The Myth of Digital Democracy* (Princeton, NJ: Princeton University Press, 2009); and Kay Lehman Schlozman, Sidney Verba, and Henry E. Brady, "Weapon of the strong? Participatory inequality and the Internet," *Perspectives on Politics* 8 (2010): 487–510.

38. Francis Schaeffer, *Bad News for Modern Man* (Westchester, IL: Crossway Books, 1984).

## CHAPTER 2

1. See Peter Berger, *The Sacred Canopy* (Garden City, NY: Doubleday, 1967), and Peter Laslett, *The World We Have Lost* (New York: Scribner, 1966), on the history of Christianity in the West.

2. Pope John XXIII appointed a study commission to review Galileo's trial and conviction, and its report led to the Vatican's apology in 1992. http://www.beliefnet.com/News/2000/03/The-Vaticans-Turn-To-Recant.aspx.

3. Christian Smith's "Introduction" in his *The Secular Revolution* (Berkeley: University of California Press, 2003) provides an extensive bibliography of works on the treatment of religion in history of science and in philosophy.

4. Voltaire's poem *Sur la déstruction de Lisbon* (1756) and his satirical novella *Candide, or The Optimist* (1759) were widely banned as scandalous and blasphemous, but also widely read.

5. Edward Paice, *Wrath of God: The Great Lisbon Earthquake of 1755* (London: Quercus Books, 2008). The 2010 earthquake in Haiti led to similar soul-searching to try to explain why such a poor country should suffer additional hardships. The Rev. Pat Robertson blamed the sins of the Haitians themselves, citing the role of voodoo in the Haitian revolution against the French, 1791–1803, as a "pact with the Devil," www.cnn.com/2010/US/01/13/haiti...robertson/index.html.

6. Charles Taylor, in *A Secular Age* (Cambridge, MA: Belknap Press of Harvard University Press, 2007), documents the increasing dominance of secular perspectives in philosophy, the arts, science, and academia in the United States as well as Europe.

7. See Pippa Norris and Ronald Inglehart, *Sacred and Secular: Religion and Politics Worldwide* (New York: Cambridge University Press, 2004), chapter 1, for a summary and critique of the major theories of secularization. They discount religious competition and lack of establishment as explanations for the distinctive American pattern, which they argue is based on high levels of economic insecurity in a capitalist country with a weak welfare state.

8. Norris and Inglehart, *Sacred and Secular*, chap. 4. See also Berger, Davie, and Fokas, *Religious America, Secular Europe?*.

9. Susan Jacoby, *Freethinkers: A History of American Secularism* (New York: Metropolitan Books, 2004).

10. David L. Holmes, in *Faiths of the Founding Fathers* (New York: Oxford University Press, 2006), lists Benjamin Franklin and Thomas Jefferson among the prominent critics of churches and Christianity. Bruce A. Barron, in *Heaven on Earth? The Social and Political Agendas of Dominion Theology* (Grand Rapids, MI: Zondervan, 1992), describes efforts by the Religious Right to define the United States as a Christian nation in which only Christians could hold public office.

11. Alexis de Tocqueville, *Democracy in America*, trans. Gerald Bevan (New York: Penguin Putnam, 2004; originally published 1832).

12. See Mark E. Deforrest, "An overview and evaluation of state Blaine amendments: Origins, scope, and first amendment concerns," *Harvard Journal of Law and Public Policy* 26 (2003).

13. See James Reichley, *Religion in American Public Life* (Washington, DC: Brookings, 1985), for a history of religion in America and trends in membership of the various denominations over time. Wilcox and Robinson, in *Onward Christian Soldiers?*, describe the origins and political involvement of fundamentalist churches.

14. James D. Hunter, in *Culture Wars: The Struggle to Define America* (New York: Basic Books, 1991), and Michael Lienesch, in *In the Beginning: Fundamentalism, the Scopes Trial, and the Making of the Antievolution Movement* (Chapel Hill: University of North Carolina Press, 2007), describe the religious and political reactions to the Scopes trial.

15. Leege and Kellstedt, *Rediscovering the Religious Factor*, provide an intellectual history of the treatment of religious beliefs and behavior by American social scientists. George Gallup and David Poling, in *The Search for America's Faith* (Nashville, TN: Abingdon, 1980), summarize early poll results on American religiosity.

16. See Norris and Inglehart, *Sacred and Secular*, chap. 1, for comparative data on American and European religiosity.

17. Membership data by denomination and decade is available through the Association of Religious Data Archives, www.thearda.com.

18. See Wilcox and Robinson, *Onward Christian Soldiers?*, 144–50, on motivations for involvement in conservative churches and the Christian Right.

19. Analyses of the resurgence of the Religious Right include Leege and Kellstedt, *Rediscovering the Religious Factor*; Wilcox and Robinson, *Onward Christian Soldiers?*; and Deal Wyatt Hudson, *Onward Christian Soldiers: The Growing Political Power of Catholics and Evangelicals in the United States* (New York: Threshold Editions, 2008).

20. Andrew Kohut, *The Diminishing Divide: Religion's Changing Role in American Politics* (Washington DC: Brookings, 2000); Melissa Deckman, in *School Board Battles* (Washington, DC: Georgetown University Press, 2004), analyzes the role of religious conservatives in local and school politics.

21. See Amy E. Black, Douglas L. Koopman, and David K. Ryden, *Of Little Faith: The Politics of George W. Bush's Faith-Based Initiatives* (Washington, DC: Georgetown University Press, 2004), for analysis of the development of faith-based initiatives under Presidents George W. Bush and Bill Clinton. Mooney, in *Republican War on Science*, describes efforts by the Religious Right to influence policies, appointments, and appropriations for federal agencies.

22. The American National Election Studies (ANES) and Pew surveys show very similar trends of declines in frequency of reported church attendance. Based on GSS data, the proportion of people who say they attend church "less than once a year" is about 7 percent, but with little change over time.

23. Norris and Inglehart, in *Sacred and Secular*, 267, cite several scholarly analyses that question the accuracy of self-reports of church attendance. The *Skeptic* survey is described by Lauri Lebo in "The social cost of atheism," *Religion Dispatches*, June 10, 2010, www.religiondispatches.org/dispatches/laurilebo/22783.

24. Norris and Inglehart, *Sacred and Secular*, table 4.3, p. 91.

25. Pew Forum on Religion and Public Life, "Religion among the Millennials," February 2010, pewforum.org/Age/Religion-Among-the-Millennials.aspx.

26. The specific GSS questions were as follows: "Should an anti-religionist be allowed to speak in public? . . . Teach in a college or university?" "Should an anti-religious book be removed from the public library?" Clyde Wilcox and Ted Jelen, in "Evangelicals and political tolerance," *American Politics Research* 18 (1990): 25–46, analyze the impact of religiosity and evangelical beliefs on tolerance.

27. James Jones, "Americans unlikely to support a Mormon for president," *Gallup Report*, December 2007.

28. The percentage of the GSS sample identifying as liberal or extremely liberal in political terms increased from 11 to 15 percent between 1980 and 2008; conservative or extremely conservative responses grew from 15 to 21 percent over the same period.

29. On the responsiveness of mass opinion to elite cues, see John R. Zaller, *The Nature and Origins of Mass Opinion* (New York: Cambridge University Press, 1992); and Thomas Carsey and Geoffrey Layman, "Changing sides or changing minds? Party identification and policy preferences in the American electorate," *American Journal of Political Science* 50 (2006): 464–77.

30. Michael Hout and Claude S. Fischer, "Why more Americans have no religious preference: Politics and generations," *American Sociological Review* 67 (2002): 165–90; Bolce and De Maio, "Secularists."

31. For analyses of the Supreme Court's *Engel v. Vitale* school prayer decision and its social and political impact, see Robert S. Alley, *School Prayer: The Court, the Congress, and the First Amendment* (Buffalo, NY: Prometheus Books, 1994). The GSS question is "How much confidence do you have in organized religion? A great deal, only some, or hardly any?"

32. Norris and Inglehart, in *Sacred and Secular*, 110, use World Values Survey data to show a moderate negative relationship in the United States between income and both frequency of prayer and belief that religion is important. The latter question is not available on the GSS.

33. GSS data show that Pearson correlations between family income (in constant dollars) and indicators of religiosity, 1972–2008, are very low (less than +/− 0.10); the only modest exception is the negative correlation between income and frequency of prayer (r = −.16).

34. Data on trends in educational achievement and minority populations from annual editions of the *Statistical Abstract of the U.S.*

35. The ideal way to test for cohort vs. age effects is to use panel surveys interviewing the same respondents over time. Since this is very expensive and impractical for longer time periods, the use of birth cohorts is a reasonable substitute. See discussion in Norris and Inglehart, *Sacred and Secular*, 33.

36. On increasing interest in the afterlife and reincarnation across different religious traditions, see the Pew Forum survey report, "Many Americans mix multiple faiths," December 2009, www.pewforum.org; and Lisa Miller, "Interest in reincarnation is growing," *New York Times*, August 27, 2010.

37. Larry M. Bartels, in *Unequal Democracy: The Political Economy of the New Gilded Age* (Princeton, NJ: Princeton University Press, 2008), chapter 1, summarizes evidence of declines in family income and social mobility.

38. Charles M. Blow, in "The rise of the Religious Left," *New York Times*, July 1, 2010, notes the growing presence of religious Hispanics and African Americans within the Democratic Party.

39. Before 1980 the only GSS categories for race were white, black, and other. A question on Hispanic ethnicity was added beginning in 2000.

40. Multivariate analysis assesses how well various predictor variables (age, education, income, race) account for indicators of religious behavior. Ordinary least squares (OLS) regression is used for two dependent variables: frequency of church attendance (ranging from 1, never, to 5, weekly), and frequency of prayer (ranging from 1, never, to 7, daily). Logit is used for the other dichotomous dependent variables.

41. Norris and Inglehart, in *Sacred and Secular*, 13–17, note the connection between religiosity and insecurity. See also the Barna Group, "How Americans' faith has changed since 9/11," www.barna.org/barna-update/article/5-barna-update/63-how-americas-faith-has-changed-since-9-11.

42. A CNN poll in 2010 found majority support for gay marriage, which only 25 percent of Americans supported when the Defense of Marriage Act was passed in 1996. Andrew Gelman, Jeffrey Lax, and Justin Phillips, "Over time, a gay marriage groundswell," *New York Times*, August 21, 2010.

43. Brian J. McCabe, "Public opinion on Don't Ask, Don't Tell," November 30, 2010, http://fivethirtyeight.blogs.nytimes.com/2010/11/30/public-opinion-on-dont-ask-dont-tell/.

44. Dagmar Herzog, *Sex in Crisis: The New Sexual Revolution and the Future of American Politics* (New York: Basic Books, 2008).

45. Lydia Saad, "More Americans pro-life than pro-choice for the first time," www.gallup.com/poll/118399/more-americans-pro-life-than-pro-choice-first-time.aspx.

46. The stability in American attitudes toward evolution is explored in Michael Berkman and Eric Plutzer, *Evolution, Creationism, and the Battle to Control America's Classrooms* (New York: Cambridge University Press, 2010).

47. Cited in Norris and Inglehart, *Sacred and Secular*, 3.

48. Penny Edgell, Joseph Gerteis, and Douglas Hartmann, "Atheists as 'Other': Moral boundaries and cultural membership in American society," *American Sociological Review* 71 (April 2006): 211–34.

49. Hout and Fischer, "Why more Americans have no religious preference."

# CHAPTER 3

1. Geoffrey Layman, in *The Great Divide: Religious and Cultural Conflict in American Party Politics* (New York: Columbia University Press, 2001), describes party polarization along religious lines. Other authors emphasize institutional reasons for increasing party divergence in Congress: growth in incumbency, decline in the number of competitive or marginal House districts, increased correspondence of party and ideology, and use of House or Senate procedural rules to control the agenda. See Jacob S. Hacker and Paul Pierson, *Off Center: The Republican Revolution and the Erosion of American Democracy* (New Haven, CT: Yale University Press, 2005), and Nolan M. McCarty, Keith T. Poole, and Howard Rosenthal, *Polarized America: The Dance of Ideology and Unequal Riches* (Cambridge, MA: MIT Press, 2008).

2. For evidence of the political impact of church attendance, see Green, *Faith Factor*; Putnam and Campbell, *American Grace*; and Kenneth D. Wald and Allison Calhoun-Brown, *Religion and Politics in the United States*, 5th ed. (Lanham, MD: Rowman & Littlefield, 2007).

3. Bolce and De Maio, "Secularists." Further subdivisions of seculars (atheists/agnostics, nonreligious affiliated, unaffiliated nonreligious) are analyzed by Lyman A. Kellstedt on the basis of a larger 2004 National Survey of Religion and Politics, in "Seculars and the American presidency."

4. The range of ANES responses to views of the Bible have changed somewhat over time, but the first response offered ("The Bible is the Word of God, and all it says is true") has been consistent since 1980. Only respondents agreeing with that viewpoint are classified as traditionalists. Other questions that could be used to differentiate seculars from the religious (frequency of personal prayer, being "born again") have only been asked occasionally since 1980.

5. Green, *Faith Factor*; chapters in Espinosa, *Race, Religion and the American Presidency*, on the opinions and voting of Catholics, Jews, mainline Protestants, evangelicals, and minorities.

6. Bolce and De Maio, in "Secularists," 259, also exclude African Americans from their analysis because they argue that the "culture war" is mostly among whites.

7. Green, *Faith Factor*, appendix A, lists the percentage of Hispanic Catholics by state. See *Latino Religions and Civic Activism in the United States*, ed. Gaston Espinosa, Virgilio P. Elizondo, and Jesse Miranda (New York: Oxford University

Press, 2005) on links between Hispanic religious involvement and civic activism.

8. On trends in African American religious involvement, see Darren E. Sherket, "African-American religious affiliation in the late 20th century: Cohort variations and patterns of switching, 1973–1998," *Journal for the Scientific Study of Religion* 41 (2002): 485–93; and Allison Calhoun-Brown, "African-American churches and political mobilization," *Journal of Politics* 58 (1996): 935–53.

9. Hanna Rosin, in "Did Christianity cause the crash?" *Atlantic*, December 2009, describes the appeal of the "Prosperity Gospel" to minority congregations. She notes that the geographic location of Prosperity Gospel churches closely overlaps the distribution of subprime mortgages. Some pastors actively encouraged their congregants to take out risky loans, either because "God will provide" or because the pastors received sizable contributions from mortgage companies.

10. Sherket, "African-American religious affiliation," 491. For critical assessment of the decline in African American civic involvement since the civil-rights era, see R. Drew Smith, *New Day Begun: African American Churches and Civic Culture in Post–Civil Rights America* (Durham, NC: Duke University Press, 2003).

11. Since 1992, the ANES codes for "evangelical Protestants" include subsets of mainline denominations (Missouri Synod Lutherans, Evangelical Presbyterians, Southern Baptists), historic black churches (AME Zion), fundamentalists, Pentecostals, Jehovah's Witnesses, Holiness churches (Church of God, Salvation Army), and Anabaptists (Amish, Mennonites). Many of these detailed categories were not available in earlier years, so coding of "evangelicals" in 1980 is only approximate. See David Leege, Kenneth Wald, and Lyman Kellstedt, "Religion and politics: A report on measures of religiosity in the 1989 NES pilot study" (Inter-University Consortium for Political Research, 1990).

12. John M. McTague and Geoffrey C. Layman, in "Religion, parties, and voting behavior: A political explanation of religious influence," summarize the literature on both major parties and survey the religious profiles of national convention delegates through 2004. In Corwin Smidt, Lyman A. Kellstedt, and James L. Guth, eds., *The Oxford Handbook of Religion and American Politics* (New York: Oxford University Press, 2009), 3–42. The 2008 delegate survey is discussed in chapter 5.

13. Christopher P. Gilbert, in *Religious Institutions and Minor Parties in the United States* (Westport, CT: Praeger, 1999), provides a historical analysis of support for third parties as a function of the religious profile of states, counties, and regions. Western states have been both more secular and more supportive of third parties since the Populist and Progressive eras.

14. See Melody Rose, *Safe, Legal, and Unavailable? Abortion Politics in the United States* (Washington, DC: CQ Press, 2007), appendix A, for the Democratic and Republican party platform statements on abortion, 1980–2004.

15. See Rose, *Safe, Legal, and Unavailable?*, for an overview of trends in public opinion concerning abortion and support for various restrictions on funding or access. Very different opinions can be elicited depending on the question wording and on the specific restrictions proposed.

16. In 2008 half the sample was asked whether abortion was an important issue or not so important; only 43 percent of seculars, compared with 64 percent of traditionalists, considered it "very" or "extremely" important. The other half of the sample was asked the detailed questions concerning abortion under particular

circumstances. On average, only 4 percent of seculars, compared with 25 percent of traditionalists, expressed "strong" opposition under each circumstance.

17. See Putnam and Campbell, *American Grace*, chap. 14, for more detailed analysis of how seculars and members of various religious groups view themselves and each other.

18. Bolce and De Maio, "Secularists"; Karen M. Kaufmann, John R. Petrocik, and Daron R. Shaw, *Unconventional Wisdom: Facts and Myths about American Voters* (New York: Oxford University Press, 2008).

19. E. E. Schattschneider, *The Semi-Sovereign People* (Hinsdale, IL: Dryden, 1960), 67.

20. Laura R. Olson, in "Clergy and American politics," 371–93, summarizes research on the political influence of clergy.

21. "Moral issues" actually had less overall influence in 2004 than opinions on the economy or national security, but may have been decisive in swing states such as Ohio. D. Sunshine Hillygus and Todd G. Shields, "Moral issues and voter decision making in the 2004 presidential election," *PS: Political Science and Politics* 38 (2005), 201–9.

22. Jesse McKinley and Kirk Johnson, "Mormons tipped scale in ban on gay marriage," *New York Times*, November 11, 2008.

23. Putnam and Campbell, *American Grace*, chap. 7.

24. Interviewer assessments compare favorably to other measures of political knowledge. See Michael X. Delli Carpini and Scott Keeter, *What Americans Know about Politics and Why It Matters* (New Haven, CT: Yale University Press, 1996).

25. According to Census of Population surveys, turnout by youth and African Americans increased considerably between 2004 and 2008, but overall turnout changed little. Michael McDonald, "Current population survey voting and registration supplement," U.S. National Election Project, on alternative indicators of voter turnout, http://elections.gmu.edu/CPS_2008.html.

26. Using snowball samples to contact both political proselytizers and the people they tried to influence demonstrated the impact of political proselytizing. R. Robert Huckfeldt and John D. Sprague, *Citizens, Politics, and Social Communication: Information and Influence in an Election Campaign* (New York: Cambridge University Press, 1995).

27. Peter Wielhouwer documents the impact of political contacting, especially by Republicans and among churchgoers. "Religion and American political participation," in *The Oxford Handbook of Religion and American Politics*, 394–426. Kellstedt, in "Seculars and the American presidency," 97, shows that based on the 2004 Religions and Public Life survey, secular respondents reported high levels of contacting by the candidates, environmentalists, and liberal issue groups.

28. MoveOn.org remained a major player in the 2010 midterm elections, raising hundreds of thousands of dollars for Democratic candidates and incumbents around the country. Sean J. Miller, "MoveOn.org brings in big money for embattled Dems," September 30, 2010, www.TheHill.com.

29. Separate regressions for 1980–1988, 1992–2000, and 2004–2008 showed that the impact of church attendance has lessened since 2000; it was still positive but no longer a statistically significant predictor of campaign activism or vote choice as in previous decades. Wielhouwer, in "Religion and American political partici-

pation," likewise found that the impact of church attendance on voter turnout has lessened in recent years.

30. David E. Campbell, "Religious 'threat' in contemporary presidential elections," *Journal of Politics* 68 (2006): 104–16.

31. David C. Leege, Kenneth D. Wald, Brian S. Krueger, and Paul D. Mueller, in *The Politics of Cultural Differences: Social Change and Voter Mobilization Strategies in the Post–New Deal Period* (Princeton, NJ: Princeton University Press, 2002), model the impact of values issues on defection as well as mobilization and vote choice.

32. Morris Fiorina, Samuel J. Abrams, and Jeremy C. Pope, *Culture War? The Myth of a Polarized America*, 3rd ed. (New York: Pearson Longmans, 2010); Putnam and Campbell, *American Grace*, 516.

33. David Barstow, "Tea Party lights fuse for rebellion on the right," *New York Times*, February 15, 2009. As Kyle Smith notes, "The morality armies have failed to inspire their children to join the crusade." Smith, "End of the culture wars?" *New York Post*, June 27, 2010.

34. Kellstedt, "Seculars and the American presidency," 99; "Catholic voters heavily favored Obama, analysis showed," *Washington Times*, November 7, 2008, www.washingtontimes.com/news/2008/nov/07/catholic-voters-heavily-favored-obama-analysis.

35. David E. Campbell and Steven J. Yonish, "Religion and volunteering in America," in *Religion as Social Capital: Producing the Common Good*, ed. Corwin Smidt (Waco, TX: Baylor University Press, 2003).

## CHAPTER 4

1. Critiques of Hunter's culture-war thesis include Fiorina, Abrams, and Pope, *Culture War?*; and Pietro S. Nivola and David W. Brady, eds., *Red and Blue Nation? Characteristics and Causes of America's Polarized Politics* (Washington, DC: Brookings, 2006). These scholars claim that differences between Red and Blue states are relatively minor, with large within-state variations.

2. Layman, in *The Great Divide*, describes the increasingly sharp party divisions along religious lines. See also Nolan McCarty, Keith T. Poole, and Howard Rosenthal, *Polarized Politics: The Dance of Ideology and Unequal Riches* (Cambridge, MA: MIT Press, 2006).

3. On the importance of elite cues for public opinion formation, see John R. Zaller, *The Nature and Origins of Mass Opinion* (New York: Cambridge University Press, 1992), and Marc J. Hetherington, "Resurgent mass partisanship: The role of elite polarization," *American Political Science Review* 95 (2001): 619–31.

4. The abortion response options for ANES respondents' own views and their placements of the parties or candidates range from 1, "By law, abortion should never be permitted," to 4, "By law, a woman should always be able to obtain an abortion as a matter of personal choice." Differences in perceptions of party or candidate positions were calculated by subtracting the Democratic scale placement from the Republican placement. A score of zero equals no difference; a positive score means that the Republican Party or candidate was perceived as more pro-choice than the Democrat. This may be an accurate perception in a state

such as Pennsylvania, which in 2008 had pro-choice Republican senator (Arlen Specter) and a pro-life Democratic senator (Robert Casey), but is clearly erroneous with respect to Bush, Kerry, or the national parties.

5. Wording of the other ANES issue questions (seven-point scales; midpoint 4 is neutral):

*Jobs/incomes*
  1. The government should guarantee jobs and a good standard of living.
  7. Each person should get ahead on his own.
*Defense spending*
  1. We should spend much less on defense.
  7. We should greatly increase defense spending.
*Spending on social services (health, education)*
  1. Government should provide many fewer services; reduce spending a lot.
  7. Government should provide many more services; increase spending a lot.
*Women's role*
  1. Women and men should have an equal role.
  7. Woman's place is in the home.
*Aid to blacks*
  1. Government should make every effort to improve the social and economic position of blacks.
  7. Government should not make any special effort to help blacks; they should help themselves.
*Environment*
  1. It is important to protect the environment even if it costs some jobs or otherwise reduces our standard of living.
  7. Protecting the environment is not as important as maintaining jobs and our standard of living.
*Intervention in foreign affairs*
  1. Should solve with diplomacy.
  7. Must be ready to use military force.

6. Morton summarizes the empirical problems with rational-choice theories of voting behavior: people do vote, even if their chance of affecting the outcome is too minuscule to offset the costs of voting, and the parties have increasingly diverged from the median-voter position. Rebecca B. Morton, "Groups in rational turnout models," *American Journal of Political Science* 35 (1991): 758–76.

7. Because the dependent variable (voted/did not vote) is a dichotomy, logistic regression was used. Of course, numerous other factors affect the likelihood of voting, including age, minority status, home ownership, and state laws concerning registration and voting. For comparison of voters and nonvoters, see Benjamin Highton and Raymond E. Wolfinger, "Political implications of higher turnout," *British Journal of Political Science* 31 (2002): 179–223.

8. Jan E. Leighley, "Group membership and the mobilization of political participation," *Journal of Politics* 58 (1996): 447–63.

9. Corwin Smidt, ed., *Religion as Social Capital: Producing the Common Good* (Waco, TX: Baylor University Press, 2003), 4. Other chapters summarize the

positive impact of religious involvement on charitable giving, volunteering, and political activism. See also Paul Djupe and Christopher Gilbert, "The resourceful believer: Generating civic skills in church," *Journal of Politics* 68 (2006): 116–27.

10. Sidney Verba, Kay Lehman Schlozman, and Henry E. Brady, *Voice and Equality: Civic Voluntarism in American Politics* (Cambridge, MA: Harvard University Press, 1995).

11. Jan E. Leighley and Jonathan Nagler, "Unions, voter turnout, and class bias in the U.S. electorate, 1964–2004," *Journal of Politics* 69 (2007): 430–44.

12. John C. Green, Mark J. Rozell, and Clyde Wilcox, eds., *The Values Campaign? The Christian Right and the 2004 Elections* (Washington, DC: Georgetown University Press, 2006).

13. Stephen Mockabee, "Catholics and the presidency," in *Religion, Race, and the American Presidency*, ed. Gaston Espinosa (Lanham, MD: Rowman & Littlefield, 2010).

14. Jacob Hacker and Paul Pierson, *Off Center: The Republican Revolution and the Erosion of American Democracy* (New Haven, CT: Yale University Press, 2005).

15. See Morton, "Groups in rational turnout models," on the impact of organizations on the calculus of voting.

16. Wielhouwer summarizes the research on the impact on voting of personal contact by political parties or other organizations (including churches). Paul Allen Beck, Russell J. Dalton, Steven Greene, and Robert Huckfeldt, "The social calculus of voting: Interpersonal, media, and organizational influences on presidential choices," *American Political Science Review* 96 (2002): 57–73.

17. James G. Gimpel, Karen M. Kaufmann, and Shanna Pearson-Merkowitz, "Battleground states versus blackout states: The behavioral implications of modern presidential campaigns," *Journal of Politics* 69 (2007): 786–97.

18. Anthony J. Nownes, Clive S. Thomas, and Richard Hrebenar, "Interest groups in the states," in *Politics in the American States: A Comparative Analysis*, 9th ed., ed. Virginia Gray and Russell L. Hanson (Washington, DC: CQ Press, 2009), 98–126.

19. James G. Gimpel, J. Celeste Lay, and Jason E. Schuknecht, *Cultivating Democracy: Civic Environments and Political Socialization in America* (Washington, DC: Brookings, 2003), 125.

20. Gimpel, Lay, and Schuknecht, *Cultivating Democracy*, 125.

21. Diana C. Mutz and Jeffrey J. Mondak, "The workplace as a context for cross-cutting political discourse," *Journal of Politics* 68 (2006): 140–55.

22. Campbell, "Religious 'threat.'"

23. Michael McDonald, "America goes to the polls 2008," http://elections.gmu.edu/voter_turnout.html.

24. D. Sunshine Hillygus and Todd G. Shields, *The Persuadable Voter* (Princeton, NJ: Princeton University Press, 2008).

25. Parish-level studies include Gregory Allen Smith, *Politics in the Parish: The Political Influence of Catholic Priests* (Washington, DC: Georgetown University Press, 2008), and Djupe and Gilbert, "The resourceful believer."

26. The ANES sample for 2004 included only twenty-eight states, but these varied considerably in religious composition based on Green, *Faith Factor*, appendix A.

27. ANES respondents were also asked where they would place the parties on these issues; the results (not shown) were very similar to those for perceived candidate differences.

28. Evangelicals were defined as respondents affiliated with churches so categorized by Green, *Faith Factor*, appendix A, as in the evangelical tradition.

29. Verba, Schlozman, and Brady, *Voice and Equality*, 234.

30. On the impact of age on political information processing, see Richard R. Lau and David P. Redlawsk, "Older but wiser? The effects of age on political cognition," *Journal of Politics* 70 (2008): 168–85.

31. Green, *Faith Factor*, appendix B, using church membership data from the Association of Religious Data Archives. His estimates for the secular "no religion" category for 2000 are based on the proportion of a state's population with no religious affiliation as well as General Social Survey data on the proportion of people in a state who claim that they have no religious involvement. See also "How religious is your state?" Pew Forum, December 21, 2009, http://pewforum.org/How-Religious-Is-Your-State-.aspx.

32. Since the dependent variables are categorical, logistic regression was appropriate for analyzing the dichotomous indicator of whether the Democratic and Republican parties differed significantly. Ordered logit was used to analyze perceived placements on the abortion scales for parties and candidates in 2004. Robust standard errors were calculated to correct for the state-clustered structure of the data.

33. Separate regressions were run to test whether Catholics or evangelicals who were frequent church attenders were more aware of party or candidate differences, but this was not the case; interaction terms with church attendance for Catholics or evangelicals had only marginal impact in any of these three models.

34. Campbell, "Religious 'threat.'"

35. Given the considerable social and theological differences between African American churches and other evangelical denominations, these equations were also estimated for whites only. The general patterns of the impact of religiosity and state context were broadly similar, although somewhat attenuated because of the smaller N. Catholicism and the state proportion of seculars still had the same significant impact on perception of candidate differences shown in table 4.1.

36. A Herfindahl index of religious diversity was calculated for each state based on the Green (*Faith Factor*) coding; it comprises the sum of the squared percentages of each religious subgroup. A high score on this index (such as Utah, 57 percent Mormon) indicates less diversity.

37. Estimates are based on stochastic simulations performed using Clarify software. Michael Toms, Jason Wittenberg, and Gary King, "CLARIFY: Software for Presenting and Interpreting Statistical Results, Version 2.1" (Cambridge, MA: Harvard University Press, 2003). All other independent or control variables were set at their means, except for age (median) and the modal category of non-Hispanic whites.

38. David Yamane, *The Catholic Church in State Politics* (Lanham, MD: Rowman & Littlefield, 2005).

39. David C. Barker, Jon Hurwitz, and Traci L. Nelson, "Crusades and culture wars: 'Messianic' militarism and political conflict in the United States," *Journal of Politics* 70 (2008): 307–22.
40. Campbell, "Religious 'threat.'"
41. Verba, Schlozman, and Brady, *Voice and Equality*, 234.
42. Barbara Arneil, *Diverse Communities: The Problem with Social Capital* (New York: Cambridge University Press, 2006).

## CHAPTER 5

1. Richard Viguerie and David Franke, *America's Right Turn: How Conservatives Used New and Alternative Media to Take Power* (Chicago: Bonus Books, 2004).
2. Razelle Frankl, *Televangelism: The Marketing of Popular Religion* (Carbondale: Southern Illinois University Press, 1987).
3. Barker, *Rushed to Judgment*.
4. Bob Lochte, in *Christian Radio: The Growth of a Mainstream Broadcasting Force* (Jefferson, NC: McFarland, 2005), documents the dramatic surge in Christian radio.
5. Scott Thumma and Dave Travis, *Beyond Megachurch Myths: What We Can Learn from America's Largest Churches* (San Francisco: Jossey-Bass, 2007).
6. Recent political-mobilization efforts are described in Formicola, *The Politics of Values*.
7. Allen Hertzke, "Religious interest groups in American politics," in *The Oxford Handbook of Religion and American Politics*, ed. Corwin E. Smidt, Lyman A. Kellstedt, and James L. Guth (New York: Oxford University Press, 2009), 299–329. People for the American Way maintains a "Right Wing Watch" on its website, with descriptions and links to many Religious Right as well as conservative groups: www.rightwingwatch.org/.
8. Edward L. Cleary and Allen D. Hertzke, eds., *Representing God at the Statehouse: Religion and Politics in the American States* (Lanham, MD: Rowman & Littlefield, 2005); Yamane, *The Catholic Church in State Politics*.
9. See Wilcox and Robinson, *Onward Christian Soldiers?*, on the recent organizational difficulties and possible future scenarios for the Christian Right.
10. Kyle Smith, "Christian Coalition 2.0, or the triumphant return of Ralph Reed," June 23, 2009, www.rightwingwatch.org. Rick Santorum has been associated with Fox News and the Ethics and Public Policy Center.
11. See Mooney, *The Republican War on Science*, for detailed and highly critical analysis of these quasi-science groups and their political tactics.
12. Reva B. Siegel, "The Right's reasons: Constitutional conflict and the spread of woman-protective antiabortion argument" (2008). *Faculty Scholarship Series.* Paper 1135. http://digitalcommons.law.yale.edu/fss_papers/1135.
13. Reporter A. A. Gill, in "Roll over, Charles Darwin!" *Vanity Fair*, February 2010, critiques the museum's displays, staff, faulty science, and overt religious messages.
14. Their website www.discovery.org lists books, articles, press releases, and examples of news coverage.

15. Mooney, in *Republican War on Science*, chap. 6, describes the "sound science" strategy.

16. Mooney, *Republican War on Science*, 205.

17. Elizabeth Kolbert, "Uncomfortable climate," *New Yorker*, November 22, 2010, 53–54.

18. Peter Boyle, "The Covenant," *New Yorker*, September 6, 2010; George C. Cunningham, *Decoding the Language of God: Can a Scientist Really Be a Believer?* (New York: Prometheus Books, 2011).

19. Steven P. Brown, in *Trumping Religion: The New Christian Right, the Free Speech Clause, and the Courts* (Tuscaloosa: University of Alabama Press, 2003), describes the range of such groups and examines several of the largest in detail.

20. HSLDA also founded Patrick Henry College in 2000 to provide higher-education opportunities, internships with public officials, and "moral leadership" training to home-schooled students; see www.hslda.org/about.

21. Brown, in *Trumping Religion*, describes some significant legal victories of the free-speech defense of religious expression but also notes its drawbacks (granting free speech to other religious minorities or viewpoints not favored by the Religious Right).

22. Paul J. Wahlbeck, "Religion and judicial politics," in *The Oxford Handbook of Religion and American Politics*, 518–45.

23. *Wikipedia*, s.v. "Justice Sunday," last modified August 28, 2010, en.wikipedia.org/wiki/Justice_Sunday_(conservative_Christian_event).

24. A. G. Sulzberger, "Ouster of Iowa judges sends signal to bench," *New York Times*, November 4, 2010, A1.

25. Putman and Campbell, *American Grace*, chapter 14.

26. Melissa Deckman, *School Board Battle: The Christian Right in Local Politics* (Washington, DC: Georgetown University Press, 2004), 173–74.

27. "Madalyn Murray: Scrappy atheist in a hurry, the most hated woman in America," *Life* magazine, June 19, 1964, 91–96. See also Ted Dracos, *Ungodly: The Passions, Torments, and Murder of Atheist Madalyn Murray O'Hair* (New York: Berkley Books, 2004).

28. James C. McKinley, "For atheist ads on buses, equally mobile reaction," *New York Times*, December 14, 2010, A19. After Christian groups complained, the city decided to ban all religious advertising from public transit.

29. The AAI website, www.atheistalliance.org, has links to its magazine *Secular World* and to its policy positions on issues. They sponsor a secular charity, Foundation Beyond Belief.

30. David Waters, "National Day of Prayer ruled unconstitutional," *Washington Post*, April 15, 2010.

31. Secular Coalition of America mission statement, www.secular.org/about/main.

32. Paul A. Djupe and Christopher P. Gilbert, in *The Political Influence of Churches* (New York: Cambridge University Press, 2009), describe the many reasons people give for joining churches and considerable opposition to overtly political messages from clergy or fellow parishioners. Author's interviews with members of Student Secular Alliance, University of Pittsburgh, Fall 2010.

## Notes

33. PAW's website has links to reports documenting the influence of the Religious Right on recent policy debates (health care reform, immigration) and election results, www.pfaw.org/issues/fighting-the-right.

34. www.hrc.org/about_us/who_we_are.asp.

35. The range of GLBT interest groups is analyzed by Craig A. Rimmerman in "Beyond political mainstreaming: Gay and lesbian interest groups and the grassroots," *The Politics of Gay Rights*, ed. Craig Rimmerman, Kenneth D. Wald, and Clyde Wilcox (Chicago: University of Chicago Press, 2000), 54–78. On legal gains, see Richard Mohr, *The Long Arc of Justice: Lesbian and Gay Marriage, Equality, and Rights* (New York: Columbia University Press, 2005).

36. http://www.adl.org.

37. Robert C. Lieberman, "The 'Israel Lobby' and American politics," *Perspectives on Politics* 7 (June 2009): 235-82.

38. Karl Vick and Ashley Surdin, "Most of California's black voters backed gay-marriage ban," *Washington Post*, November 7, 2008.

39. The court's decision was "shameful and incomprehensible," ignorant of medical consensus, and chilling for the medical profession. "ACOG statement on the U.S. Supreme Court decision upholding the Partial-Birth Abortion Ban Act of 2003" (press release, April 18, 2007, http://www.acog.org/from_home/publications/press_releases/nr04-18-07.cfm).

40. Mooney, in *Republican War on Science*, 207, describes the National Cancer Institute's protests of the Breast Cancer Prevention Institute's claims as "an unprecedented mobilization of scientists" against the Bush administration and its manipulation of science.

41. Bruce Alberts, "The evolution controversy in our schools," March 4, 2005, www.nasonline.org; "Climate change and the integrity of science," *Science*, May 7, 2010.

42. Mooney, *Republican War on Science*, 249.

43. Mooney, *Republican War on Science*, 224–37.

44. Jerry Falwell, "'Global warming' fooling the faithful," February 24, 2007, www.worldnetdaily.com/news/article.asp?ARTICLE_ID=54413.

45. NCSE describes itself as a "not-for-profit membership organization providing information and resources for schools, parents, and concerned citizens working to keep evolution in public school science education," www.ncse-com/about. The mission statement is from the Richard Dawkins Foundation website, http://richarddawkinsfoundation.org/.

46. Mooney, *Republican War on Science*, 252–53.

47. Angelo N. Ancheta, *Scientific Evidence and Equal Protection of the Law* (New Brunswick, NJ: Rutgers University Press, 2006), 11.

48. Ancheta, *Scientific Evidence*, 4.

49. Justice Thomas's dissent, in the *Bollinger* and *Grutter* affirmative-action cases at the University of Michigan, was openly skeptical about social-science claims of the educational advantages of diversity.

50. *CBS Evening News*, February 9, 1988 (television news archive, Vanderbilt University, www.tvnews.vanderbilt.edu).

51. S. Robert Lichter, Stanley Hoffman, and Linda Lichter, *The Media Elite: America's New Powerbrokers* (Bethesda, MD: Adler and Adler, 1986).

52. Mark Silk, *Unsecular Media: Making News of Religion in America* (Urbana: University of Illinois Press, 1995); Jeff Cohen, "Media coverage of religion: An overview," December 1999, www.fair.org/articles/media-religion.html.

53. Doris Graber, Dennis McQuaid, and Pippa Norris, *The Politics of News: The News of Politics* (Washington, DC: CQ Press, 2008).

54. C. Danielle Vinson, "Religion and politics and the media," in *The Oxford Handbook of Religion and American Politics*, 249–74; Peter A. Kerr, "The framing of fundamentalist Christians: Network television news, 1980–2000," *Journal of Media and Religion* 2 (2003): 203–35.

55. Louis Bolce and Gerald De Maio, "Secularists, antifundamentalists, and the new religious divide in the American electorate," in *From Pews to Polling Places: Faith and Politics in the American Religious Mosaic*, ed. J. Matthew Wilson (Washington, DC: Georgetown University Press, 2007), 251–76.

56. Terry Mattingly, "Getting religion in the newsroom," in *Blind Spot: When Journalists Don't Get Religion*, ed. Paul Marshall, Lela Gilbert, and Roberta G. Ahmanson (New York: Oxford, 2009), 148.

57. C. Danielle Vinson and James L. Guth, "'Misunderestimating' religion in the 2004 presidential campaign," in *Blind Spot: When Journalists Don't Get Religion*, 87–106.

58. Recent critical assessments of the political impact of the Internet include Mossberger, Tolbert, and McNeal, *Digital Citizenship*; and Matthew S. Hindman, *The Myth of Digital Democracy* (Princeton, NJ: Princeton University Press, 2009).

59. Kay Lehman Schlozman, Sidney Verba, and Henry E. Brady, "Weapon of the strong? Participatory inequality and the Internet," *Perspectives on Politics* 8(2): 487–510.

60. Paul Starr, "The Republicans' senior moment," *American Prospect*, January-February 2011, 3.

61. The Christian Coalition website, www.cc.org, now offers links to blogs, Facebook, Twitter feeds, and mobile phone apps.

62. Kimberly H. Conger, *The Christian Right in Republican State Politics* (New York: Palgrave Macmillan, 2009).

63. Boice and De Maio, "Secularists"; Gary Miller and Norman Schofield, "The transformation of the Republican and Democratic party coalitions in the U.S.," *Perspectives on Politics* 6(3): 433–50.

64. Green, *Faith Factor*, 157.

65. Data for 2004, Green, *Faith Factor*; data from the 2008 Convention Delegate Survey, personal communication from John C. Green, November 2010.

66. Jim Wallis, *God's Politics: Why the Right Gets It Wrong and the Left Doesn't Get It* (San Francisco: HarperCollins, 2005).

67. "Growing number of Americans say Obama is a Muslim," Pew Forum on Religion and Public Life, August 18, 2010, http://pewforum.org/Politics-and-Elections/Growing-Number-of-Americans-Say-Obama-is-a-Muslim.aspx.

68. James D. Hunter, *To Change the World: The Irony, Tragedy, and Possibility of Christianity in the Late Modern World* (New York: Oxford University Press, 2010), 139.

69. Definitions and membership data from Laura R. Olson, "Whither the Religious Left? Religiopolitical progressivism in twenty-first-century America," in

Wilson, *From Pews to Polling Places*, 58–65. Self-identification data is from Clyde Wilcox and Greg Fortelny, "Religion and social movements," in *The Oxford Handbook of Religion and American Politics*.

70. Olson, "Whither the Religious Left?," 72–75.

71. *Tikkun olam* in Hebrew means "to heal the world." Rabbi Michael Lerner is also author of *The Left Hand of God: Taking Our Country Back from the Religious Right* (San Francisco: Harper, 2006). The liberal Jewish group J Street opposes American Israel Public Affairs Committee (AIPAC) and advocates for a democratic, peaceful two-state solution for Israel and Palestine, www.jstreet.org/about/about-us.

72. For biographies and publications of these leaders, see www.beliefnet.com/News/Politics/2005/02/Beliefnet-Whos-Who-Leaders-Of-The-Religious-Left.aspx.

73. Cited in Hunter, *To Change the World*, 14.

74. Richard Dawkins, *The God Delusion* (New York: Houghton Mifflin, 2006). Psychologist Steve Pinker, in "Evolution and Ethics," summarizes anthropological and biological evidence for the evolution of morality as a survival advantage, not a legacy of religion. In *Intelligent Thought: Science versus the Intelligent Design Movement*, ed. John Brockman (New York: Vintage Books, 2006), 142–52.

75. Olson, "Whither the Religious Left?," 74–75. Djupe and Gilbert, in *Political Influence of Churches*, describe similar hesitation among mainline and liberal Episcopalians and Lutherans, although some of the congregations they analyzed were politically engaged. Putnam and Campbell, in *American Grace*, 429, find *more* explicit political messages in sermons in liberal rather than conservative churches.

76. Olson, "Whither the Religious Left?," 77.

77. Sonia Sikka, "Liberalism, multiculturalism, and the case for public religion," *Politics and Religion* 3 (2010): 580–609.

78. Gaston Espinosa, "Religion, race, and the 2008 presidential election," in *Religion, Race, and the American Presidency*, ed. Gaston Espinosa (Lanham, MD: Rowman & Littlefield, 2010), 275–86.

79. See Cleary and Hertzke, *Representing God*, on state lobbying by religious liberals and seculars.

80. Allen Hertzke, "Religious interest groups in American politics," in *The Oxford Handbook of Religion and American Politics*, 322.

81. Jon Shields, *The Democratic Virtues of the Christian Right* (Princeton, NJ: Princeton University Press, 2009); William Galston and Elaine Kamarck, "The still-vital center: Moderates, Democrats and the renewal of American politics," *Moderate Politics*, February 2010.

## CHAPTER 6

1. Gay, lesbian, bisexual, and transgender (GLBT) advocates have debated the relative virtues of political strategies based on accommodation versus legal equality; an explicit focus on gay marriage is a recent development. See Patrick Egan and Kenneth Sherrill, "Marriage and the shifting priorities

of a new generation of lesbians and gays," *PS: Political Science and Politics* 38 (2005): 229–33.

2. Many public-policy exceptions to Full Faith and Credit doctrines have been upheld by federal courts, such as states' refusal to accept marriages involving first cousins. See Heather Hamilton, "The Defense of Marriage Act: A critical analysis of its constitutionality under the Full Faith and Credit Clause," *DePaul Law Review* 47 (Summer 2008).

3. President Clinton's statement issued September 20, 1996, is available at http://www.cs.cmu.edu/afs/cs/user/scotts/ftp/wpaf2mc/clinton.html.

4. Patrick J. Egan and Nathanial Persily, in "Court decisions and trends in support for same-sex marriage," *Polling Report*, August 17, 2009, document trends over time in support of gay marriage. As of 2010, supporters outnumbered opponents for the first time; see http://www.pollingreport.com/penp0908.htm.

5. Christine Vestal, "Gay marriage legal in six states," www.stateline.org, June 4, 2009, http://www.stateline.org/live/details/story?contentId=347390.

6. Voters in Arizona initially rejected the ban in 2006 (probably because of confusing wording on the ballot) but approved a ban using simpler language in 2008.

7. On strategic use of "values" issues by political elites, see Formicola, *The Politics of Values*, and Leege, Wald, Krueger, and Mueller, *The Politics of Cultural Differences*.

8. *In re Marriage Cases*, 43 Cal.4th 757 (2008). "California Supreme Court rules in marriage cases," Judicial Council of California news release 26, May 15, 2008.

9. "Donors pump $83 million to Calif. gay marriage campaign," Associated Press, January 2, 2009, www.abcnews.go.com/US/wirestory?id=6790538.

10. *San Francisco Chronicle*, "Californians should reject Proposition 8," October 1, 2008, http://www.sfgate.com/cgi-bin/article.cgi?f=/c/a/2008/10/01/ED7T1390OF.DTL.

11. Equality for All was the lead organization opposing Prop. 8. Other opponents included the League of Women Voters, NAACP, Amnesty International, Google, and a coalition of Silicon Valley executives, *Wikipedia*, s.v. "California Proposition 8 (2008)," accessed September 7, 2010, http://en.wikipedia.org/wiki/Proposition_8.

12. Mark DiCamillo, "Why Prop. 8 confounded pre-election pollsters," *San Francisco Chronicle*, November 10, 2008, http://www.sfgate.com/cgi-bin/article.cgi?f=/c/a/2008/11/10/EDGQ140F5R.DTL.

13. Katie Maloney, "Did Prop 8 voters know what they were voting for?" *Newsweek*, August 3, 2010. San Francisco mayor Gavin Newsom's statement in a commercial about Prop. 8—"The door's wide open now. It's going to happen, whether you like it or not"—was also blamed for a shift in the polls in favor of Prop. 8.

14. "Reneging on a right," *Los Angeles Times*, August 8, 2008, http://articles.latimes.com/2008/aug/08/opinion/ed-marriage8.

15. Green, *Faith Factor*, appendix A.

16. Joe Pyrah, "LDS donate millions to fight gay marriage," *Daily Herald*, September 16, 2008, www.heraldextra.com/content/view/280669/17/.

17. Jesse McKinley and Kirk Johnson, "Mormons tipped scale in ban on gay marriage," *New York Times*, November 11, 2008, http://www.nytimes.com/2008/11/15/us/politics/15marriage.html?_r=1.

18. "Church readies members on Proposition 8," *Newsroom*, October 10, 2008, http://beta-newsroom.lds.org/article/church-readies-members-on-proposition-8.

19. Ben Sayre, Leticia Bode, Dhavan Shah, Dave Wilcox, and Chirag Shah, "Agenda setting in a digital age: Tracking attention to California Proposition 8 in social media, online news and conventional news," *Policy & Internet* 2 (2010). See also Richard Viguerie and David Franke, *America's Right Turn: How Conservatives Used New and Alternative Media to Take Power* (Chicago: Bonus Books, 2004) on use of the new media by conservatives.

20. Marcos Breton, "Faith was key factor in Prop. 8 vote," *Sacramento Bee*, November 9, 2008; Patrick Egan and Kenneth Sherrill, "California's Proposition 8: What happened and why," National Gay and Lesbian Task Force report, www.thetaskforce.org/downloads/issues/egan_Sherrill_prop8_1_6_09.pdf (accessed August 24, 2010).

21. Rubin Vives, "Mormon church to be fined by state political commission over Proposition 8," *Los Angeles Times*, June 9, 2010; Sayre et al., "Agenda setting in a digital age"; Ann Morgan, "Ad campaign re-branding Mormons as regular folks," *Pittsburgh Post-Gazette*, August 22, 2010.

22. *Strauss v. Horton* 46 Cal.4th 364 (2009).

23. *Perry et al. v. Schwarzenegger et al.*, 704 F. Supp. 2d 921 (N.D. Cal. 2010).

24. Opinion of Judge Walker, *Perry et al.*, 135.

25. Donald P. Haider-Markel, Alana Querze, and Kara Lindaman, "Win, lose, or draw? A reexamination of direct democracy and minority rights," *Political Research Quarterly* 60 (2007): 304–14.

26. Lincoln Caplan, "Forget the tone, it's dissent that matters," *Washington Post*, July 6, 2003.

27. Dahlia Lithwick, "A brilliant ruling: Judge Walker's decision to overturn Prop 8 is factual, well-reasoned, and powerful," Slate.com, August 4, 2010, http://www.slate.com/id/2262766/ (accessed August 30, 2010).

28. Egan and Persily, "Court decisions."

29. Darren E. Sherkat, Kylan M. de Vries, and Stacia Creek, "Race, religion, and opposition to same-sex marriage," Southern Illinois University working papers, 2009, http://opensiuc.lib.siu.edu/ps.wp/5.

30. *The Fundamentals*, published by the Bible Institute of Los Angeles, included an essay in volume VII by Harry Beach on "The Decadence of Darwinism." Edward Larson, in *Summer for the Gods: The Scopes Trial and America's Continuing Debate over Science and Religion* (New York: Basic Books, 2006), 31–43, describes the fundamentalist reaction to trends in modernist thought during the nineteenth century among mainline Protestants. His detailed history of the background, events, and consequences of the Scopes trial won the Pulitzer Prize in history in 1998.

31. Larson, *Summer for the Gods*, 24–25.

32. George M. Thomas, Lisa R. Peck, and Channin G. De Haan, "Reforming education, transforming religion," in *The Secular Revolution: Power, Interests, and Conflict in the Secularization of American Public*, ed. Christian Smith (Berkeley: University of California Press, 2003), chap. 8.

33. Larson, in *Summer for the Gods*, 43, describes Bryan's campaign and actions against evolution considered in other states before the Scopes trial.

34. Larson, in *Summer for the Gods*, 45–48, describes the legislative debate over the Butler bill and the role of the governor and university president.

35. The ACLU originally defended labor unions and freedom of speech; the Scopes trail represented its first foray into the issue of establishment of religion. It challenged the Tennessee law on all three grounds (Larson, *Summer for the Gods*, 60–75).

36. Larson, in *Summer for the Gods*, chapters 4 through 7, provides a detailed account of all aspects of the trial and of Darrow's attack on Bryan's support for biblical literalism.

37. Cited in P. C. Kemeny, "Power, ridicule, and the destruction of religious moral reform politics in the 1920s," in Smith, ed., *The Secular Revolution*, 231.

38. Larson, in *Summer for the Gods*, chap. 9, critiques the play and movie versions of the Scopes trial. As he notes, the play's authors, Jerome Lawrence and Robert E. Lee, took liberties with the story in order to highlight the dangers of McCarthyism during the 1950s.

39. For discussion of these cases, see John Witte and Joel A. Nichols, *Religion and the American Constitutional Experiment*, 3rd ed. (Boulder, CO: Westview Press, 2011).

40. On state laws and court challenges since the Scopes trial, see Dorothy Nelkin, *The Creation Controversy: Science or Scripture in the Schools* (Boston: Beacon Press, 2002); and Lenny Flack, "Creationism: A short legal history," www.talkreason.org/articles/historyID.cfm.

41. Frank Schaeffer's influential book *Bad News for Modern Man* (Westchester, IL: Crossway Books, 1984) argues that "secular elites" are moving the country away from Christianity and attacking traditional values.

42. These arguments of the Discovery Institute are summarized at http://www.designinference.com/inteldes.htm. John Brockman's edited book *Intelligent Thought: Science versus the Intelligent Design Movement* (New York: Vintage Books, 2006) provides a detailed summary and critique of ID claims by prominent scientists.

43. *Edwards v. Aguillard*, 482 U.S. 578 (1987). On the "wedge," see Gordy Slack, *The Battle over the Meaning of Everything: Evolution, Intelligent Design, and a School Board in Dover, PA* (San Francisco: Jossey-Bass, 2007), 76–77, and Barbara Forrest and Paul Gross, *Creationism's Trojan Horse: The Wedge of Intelligent Design* (New York: Oxford University Press, 2007).

44. Slack, *The Battle over the Meaning of Everything*, 15.

45. Slack, *The Battle over the Meaning of Everything*, 18.

46. Slack, *The Battle over the Meaning of Everything*, 13. See also William P. Davis, Dean H. Kenyon, and Charles B. Thaxton, *Of Pandas and People: The Central Question of Biological Origins*, 2nd ed. (Dallas, TX: Haughton Publishing Company, 1993).

47. Full statement in Slack, *The Battle over the Meaning of Everything*, 98.

48. Slack, *The Battle over the Meaning of Everything*, 63.

49. Slack, *The Battle over the Meaning of Everything*, 156.

50. For details of testimony by both sides at the trial, see Slack, *The Battle over the Meaning of Everything*, chapters 7–12, and the 2008 *Nova* broadcast on PBS, "Judgment day: Intelligent design on trial," http://www.pbs.org/wgbh/nova/programs/.

51. Slack, *The Battle over the Meaning of Everything*, 143.
52. Slack, *The Battle over the Meaning of Everything*, 153.
53. Judge Jones's decision is *Kitzmiller v. Dover Area School District* (400 FSupp 2d.707 M. D. PA., 2005).
54. For the Discovery Institute reactions to Jones's ruling, see their book *Traipsing into Evolution: Intelligent Design and the* Kitzmiller vs. Dover *Decision* (Seattle, WA: Discovery Institute Press, 2006).
55. Glenn Branch and Eugenie Scott, "The latest face of creationism in the classroom," *Scientific American*, January 2009.
56. Eric Plutzer and Michael Berkman report on a nationwide teacher survey funded by the National Science Foundation in "Trends: Evolution, creationism, and the teaching of human origins in schools," *Public Opinion Quarterly* 72 (2008): 540–53.
57. Michael Berkman and Eric Plutzer, *Evolution, Creationism, and the Battle to Control America's Classrooms* (New York: Cambridge University Press, 2010).
58. "Authors scramble to make textbooks conform to Texas science standards," *Science* 324 (2009): 1385.
59. Pat Robertson, "God may smite down town that voted out anti-evolution school board," Associated Press, November 11, 2005.
60. *Nova* executive producer Paula Ansell (2007) explains why PBS covered such a controversial case at www.pbs.org/wgbh/nova/evolution/why-nova-covered-case.html.
61. Pew Research Center, "Pew Research Center Pollwatch: Reading the polls on evolution and creationism," September 28, 2005, http://www.pewtrusts.org/our_work_report_detail.aspx?id=23428.
62. Frank Newport, "Majority of Republicans doubt theory of evolution," Gallup News Service, June 11, 2007, www.gallup.com/poll/27847/Majority-Republicans-Doubt.
63. The 2008 GSS found that 40 percent of respondents had "a great deal" of confidence in science (a decline of 4 percent since 1980), but only 20 percent expressed such confidence in organized religion (a decline from 36 percent in 1980). Other polls show recent declines in beliefs that global warming is occurring or is attributable to human action, and increases in views that its effects have been exaggerated (www.pollingreport.com/enviro.htm).
64. Todd Woody, "Foes outspend backers of Proposition 23," *New York Times*, October 11, 2010. The initiative would suspend a state law to cut greenhouse gas emissions.
65. George J. Annas, "Intelligent judging—evolution in the classroom and courtroom," *New England Journal of Medicine* 354, no. 21 (2006): 2277–81. See also David K. DeWolf, "The 'Teach the Controversy' controversy," *University of St. Thomas Journal of Law and Public Policy* IV (2010): 320–34.
66. Berkman and Plutzer, *Evolution, Creationism*, chap. 9.
67. Berkman and Plutzer, *Evolution, Creationism*, 218.
68. Assessment of Christian Right influence is based on the proportion of the state's Republican Party committee who are members or supporters of the Christian Right. Wilcox and Robinson, *Onward Christian Soldiers?*, 105.

69. Turnout in direct-democracy states is, on average, 4 percent higher than in states lacking initiatives or referenda. Caroline Tolbert, John Grummel, and Daniel Smith, "The effect of direct democracy on turnout in the American states," *American Politics Research* 29 (2001): 625–48.

70. Green, *Faith Factor*, appendix B.

71. The Alan Guttmacher Institute, the research arm of Planned Parenthood, provides information on state abortion regulations, www.guttmacher.org/pubs/sfaa/south_dakota.html.

72. Data on state abortion rates in 2005 from the Guttmacher Institute State Data Center, www.guttmacher.org/datacenter/profiles/SD.jsp. The Yes For Life website describes alternatives to abortions it provides through Pregnancy Resource Centers, www.voteyesforlife.com.

73. "Report of the South Dakota Task Force to Study Abortion," December 2005. http://voteyesforlife.com.antlia.makeko.com/docs/Task_Force_Report.pdf.

74. http://ballotpedia.org/wiki/index.php/South_Dakota_Abortion_Ban,_Initiated_Measure_11_(2008)

75. Shawn Bowler and Todd Donovan, "Measuring the effects of direct democracy on state policy," *State Politics and Policy Quarterly* 4 (2004): 345–63.

76. The Pew Research Center report "Abortion, the court, and the public" (October 5, 2005) summarizes recent survey data on abortion and the impact of question wording on opinions, http://people-press.org/2005/10/03/abortion-the-court-and-the-public/.

77. Governor Rounds's popularity rebounded after the abortion ban was repealed in 2006, and he was reelected in 2008 (www.ballotpedia.org/wiki/index.php/Mike_Rounds).

78. http://ballotpedia.org/wiki/index.php/South_Dakota_Abortion_Ban,_Initiated_Measure_11_(2008)

79. Judy Keen, "Republicans opposed to abortion ban lose in S.D.," *USA Today*, June 7, 2006.

80. Jeffrey Rosen, "The day after *Roe*," *Atlantic*, June 2006.

81. Democracy Now, Sarah Stoesz interview, March 28, 2006, www.democracynow.org/2006/3/28/south_dakota_abortion_ban_draws_fiery.

82. Data on contributions from http://ballotpedia.org/wiki/index.php/South_Dakota_Abortion_Ban,_Initiated_Measure_11_(2008).

83. Kelsey Burke, "The Role of Risk in Social Movement Activities and Activist Identity: A Case Study of South Dakota Pro-Choice Clergy" (graduate research paper, Department of Sociology, University of Pittsburgh, 2009).

84. Religious Coalition for Reproductive Choice, "South Dakota pastors urge voters to repeal state abortion ban," October 10, 2006, www.rcrc.org/news/Pastorsphoto.cfm.

85. Data on contributions from http://ballotpedia.org/wiki/index.php/South_Dakota_Abortion_Ban,_Initiated_Measure_11_(2008). Healthy Families brought suit to find out the name of an "anonymous" contributor of $750,000 to Yes for Life, but the case was settled and the donor remained secret. "SD officials reach deal in abortion donation case," Sioux Falls *Argus Leader*, November 25, 2009.

86. 2006 Ballot Question Pamphlet compiled by the South Dakota secretary of state Chris Nelson, www.sdsos.gov/electionsvoteregistration/electvoterpdfs/2006/%20Pamphlet&Cover.pdf.

87. Kevin Wooster, "Doctors association joins abortion fray," *Rapid City Journal*, October 9, 2008.

88. Hotline on Call, "Allen, Romney, and McCain on the South Dakota abortion ban," February 28, 2006, www.hotlineoncall.nationaljournal.com/archives/2006/02/allen_romney_an.phpBush/McCain.

89. "Going too far," *Rapid City Journal*, October 28, 2006; "Abortion ban, death penalty debates should be separate," *Madison Daily Leader*, October 21, 2006; *Aberdeen News*, "HB1215 won't stop abortions," October 24, and "Abortion not the answer to unwanted pregnancy," October 26, 2006.

90. "South Dakota paper bans abortion opinions," *Editor & Publisher*, March 10, 2006, www.editorandpublisher.com/eandp/search/article_display.jsp?vnu_content_id=1002155681.

91. Data on turnout and election results from the Office of the South Dakota Secretary of State, www.sdsos.gov/electionsvoteregistration/pastelections.

92. Denise Ross, "Why won't South Dakota ban abortion?" *New Republic*, December 2, 2006.

93. Survey conducted October 2006 by Mason-Dixon Polling and Research for Sioux Falls *Argus Leader* and KELO-TV, reported in Steven Erteit, "SD abortion ban tied among state voters," October 27, 2006, www.lifenews.com/state3589.html.

94. Ben Dunsmoor, "South Dakota legislative committee kills abortion ban bill," KELO News, February 21, 2007, www.keloland.com/NewsDetail6162.cfm?Id=54884.

95. Wooster, "Doctors' association joins abortion fray."

96. Eric Ostermeier, "Minnesota leads nation in voter turnout," Smart Politics, December 16, 2008, blog.lib.umn.edu/cspg/smartpolitics/2008/12/minnesota_leads_nation_in_vote_1.phple.

97. Associated Press, "8th Circuit: S. D. can enforce abortion counseling law," June 30, 2008, www.firstamendmentcenter.org/news.aspx?id=20242.

98. Ross, "Why won't South Dakota ban abortion?"; Pamela Carriveau and Laura Colmenero-Chilberg, "Voters reframe the abortion policy debate: A theoretical analysis of abortion attitudes in South Dakota," *Journal of the Great Plains Sociological Association* (December 2010).

99. William Saletan, *Bearing Right: How Conservatives Won the Abortion War* (Berkeley: University of California Press, 2003).

100. Opinion Dynamics/Fox News Poll, as reported by Angus Reid Public Opinion (2005) at www.angus-reid.com/polls/11766/most_americans_decry_south_dakota_abortion_ban/.

101. Thomas Stratmann, "Is spending more potent for or against a proposition?" *American Journal of Political Science* 50 (2006): 788–801.

102. Ballotpedia.org provides links by year to outcomes of state elections and ballot measures.

103. Rosen, "The day after *Roe*"; Dale A. Osterle (2006), "The South Dakota referendum on abortion: Lessons from a popular vote on a controversial right," *Yale*

*Law Journal Pocket Part* 116(22): 122–25, http://thepocketpart.org/2006/11/1/oesterle.htm/.

104. Haider-Markel, Querze, and Lindaman, "Win, lose or draw?"

105. Jongho Roh and D. Donald Haider-Markel, "All politics is not local: National forces in state abortion initiatives," *Social Science Quarterly* 84 (2003): 15–31.

106. Data on contributions from the National Center on Money in State Politics, http://www.followthemoney.org/.

107. Patrick M. Garry, Derek A. Nelsen, and Candace J. Spurlin, "Raising the question of whether out-of-state political contributions may affect a small state's political autonomy: A case study of the South Dakota voter referendum on abortion," *South Dakota Law Review* 35 (2010).

108. *Citizens United v. Federal Election Commission*, 130 S.Ct. 876 (2010).

## CHAPTER 7

1. Chapters in David E. Campbell, ed., *A Matter of Faith: Religion in the 2004 Presidential Election* (Washington, DC: Brookings, 2007), critically evaluate the impact of evangelicals and "moral issues" voters in 2004.

2. Bolce and De Maio, "Secularists."

3. For a similar conclusion based on GSS data to 1999, see Hout and Fischer, "Why more Americans have no religious preference."

4. Divorce rates as a function of state economic conditions are considered in Hansen, *Globalization and the Politics of Pay*, chapter 5; Pew Social Trends Staff, "The decline of marriage and rise of new families," www.pewsocialtrends.org, November 18, 2010.

5. Faith Matters survey cited in Putman and Campbell, *American Grace*; Darren Sherkat, "Beyond believing but not belonging," The Immanent Frame blog, February 17, 2010, www.blogs.ssrc.org/tif/2010/02/17/beyond-believing-but-not-belonging.htm.

6. Robert Wuthnow, *After the Baby Boomers: How Twenty- and Thirty-Somethings Are Shaping the Future of American Religion* (Princeton, NJ: Princeton University Press, 2007).

7. Darren Sherkat, Kylan M. de Vries, and Stacia Creek, "Race, religion, and opposition to same-sex marriage," *Social Science Quarterly* 91 (2010): 80–98. Their analysis of GSS data shows very similar trends in support for gay marriage among recent cohorts of whites and African Americans.

8. Taeku Lee, *Mobilizing Public Opinion: Black Insurgency and Racial Attitudes in the Civil Rights Era* (Chicago: University of Chicago Press, 2002).

9. Clem Brooks, "Religious influence and the politics of family decline concern," *American Sociological Review* 67 (2002): 191–211.

10. Herzog, *Sex in Crisis*.

11. On the strategic use of issues by the Religious Right, see Formicola, *The Politics of Values*. According to the Pew Research Center, only 40 percent of evangelicals under thirty considered themselves Republican in 2008, but in 2006, 55 percent of them did. More conservative views, based on a 2002 survey, are

reported by Buster G. Smith and Byron Johnson, "The liberalization of young evangelicals: A research note," *Journal for the Scientific Study of Religion* 49 (2010): 351–60.

12. Kate Zernike, "Tea Party avoids divisive social issues," *New York Times*, March 10, 2010. She notes that some Tea Party groups, such as the 9/12 faction led by Glenn Beck, a Mormon, did support traditional Christian values.

13. "NAE begins search of Cizik's replacement," People for the American Way, Right Wing Watch, January 28, 2009, www.rightwingwatch.org/category/individuals/richard-cizik.

14. Wilcox and Robinson, *Onward Christian Soldiers?*, 184.

15. Herzog, *Sex in Crisis*, 72.

16. Ben Smith, "Tea Parties stir evangelical fears," Politico.com, March 12, 2010, www.politico.com/news/stories/0310/34291.html.

17. Zachary Courser, "The Tea Party at the election," *The Forum* 8 (2010): article 5, www.bepress.com/forum.vol8/iss4/art5.

18. Linda Hirshman, "Unnecessarily evil: Reclaiming the morality of abortion and the overdue change to the Democratic platform," Slate.com, August 12, 2008, www.slate.com/id/2197363. The role of abortion in health care reform is described in Lawrence R. Jacobs and Theda Skocpol, *Health Care Reform and American Politics* (New York: Oxford University Press, 2010).

19. Herzog, in *Sex in Crisis*, 177–79, provides examples of state or local resistance to abstinence education, including refusal by some states to accept federal funding for it.

20. Jane Mayer, "Covert operations: The billionaire brothers who are waging a war against Obama," *New Yorker*, August 30, 2010. Contributions for Haiti were solicited online at www.richarddawkinsfoundation.org.

21. "Religion in the 2010 elections: A preliminary look," Pew Forum, November 3, 2010, www.pewforum.org/Politics-and-Elections/Religion-in-the-2010-elections.htm.

22. Michael P. McDonald, "Voter turnout in the 2010 midterm election," *The Forum* 8 (2010): article 8, www.bepress.com/forum.vol8/iss4/art8.

23. David Gibson, "Tea Party is much like the Religious Right—only more so, survey finds," www.politicsdaily.com/2010/10/05/tea-party-is-much-like-the-religious-right.htm.

24. Courser, "The Tea Party at the election."

25. Robert Pear, "Push for stricter abortion limits is expected in House," *New York Times*, December 12, 2010; Eric Eckholm, "Across country, lawmakers push abortion curbs," *New York Times*, January 22, 2011, A1.

26. "Impeachment as intimidation," editorial, *New York Times*, January 12, 2011; Eve Conant, "I do? I don't! Brian Brown is leading the fight against gay marriage. And succeeding," *Newsweek*, November 22, 2010, 38–39.

27. Tom Smith, "Changes in family structure, family values, and politics, 1973–2006," in *Red, Blue, and Purple America*, ed. Ruy Teixeira (Washington, DC: Brookings, 2008), 147–93.

28. Hanna Rosin, "Did Christianity cause the crash?" *Atlantic*, December 2009.

29. National Association of Latino Elected and Appointed Officials, "Record number of Latino Republicans to join new Congress," www/naleo.org/

pr/pr11-03-10.html; Pew Research Center Publication, "The Latino vote in the 2010 elections," http://pewresearch.org/pubs/1790/2010-midterm-elections-exit-poll-hispanic-vote.html.

30. Pew Research Center Forum on Religion and Public Life, "Faith on the Hill: The religious composition of the 112th Congress," January 5, 2011, www.pewforum.org/Government/Faith-on-the-Hill. Cited in Charles M. Blow, "Religion and representation," *New York Times*, January 7, 2011.

31. Witte and Nichols, in *Religion and the American Constitutional Experiment*, describe the separationist and accommodationist perspectives on church/state relations.

32. Ralph Reed is the executive director of the Judicial Confirmation Network. Federal judicial appointments by recent presidents are summarized in *Wikipedia*, s.v. "Judicial appointment history for the United States federal courts," http://en.wikipedia.org/wiki/Judicial_appointment_history_for_United_States_federal_courts.

33. Anita L. Allen, "Atmospherics: Abortion law and philosophy," *Scholarship at Penn Law*, Paper 180 (2007), http://lsr.nellco.org/upenn_wps/180.

34. Gardner Harris, "U.S. judge rules against Obama's stem cell policy," *New York Times*, August 24, 2010. The ruling was later stayed by the Federal Circuit Court, and embryonic stem-cell research is continuing on appeal by Obama and NIH.

35. Putnam and Campbell, in *American Grace*, 406–14, consider reasons for recent declines in support for abortion by the "Juno generation" of younger Americans.

36. Rosen, "The day after *Roe*"; Tamar Lewin, "Falling for years, abortion rate levels off, with more choosing medication over surgery," *New York Times*, December 2010.

37. John Schwartz, "The federal courts: Movement is seen on gay rights issues," *New York Times*, September 22, 2010, A18.

38. Paul Brace and Brent Boyea, "State public opinion and the practice of electing judges," *American Journal of Political Science* 52 (2008): 360–72.

39. Putnam and Campbell, *American Grace*.

40. Lawrence R. Jacobs and Theda Skocpol, eds., *Inequality and American Democracy: What We Know and What We Need to Learn* (New York: Russell Sage, 2005), chap. 2: "Inequalities of political voice."

41. Wilcox and Robinson, *Onward Christian Soldiers?*, 203.

42. Jennifer Aaker, Andy Smith, and Carlye Adler, *The Dragonfly Effect: Quick, Effective, and Powerful Ways to Use Social Media to Drive Social Change* (San Francisco: Jossey-Bass, 2010). For a more critical perspective on social networks, see Malcolm Gladwell, "Small change: Why the revolution will not be tweeted," *New Yorker*, October 4, 2010.

43. Michael Shermer, "Political science: Psychological research reveals how and why liberals and conservatives differ," *Scientific American*, December 2009, 38.

44. Putnam and Campbell, *American Grace*, chap. 13: "Religion and good neighborliness." More liberal policy views are also held by another fast-growing segment of Americans: people who claim to be "spiritual" but have no formal religious ties. Laura R. Olson, "The Politics of 'Spiritual but Not Religious' America" (paper presented at the Midwest Political Science Association, Chicago, April 2011).

45. Clyde Wilcox and Ted G. Jelen, "Evangelicals and political tolerance," *American Politics Quarterly* 18 (1990): 25–46; Marie A. Eisenstein, "Religion and political tolerance in the United States," in *The Oxford Handbook of Religion and American Politics*, 427–50; Putnam and Campbell, *American Grace*.

46. Speech at inauguration, January 20, 2009. Studies in Gaston Espinosa, ed., *Religion, Race, and the American Presidency* (Lanham, MD: Rowman & Littlefield, 2010) describe the increasingly important role religion plays in presidential elections and public policy.

47. Sharyl Attkisson, "Quran burning 'ugly' but free speech," *CBS News Investigates*, September 9, 2010, www.cbsnews.com/8301-31727_162-20016003-10391695.html; Adelle Banks, "Florida pastor oversees Quran burning," *USA Today*, March 21, 2011.

48. William Martin, *Secular State, Religious People: The American Model*, Rice University, Baker Institute for Public Policy, April 2006.

49. Charles Blow, "Religion and representation."

# Index

AAI. *See* Atheist Alliance International
*Aberdeen News*, 138
abortion, 2, 23, 51, 54, 74–75, 82–83, 86, 96, 105, 113; ANES questions on, 54, 67, 70, 76–78, 93–95, 142, 148, 150–52, 155; candidate positions on, 66–67, *68*, 76, 78, 152; claims of health risks, 94–95, 104, 135, 138; party positions on, 66–67, *68*, 69, 75–76, 78, 81, 159; rate of, 135, 157; secular attitudes toward, 52, 54–55, 62; South Dakota referenda, 117, 134–41; state restrictions on, 115, 135–36, 140, 143, 154; trends in attitudes toward, 19, 37–38, 39, *52*, *53*, 62, 87, 136, 140–41, 157
Abramoff, Jack, 93
abstinence education, ix, 24, 30–31, 93, 97, 101, 106, 115, 135, 143, 152
ACLU Foundation. *See* American Civil Liberties Union
Acquired Immune Deficiency Syndrome (AIDS), 17, 93, 150, 158
ADF. *See* Alliance Defense Fund
ADL. *See* Anti-Defamation League
Affordable Health Care Act, 151
African Americans, 33, 47, 52, 59–62, 67, 102, 103–4, 121–22, 134, 146–47, 149, 155; church affiliations, 44–45, 71, 84; Democratic voting by, 49, 61, 109, 123; and public policies, 84, 146–48; religious beliefs, 33, 35, 43, 45, 47, 60, 103, 121, 147–48
age: and religious beliefs, 30–33, 35, 37, 39, 45, 60, 62, 77, 86, 145–48, 151, 153
agnostics, 8, 14, 22, 25–26, 52, 100, 155, 162
AIDS. *See* Acquired Immune Deficiency Syndrome
AIPAC. *See* American-Israeli Political Action Committee
Alabama, 73, 77, 102
Alan Guttmacher Institute, 135
Alaska, 8
Alberts, Bruce, 104
Alliance Defense Fund (ADF), *92*, 95–96, 157
AMA. *See* American Medical Association
American Atheists, 1, 89, *98*, 99–100
American Civil Liberties Union (ACLU), x, 1, 14–15, 90, 95, *98*, 101, 103, 106, 115, 125, 128–32, 137, 156, 162
American College of Obstetrics and Gynecology (ACOG), 104, 135, 156

American Humanist Association (AHA), *98*, 100
American-Israeli Political Action Committee (AIPAC), 113, 181n71
American Medical Association (AMA), 11, 156
American National Election Studies (ANES), xii, 5–7, 20, 26, 28, 37, 42–43, 45, 47–49, 51–53, 56–59, 63, 67–70, 75–77, 82–83, 145–46, 148; thermometer scores, 51, 54–55, 61, 64, 99, 103, 108
American Political Science Association (APSA), 7, 11
American Psychological Association (APA), 135
American Revolution, 21
Americans United for Separation of Church and State (AUSCS), 14, 73, *98*, 101–2, 115, 129
American Taliban, 4, 116
American Values Survey (2010), 153
Amish, 101
Anabaptists, 5
Anderson, John, 50
ANES. *See* American National Election Studies
Answers in Genesis, *92*, 94
Anti-Defamation League (ADL), *98*, 103, 115
APA. *See* American Psychological Association
APSA. *See* American Political Science Association
*Argus Leader* (Sioux Falls), 138
Arkansas, 126
Ark Encounter, 1
Asian Americans, 22, 155
*Associated Press Stylebook*, 108
Atheist Alliance International (AAI), *98*, 100
atheists, x, 6, 25–26, 39, 89, 124, 128, 155, 158, 162; as presidential candidates, 26, *27*, 146; among seculars, 8, 14, 162; organizations, 14, *98*, 99–100; public attitudes toward, 16, 19, 26, *27*, 28–29, 31, 35, 54–55, 60–61, 99–100, 145–46, 160
AUSCS. *See* Americans United for Separation of Church and State

*Bad News for Modern Man* (Schaeffer), 17, 158
Bakker, Jim, 108
Bakker, Tammy, 108
*Baltimore Sun*, 126
Baptists, 44
Behe, Michael, 127, 129
belief in God, 5, 8, *9*, 21, 23, *25*, *26*, 28–30, 32, 35, 155, 158, 162
Bible, 4–5, 8, 19, 29–30, 32, 35, 111, 147
Bible Belt, 12–13, 23, 47, 73, 77, 87, 109, 125, 145
biblical literalism, 22–23, 30–34, 43, 45, 47, 111, 126, 147–48
Black Muslims, 45
Blaine amendments, 22
Blankenhorn, David, 123
Blow, Charles M., 155, 162
Boehner, John, 154
Bolce, Louis, xi, 7, 42–43
*Bowers v. Hardwick* (1986), 118, 123
Breast Cancer Prevention Institute, *92*, 93
Brown, Jerry, 122
Bryan, William Jennings, 125–26, 132
Buchanan, John, 102
Buckingham, Bill, 130
Buddhists, 32, 112
Bush, George H. W., 49, 156
Bush, George W., ix, 3, 67–68, 69–70, 72, 74, 76, 81, 82, 84, 100, 104, 105, 108, 114, 115, 129, 131, 134, 144, 151; abortion views of, 68, 70, 105, 138; medical/scientific appointments, 24, 94, 97, 106
Butler law (Tennessee), 125

California, 17, 56, 91, 96, 101, 103, 104, 117–23, 141–42, 144, 148, 157–58, 161; constitution of, 119, 122–23
California Fair Political Practices Commission, 122
California Faith for Equality, 152

California Family Code, 119
California Field Poll, 120
campaign contributions, 10, 58, 63, 74, 119–21, 137, 142
campaign participation, *57*, 58–61, 63–64, 87, 96, 159
Campbell, David E., 86, 97
Campolo, Tony, 113
candidate differences: perceptions of, 66, 76, 82–84, *85*, 87, 152
Casey, Robert, 111
Catholic Chancery Office, 137
Catholic League, 1, 107
Catholics. *See* Roman Catholics
CBS. *See* Columbia Broadcasting System
Centers for Disease Control, 135
Central America, 114
charismatics, 5, 107
Chittester, Joan, 113
Christian Broadcasting Network, 91, *92*
Christian Coalition, 13, 91, *92*, 93, 95–97, 144, 150
Christian Democratic parties, 21
Christian fundamentalists, 29, 90, 103; and campaign activism, 60–61, 64; secular antipathy toward, 4, 14, 16–17, 54–55, 59–61, 74, 87, 97, 144, 152, 160
Christian Legal Society, *92*, 95
Christian media, 2, 13, 56, 89–91, 107, 144
Christian nation, 22, 154, 156
Christian Right, 103, 111–12, 131, 134–36, 151, 153–54
Christianity/Christians, 59–61, 87, 95, 102, 107, 113, 126, 152–54, 162; attitudes toward, 54–56; beliefs, 22, 103. *See also specific denominations*
Christmas, 1, 100, 156
Chuck Colson Prison Fellowship, 13
church attendance, ix–x, 2–3, 6–8, 10, 16, 18–21, 23–25, 28–30, 32–33, 35, 37, 38–39, 42–43, 45, 47, 56, 59–60, 63–64, 66, 68, 70–71, 75–76, 78, 81, 82, 84, 86–88, 96, *110*, 112, 133, 144, 146, 148, 152, 159

church membership, 5, 45, 56, 109, 159
Citizens for Excellence in Education, 97
*Citizens United v. Federal Election Commission* (2010), 96, 142
civil libertarians, x, 17, 90, *98*, 101–2, 155
Civil Rights Act of 1964, 12, 149
civil unions, 51, 119, 122
Cizik, Richard, 150
clergy, 6, 56, 71, 73, 101, 113, 121, 137, 141, 149
Clinton, Bill, 113, 118, 154
Code of Professional Practice and Conduct for Educators, 128
cohorts: analysis of, 32–33, 169n35; and religious beliefs, 35, *36*, 37, 39, 145, 161
Cold War, 99
Collins, Francis, 95
Colorado, 8, 141
Columbia, District of, 158
Common Cause, 12
*Common Sense* (Paine), 21
Compte, Auguste, 149
Concerned Women of America, *92*, 102
confidence in organized religion, 29, 31, 32, 35, 39
Congress, 7, 15, 17, 22–23, 48, 49, 51, 56, 65–66, 91, 99, 101, 103, 104, 107, 118, 134, 139, 145, 149, 153, 154, 155, 156
Congressional Prayer Caucus, 1
conservative Christians, ix–xi, 2, 4–6, 13, 90, 96, 103, 108, 109, 126, 128–29, 131, 152
conservative Jews, 47
constitutions, state, 118–20, 158
Constitution, U.S., 22, 118. *See also* First Amendment; Full Faith and Credit clause; Tenth Amendment
Copernicus, Nicolaus, 20
Counter-Reformation, 20
countervailing power, 90, 116–17
courts: and the Religious Right, 14, 95, 107, 154; and scientific evidence, 106, 123, 130–32, 156–58

creationism, 3, 15, 24, 38, 103, 104–5, 124, 126–33. *See also Edwards v. Aguillard*; intelligent design
Creation Museum, 1, 94
Crist, Charles, 138
culture war, 2, 37–39, 65, 160, 162; critiques of, 62, 65; and secular mobilization, 109

Darrow, Clarence, 125–26
Darwin, Charles, 22, 124–25, 128–29, 132
Darwinism, 124–28
Daschle, Tom, 134
Dawkins, Richard, 152
Dayton, Tennessee, 125–26, 132
death penalty, 6, 94, 104, 138, 160
Declaration of Independence, 22
Defense of Marriage Act (DOMA), ix, 118–19, 124, 157
defense spending, 84, 113, 160, *161*
DeGeneres, Ellen, 15
Delaware, 154
De Maio, Gerald, xi, 42–43
Dembski, William, 127
Democratic National Convention, 8, 111, 151; delegates, 8, 15, 109, *110*
Democratic Party, x, xi, 2, 4, 13, 15–17, 29, 42, 55, 59–60, 61, 62–63, 67–70, 72, 74, 76, 77, 90, 96, 109–11, 112, 114, 121, 122, 133, 134, 148, 150–51, 153, 156, 160; African Americans and, 49, 61, 109, 123; secular ties with, 41, 48–51, 60, 62–65, 74, 89–90, 108, 109, 115, 144, 162
demographics of religious groups, 29–36, 45–47
demographic trends, 17, 28–29, 39, 45, 59, 143, 145–46, 154, 161; in race/ethnicity, 33, 43–44, 46, 146–49, 154–55
deoxyribonucleic acid (DNA), 127
direct democracy, 10, 134, 141; and bans on gay marriage, 3, 14, 119, 158; impact on minorities, 123, 142; in South Dakota, x, 134, 136–40
Discovery Institute, 93–94, 104, 127, 129–33

divorce, 6, 12, 17, 45, 62, 102, 118, 145, 149, 158
DNA. See deoxyribonucleic acid
Dobson, James, 13, 92
DOMA. See Defense of Marriage Act
"don't ask, don't tell" (DADT), 1, 37, 111, 157–58
Dover decision (*Kitzmiller v. Dover Area School District*, 2007), 103, 130–32, 156
Dover, Pennsylvania, 96, 101, 117, 124, 128, 131, 152, 159
Durkheim, Emile, 21

Eagle Forum, 23
Edgar, Bob, 113
education: and religious beliefs, 28–30, 32, *34*, 35, 37, 39, 45, 47, 60, 63–64, 66, 70–71, 75, 77–78, 81, 84, 86, 94–95, 97, 106, 107, 125, 127, 132, 134, 145–46, 152, 159–60; trends in, 8, 32, 39, 87, 152, 159–60
*Edwards v. Aguillard* (1987), 126–27, 129–30
Egan, Patrick, 122
Egypt, 159
elections, presidential: 1980 election, 56, 58; 2004 election, 3, 15, 56, 58, 62–64, 68, 74–75, 81, 84, 108, 111, 114, 119, 144, 150; 2008 election, 56, 58, 61–64, 68, 74, 109, 114, 120, 140
Electoral College, 10
Elliot Institute, 93, 95
emergency contraception, 107, 135, 138
*Engel v. Vitale* (1962), 19, 91
environment, 12, 66, 68, 73, 78, 81, 84, 113, 150, 160
Environmental Protection Agency, 94
*Epperson v. Arkansas* (1968), 126
Equal Rights Amendment (ERA), 3–4, 6, 12–13, 23, 91, 115, 143
Ethical Culture Society, 100, 101, 103
Europe, 6, 20–23, 25, 31, 38, 41, 159
evangelicals, 5, 7, 12, 21–22, 43–44, 46–47, 72–77, 81–87, 90, 92, 95, 97, 105, 109, 110, 111, 112, 113, 134, 150; definitions of, 5–7

evolution, 2, 6, 14, 17, 19, 22–23, 38–39, 93–94, 105, 117, 124–26, 128; and public opinion on, 6, 19, 38–39, 115, 127, 131, 133–34, 145

Facebook, 100, 108, 109
Faith and Freedom Coalition, 93
faith-based public policies, ix, 24, 97, 100, 101, 115, 143
Faith Matters, 146
Falwell, Jerry, 12–13, 105
Family Research Council, 93
family values, 4, 65, 102, 111, 118, 145, 149, 154, 158, 160
Farris, Michael, 95
FAS. *See* Federation of American Scientists
Federal Communications Commission (FCC), 91
federalism, 138, 141–42, 155–58
Federalist Society, 95, 156
Federal Rules of Evidence, 106
Federation of American Scientists, 98, 104
Feminist Majority Foundation, 98, 102, 137
feminists, 17, 90, 102, 144, 151–52
First Amendment, 14, 22, 96, 100, 103, 127, 162
Fischer, Claude S., 39
Florida, 125, 148, 162
*Flying Blind* (report), 105
Focus on the Family, 91, 92, 96, 107, 144, 151
Forbes, James, 113
Forrest, Barbara, 130
Founding Fathers, 22
Freedom from Religion Foundation, 1, 98, 100
Freedom to Marry, 102
free-rider problem, 11–12
free thinkers, 14, 20, 21
Freethought Society, 99
Freud, Sigmund, 21
Full Faith and Credit clause, 118
fundamentalists, 5–6, 22, 29, 47, 55; beliefs of, 28, 35, 43, 103, 107, 108, 124–26, 149; churches, 12, 30, 44, 73, 90, 97, 112
fund-raising appeals, 96, 150–51, 161

Galilei, Galileo, 20–21
Gallup, George, 23
Gallup Poll, 5, 7, 25–26, 28, 38, 42, 52, 131, 133
gay, lesbian, bisexual, and transgender (GLBT), 101, 102–3, 120
gay marriage, 2, 6, 24, 74, 96–97, 102–3, 113, 117, 122, 157; public opinion on, 37, 51, 62, 118–20, 124, 145, 161; and Republican Party strategy, 72, 119, 150; state referenda on, 56, 72, 118–19, 124, 135, 139, 143, 158–59
gay rights, 37, 51, 160
gay rights organizations, 90, 98, 102, 115, 120, 123, 144, 152, 158
gays and lesbians: attitudes toward, 28, 37, 51–52, 55, 62, 102–3, 118, 145–46, 157–58
gender differences, 45, 47, 52, 60, 62, 140
General Social Survey (GSS), xii, 7, 19–20, 24–26, 28–29, 31, 33, 35, 37, 38, 39, 42–43, 45, 64, 112, 133, 145
Genesis, 124–25, 133
Georgia, 125
Gingrich, Newt, 93
Ginsberg, Ruth Bader, 156
GLBT. *See* gay, lesbian, bisexual, and transgender
global warming, x, 16, 94, 105, 106, 107, 133
Goldwater, Barry, 72
*Gonzales v. Carhart* (2007), 24, 87, 94, 104, 140, 142, 156–58
GOP. *See* Grand Old Party (Republicans)
Graham, Billy, 12
Grand Old Party (Republicans) (GOP). *See* Republican Party
GSS. *See* General Social Survey

Haggard, Ted, 92, 108
Haiti, earthquake in, 21

Harrisburg, Pennsylvania, 128, 132
Hawaii, 118
health care, 151, 160
Healthy Families, 137
Heaven, belief in, 5, 21, 23, 29–30, 32, 121
Heritage Foundation, 94
Hillygus, D. Sunshine, 74
Hindus, 54–55, 162
Hispanic Catholics, 23, 43–44, 77, 110, 146, 155
Hispanics, 33, 35, 37, 45–46, 52, 59–60, 62, 67, 121–23, 134, 147–49, 155; church affiliations, 23, 43–44, 155; generational differences, 148; growth in numbers, 146, 148; religious beliefs of, 33, 35, 37, 43, 147
Home School Legal Defense Association (HSLDA), 93, 95, 151
House of Representatives, 10, 49, 57, 154
Hout, Michael, 39
HRC. *See* Human Rights Campaign
HRCF. *See* Human Rights Campaign Fund
HSLDA. *See* Home School Legal Defense Association
Human Life Protection Act, 136
Human Rights Campaign (HRC), 102, 120
Human Rights Campaign Fund (HRCF), 102
Hume, David, 8, 21
Hunter, James D., 2, 65
Hunt, Roger, 138

ID. *See* intelligent design
Idaho, 121
immigration, 44, 73, 123, 146, 148, 154, 155
income, 29, 32, 78; and religiosity, 31, 32, 33, 35, *36*, 37; religious groups compared, 47
independents, 17, 29, 48, 58, 62, 144, 150–51
Ingersoll, Robert, 21
Inglehart, Ronald, 31, 35, 37

*Inherit the Wind* (play), 107, 126
Inquisition, 20–21
intelligent design, 93–94, 96, 101, 104–5, 117, 124, 127–33, 153
interest groups: and organization theory, 11, 74, 90, 96, 114; religious, 73, 83, 89–93, *92*, 109, 113, 115–6, 120; secular, 73, 89–90, 97, *98*, 116, 120
Interfaith Alliance, 112
Internet, 11, 15, 18, 56, 58, 64, 89–90, 108–9, 121, 132, 153, 159
Iowa, 23, 107, 119, 134; Supreme Court of, 96, 154
Iraq, 113, 160
Ireland, 25
Irish Americans, 23
Israel, 62, 103

J Street, *99*, 181n71
Jehovah's Witnesses, 23, 44, 101
Jesuits, 21
Jewish Council for Public Affairs, *98*, 103
Jewish Social Policy Action Network, *98*, 103
Jews, 17, 22–23, 26, 43, 47, 54–55, 62, 90, 102, 103, 110, 112, 115, 134, 162
Jews on First, *98*, 103
Jones, John, III, 129, 133, 156
*Journal of Science and Health Policy*, 106
judicial elections, 96, 142, 154, 158
Justice Foundation, *92*, 94–95
Justice Sunday, 96

Kant, Immanuel, 8
Kellstedt, Lyman A., x, xi
Kennedy, Anthony, 124, 156
Kentucky, 1, 94, 125, 154
Kepler, Johannes, 20
Kerry, John, 63, 67–70, 72, 76, 81, 82, 84, 108, 111, 113, 114
King James Bible, 22
*Kitzmiller v. Dover Area School District*. *See* Dover decision
Koch brothers, 13, 152
Koran, 162
Ku Klux Klan, 126

labor unions, 11, 71–72, 75, 159
Lambda Foundation, *98*, 102
Latinos. *See* Hispanics
Latter-day Saints. *See* Mormons
*Lawrence v. Texas* (2003), 123–24, 141–42, 155, 157
LDS Church. *See* Mormons
leadership: and costs of organization, 13–14, 70; of Religious Left, 113; of Religious Right, 12–13, 18, 91, 127, 149
League of Women Voters, 12
Lehigh University, 129
Lerner, Michael, 112, 113
liberal religious beliefs, 28, 112–13, 125
libertarians, 154
*Life* magazine, 7, 99
Limbaugh, Rush, 14
Lincoln Tunnel, 1, 100
Lisbon earthquake, 21
Log Cabin Republicans, 102
*Los Angeles Times*, 120
Louisiana, 73, 126
Luther, Martin, 20
Lynn, Barry, 101

*Madison Daily Leader*, 138
mainline Protestants, 5–6, 8, 22, 43–44, 112, 115, 124, 134, 137; among party convention delegates, 110; beliefs of, 124–25; declining numbers of, 23, 46–47
marriage, 45, 47, 145, 160. *See also* Defense of Marriage Act; gay marriage
Maryland, 22, 119
Massachusetts, 145
Massachusetts Bay Colony, 21
Massachusetts Institute of Technology (MIT), 105
McCain, John, 49, 58, 61, 67–69, 134, 138, 140
McGovern, George, 72, 134
media, 4, 12, 14, 16–17, 29, 58, 65, 81, 90, 105, 106, 107–9, 115, 120, 122, 143, 147, 149; coverage of Religious Right, 107, 108, 121, 123, 126, 132, 138, 141, 143–44, 149–50. *See also* new media

Medicaid, 135, 154
Medical Institute for Sexual Health, *92*, 93, 94
mega-churches, 13, 23
Mencken, H. L., 126
Mennonites, 112
Methodists, 44
Metropolitan Church, 120
midterm elections: 1998 election, 154; 2006 election, 140, 153–54; 2010 election, 3, 17, 109, 145, 149–52, 154–55, 162
mifeprestone, 102, 135, 157
Miller, Kenneth, 132
Mills, C. Wright, 38
Minnesota, 73, 134, 137
MIT. *See* Massachusetts Institute of Technology
mobilization, 6, 55–61, 65, 77, 137
morality policy, 117; link to political activism, 39; Religious Right and, 150
morality-policy cycle, 17, 64, 89, 115; definition of, 12, 14
morality politics, 10, 90, 97, 114, 117–18, 141, 143
Moral Majority, 13, 23, 91, *92*, 102, 150
Mormons, 5, 22–23, 44, 56, 73, 91, 107, 110, 112; and Proposition 8, 121–22
MoveOn.org, 109
Muslims, 20, 28, 54–55, 101, 108, 112, 162

NAACP. *See* National Association for the Advancement of Colored People
NAACP Legal Defense Fund, *98*, 103–4, 121
Nader, Ralph, 50
NARAL Pro-Choice America, *98*, 102, 137
National Academies of Sciences (NAS), 90, *98*, 104–5, 130, 132
National AeroSpace Agency (NASA), 105
National Association for the Advancement of Colored People (NAACP), *98*, 149

National Association of Evangelicals, 91, *92*, 150
National Cancer Institute, 104
National Center for Science Education (NCSE), *98*, 105–6, 130, 132
National Conservative Political Action Committee, 102
National Council of Churches, 113
National Day of Prayer, 100
National Gay and Lesbian Task Force, *98*, 102
National Institutes of Health, Medicaid, and Medicare, 95, 154, 157
National Opinion Research Center, 19
National Organization for Marriage, *92*, 154
National Organization for Women (NOW), *98*, 102, 137
National Public Radio, 150
National Religious Broadcasters, 91, *92*
National Rifle Association (NRA), 11
National Right to Life Committee, 137
Native Americans, 22, 134–35
Nazism, 162
NCSE. *See* National Center for Science Education
New Deal, 160–61
New England, 22
New Hampshire, 119
new media, 108–9, 121–22
Newton, Isaac, 20
New York, 22, 73, 119, 125, 157
*New York Times*, 162
Nietzsche, Friedrich, 21
No Child Left Behind, 134
nonattendees, 87, 133
Norris, Pippa, 31, 35, 37
Nova program on Dover case, 132–33
NOW. *See* National Organization of Women
NRA. *See* National Rifle Association

Obama, Barack, 1, 63, 67–70, 95, 104, 111, 114, 120, 122, 140, 149–51, 154, 157, 162
Obamacare, 151
occupations, 45, 47, 71

OFA. *See* Organizing for America
*Of Pandas and Peoples* (textbook), 128–30
O'Hair, Madalyn Murray, 89, 99
Oklahoma, 125
Operation Rescue, 150
Oregon, 8
organizational challenges, 10–11
organizational involvement, 56, 58, 63, 66, 70–72, 75–76, 78, 83–88, 159
Organizing for America (OFA), 109
Orthodox Jews, 6, 47, 103, 146

Paine, Thomas, 21
Palestinians, 113
parochial (religious) schools, 14, 22, 101, 150, 156. *See also* Blaine amendments
partial-birth abortion, 104, 115, 136, 140, 156. *See also Gonzales v. Carhart*
partisanship, 50, 56, 59–60, 62–64, 70–71, 75, 77–78, 81, 84, 86
party differences: partisanship and, 67; political elites and, 66, 72, 88; public awareness of, 16, 64–66, 71–76, 86–88, 144, 152, 159
party identification, 51, 59, 71
Pascal, Blaise, 21
Pastors for Moral Choices (P4MC), 137
Paul, Rand, 154
PAW. *See* People for the American Way
Peay, Austin, 125
Pentecostals, 5, 23, 44, 112, 155
People for the American Way (PAW), 73, *98*, 97, 102
Perot, Ross, 50
*Perry et al. v. Schwarzenegger et al.*, 132. *See also* Proposition 8
Pew Forum on Religion and Public Life, 7, 8, 133, 155
Pew National Surveys, 7, 10, 26, 42
Pew Religious Landscape Survey, 8
Philadelphia, 130
Phillips, Virginia, 1
Pitts, Joe, 154
Planned Parenthood, *98*, 102, 135–38, 140

*Planned Parenthood v. Casey* (1992), 136, 157
polarization, 16, 41, 43–44, 48–49, 51, 62, 64–66, 86, 160
policy shocks, 118–19, 124, 143
political elites, 28, 41, 66, 68, 72, 74, 86, 89, 117, 119, 143, 161
political ideology, 28–29, 39, 48–49, 62, 160
political information, 56–57, 63, 88, 96, 159
political parties: congressional voting by, 48, 65; contacts with voters, 56, 58–60, 63–64, 70–71, 88, 96, 112, 152; convention delegates, 8, 15, 109, *110*; platforms, 15, 23, 48, 51, 66, 70, 81, 111, 114, 150–51
political proselytizing, 58, 63, 159
polls on religious beliefs, 2, 23, 25, 28
Populist Farmers' Alliance, 134
pornography, 14, 97, 108
prayer, 1, 9, 29–36
premarital sex, 37, *38*
presidency: voting for minority candidates, 26, *27*, 146; voting by religious groups, 50
primary elections, 50, 58, 63, 136, 150, 159
Princeton University, 112
pro-choice, 84, 136–37, 139, 151–52, 157–58
Progressive Religious Partnership, *99*, 112
Prohibition, 6, 22, 126
pro-life, 4, 135, 137, 142, 157–58
Proposition 8, 91, 101, 104, 117; 2008 vote on, 17, 56, 120; African Americans and, 121–22; California newspapers and, 120, 123; court rulings on, 102–3, 122–23, 132, 152, 161
Prosperity Gospel, 45, 155
ProtectMarriage, 121
Protestant, 21–22, 47, 54–55, 73, 90, 110, 124–25, 153
Putnam, Robert D., 97

Quakers. *See* Society of Friends

racism, 149–50
*Rapid City Journal*, 138
rational choice models: and organizations, 11, 74, 90, 96; and political strategy, 64, 69, 71–72; and voting behavior, 68, 72
Reagan, Ronald, 13, 23, 49, 105
Reconstructionist Jews, 103, 112
Reed, Ralph, 13, 93
Reformation, 5, 20
Reform Judaism, 47, 112, 137
Rehnquist court, 156
religion, belief in importance of, 25, 31, 43, 147
religiosity, 51, 53, 59, 82; beliefs, 6, 8, 23; measures of, 5–7, 10, 26, 43
religious diversity, 28, 54, 74–75, 81, 99
religious language, 111, 114, 161–62
Religious Left, xi, 2, 4, 7, 14, 17, 43, 90, 97, *99*, 111–14, 115, 116; alliance with seculars, 111–12, 144, 152, 158; definition of, 111–12; leaders of, 113; political involvement, 112–14
religious moderates, 7; antipathy to Christian fundamentalists, 61, 64, 144; definition of, 43; demographics, 45, 47; partisan affiliations, 48; partisanship, 50; political involvement, 60; presidential voting by, 49, 62
Religious Right, 1, 4–5, 7, 11, 13, 15, 74, 87; history of, 2–3, 6, 12, 22–23, 143; and the judiciary, 14, 95, 107, 154; leaders of, 12–13, 18, 91, 127, 149; legal organizations, 93, 115, 151, 156; organizational advantages of, 14, 42, 56, 89–90, 97, 114, 116, 122–23, 144, 158, 162; organizations, 91, *92*, 93, 96; policy gains by, 2, 162; political strategies, 56, 119, 139, 150, 161; scandals in, 14, 29, 32, 89, 91, 93, 107–8, 114; ties to Republican Party, 41, 48, 55, 64–65, 108, 109, 134–35, 139, 141, 151
religious threat, 4, 73–74, 77, 87, 97, 99, 108, 122, 160, 162
religious traditionalists, 7; definition of, 43; demographics, 45, 47; partisan affiliations, 48, 62; partisanship,

50; political involvement, 56, 58, 60, 159; presidential voting by, 49, 63
Religious Values survey, 112
Renaissance, 20–21
reproductive rights, 102, 111, 117, 136–37, 145, 151, 160
Republican Party, 2–3, 6–7, 15, 17, 48, 51, 55, 56, 59–60, 61, 62, 63, 64, 65, 67–69, 76–78, 89, 91, 94, 107, 108, 110–11, 119, 129, 133, 134, 138, 145, 148, 150, 153–155, 156, 160; in the states, 13, 23, 72, 86, 109; religiosity and votes for, 49, *50*
Rhode Island, 73
Richard Dawkins Foundation for Reason and Science, *98*, 106, 152
Right Wing Watch, 102
Roberts, Oral, 12, 156
Robertson, Pat, 13, 23, 92, 95, 107, 132, 150
*Roe v. Wade* (1973), x, 4, 6, 23, 91, 111, 140, 149, 151; as policy shock, 12, 143; possible repeal of, 136, 141, 150, 157, 161
Roman Catholics, 4, 5, 6, 8, 20–26, 43–44, 47, 54, 55, 62, 66, 72–73, 75, 76–77, 78, *79*, 87, 90–91, 93, 103, 108, 124, 134, 146, 148, 153, 155–57; among party convention delegates, 110; bishops, 13, 72, 91, 151; voting on abortion, 81, 82, *83*, 86–87
Roosevelt, Franklin D., 161
Rounds, Mike, 136
Rove, Karl, 3, 56
Rutherford Institute, 96

*Sacramento Bee*, 120
*San Francisco Chronicle*, 120
*San Jose Mercury News*, 120
Santorum, Rick, 93
SCA. *See* Secular Coalition for America
Scalia, Antonin, 123, 157
scandals, 14, 29, 32, 89, 91, 93, 107–8, 114
Schaeffer, Francis, 17, 158
Schattschneider, E. E., 10, 56
school boards, 24, 97, 125, 128, 131–32, 151–52

school prayer, 4, 12, 14, 19, 24, 29–31, 32, 33, 35, 91, 97, 99, 101, 103, 128, 150, 155
Schwarzenegger, Arnold, 120
*Science*, 20–21, 90, 93, 99, 106, 132–33
*Scientific American*, 106
scientific organizations: mainstream, 15–16, 20, 104–6, 123, 133–34; set up by Religious Right, 90, 93–94, 96, 104, 106
Scopes, John, 125, 126, 131
Scopes trial, 22, 125–31; role of media in, 2, 107, 125–26, 132
search for extraterrestrial intelligence (SETI), 127
Seattle, Washington, 127
Second Coming of Christ, 22, 103
Secular Coalition for America (SCA), 100, 152
secular humanists, 4, 17, 60, 127, 143, 150; Religious Right critique of, 17, 158
secularism/seculars, xi, 1, 19–21, 29, 42–43, 48, 52, 75, 77, 82, 89, 111–15, 144–45, 151–52, 158; allies of, 4, 14, 16–17, 97, 115, 144, 153, 160–61; antipathy to Christian fundamentalists, 4, 14, 16–17, 54–55, 59–61, 64, 74, 87, 97, 144, 152, 160; awareness of party/issue differences, 87; definitions of, 5, 7–8, 43; demographics, 44–46; growth in numbers, 3, 7, 10, 19, 24–25, 28, 43, 63, 143, 147, 162; organizations, 4, *98*, 115, 144; partisanship, 50, 56, 59, 62–63; political mobilization by, 4, 16, 56–58, 60, 63–64, 96–97, 144, 152, 159; presidential voting by, 49, 63, 160; ties to Democratic Party, 41, 48–50, 60, 62–63, 65, 74, 89–90, 108, 109, 115, 144, 162; values of, 18, 51–55, 113, 159–60
secular threat, 4, 18–19, 74–75, 81, 84, 86, 125, 152, 159
Senate, 2, 10, 49, 57, 94, 155
separation of church and state, 18, 90, 99–100, 101–2, 111, 114, 127, 129, 143–44, 156, 160, 162

SETI. *See* search for extraterrestrial intelligence
sex education, 24, 37, 93, 97, 102, 151. *See also* abstinence education
sexual orientation, 47, 120, 145
Sherrill, Kenneth, 122
Sioux Falls, South Dakota, 135
social capital: churches and, xi, 1, 18, 43, 71, 158–59; critiques of, 87, 159; definition of, 71; and political involvement, 18, 63, 66, 75, 84, 87
Social Gospel, 22, 111
Socialist Party, 134
Social Security, 118
Society of Friends, 112, 120, 137
Sojourners, 99, 112
Soros, George, 152
Sotomayor, Sonya, 157
South Dakota, x, 17, 107, 117, 134, 142, 144; abortion restrictions in, 135–36, 138–41, 157, 159; direct democracy in, 134, 136–40; legislature, 135–37, 139–41
South Dakota State Medical Association, 138–39
Southern Poverty Law Project (SPLP), 98, 104
SSA. See Student Secular Alliance
Stark, Pete, 155
state legislatures, 107, 118–19, 123, 125, 127, 140, 153
states: electoral competition, 66, 70, 73–75, 78, 84, 86; Red/Blue state divide, 65–66, 73, 134, 148; religious composition, 8, 65–66, 73–75, 77, 78, 81, 82–88, 134, 152, 176n31; Republican Party influence in, 13, 23, 72, 86, 109
stem-cell research, 24, 94, 104, 105, 106, 115, 156–57
Stewart, Jon, 14–15
Stoesz, Sarah, 137
Stonewall Democrats, 102
Student Secular Alliance (SSA), 97, 98, 100, 101
Supreme Court, 12, 14, 24, 29, 32, 35, 87, 118, 122, 124, 126, 136, 141–43, 155–58, 161

Swaggart, Jimmy, 108

"teach the controversy," 126–27, 129, 131, 133
Tea Party, 17, 62, 89, 150–51, 153–54
teen pregnancy, 17, 93, 127, 158
televangelism, 6, 12–13, 56, 90–91, 107, 127, 144
Ten Commandments, 103
Tennessee, 125–26
Tenth Amendment, 106
Texas, 100, 125; state board of education, 132
textbooks, 24, 127–28, 132, 134
think tanks, 15, 89, 93–94, 104, 106, 151
third parties, 61, 63, 144; secular support for, 49–50, 63
Thomas More Law Center, 92, 95–96, 129, 132–33
Thomas, Clarence, 21, 107
Thompson, Richard, 132
Tikkun, 99, 112
Tocqueville, Alexis de, 22
tolerance, 28–29, 54, 97, 99, 146, 148, 160
traditionalists, 42, 54, 62, 65, 109, 145, 148, 152–54
Truman, Harry S., 100
Tunisia, 159
Twain, Mark (Samuel Clemens), 21
Twitter, 109, 121

U.S. Constitution, 22, 106, 118
unaffiliated, 8, 14, 25, 28, 32, 35, 37, 39, 47, 88, 109–11, 152–53, 161–62
Union of Concerned Scientists (UCS), 98, 105
Unitarian Universalists, 120, 137, 155
United Church of Christ, 101, 112
University of Pittsburgh, xi, 101
Utah, 73, 91, 121, 142

values issues, 2–3, 29, 51, 73, 75, 108, 133
Vatican, 20–21, 23. *See also* Roman Catholic Church
Vermont, 8, 119

Viet Nam, 114
Viguerie, Richard A., 90
Voltaire, 21
Vote Yes for Life, 137–39, 141
voter turnout, 3, 10, 56, 58–59, 61, 63–64, 74, 121, 131, 134, 139–40, 149, 152–53, 159; and awareness of party/candidate differences, 68–71, 87–88
vouchers, ix, 11, 101, 113, 145, 156

Walczak, Witold, 130
Walker, Vaughn R., 122–24, 156, 158, 161
Wallis, Jim, 112, 113
Warren court, 115, 156
Washington, D.C., 2, 8, 37, 77, 91, 100, 113, 115, 118–19
Watergate, 29
Weber, Max, 21
wedge issues, 29, 74; Discovery Institute strategy, 127, 130; Republican Party use of, 72, 74

White House, 24
whites: declining population percentage of, 146, 148; political behavior of, 43, 49, 62, 78, 84, 109, 153, 160; religious beliefs of, 43, 45, 47, 146–48, 154
Williams, Roger, 21
Willmon, Don, 13
women's roles, 24, 42, 45, 47, 52, 53, 55, 62, 68, 84, 114, 145, 160
World Christian Fundamentals Association, 22, 124
World Values Survey, 25–26, 31
Wright, Jeremiah, 111
Wuthnow, Robert, 147

Yes for Life. *See* Vote Yes for Life
younger Americans, 16, 19, 28, 37–39, 60, 62, 66, 78, 109, 145–50, 159

Zaller, John, 73–74